02.

30

26.

19

30.

In Enemy Hands

In Enemy Hands

Personal Accounts of Those
Taken Prisoner in World War II

Claire Swedberg

STACKPOLE
BOOKS

Library of Congress Cataloging-in-Publication Data

Swedberg, Claire E.
    In enemy hands : personal accounts of those taken prisoner of war in
World War II / Claire Swedberg.
        p.   cm.
    Includes bibliographical references.
    ISBN 0-8117-0900-0
    1. World War, 1939–1945—Prisoners and prisons.   2. Prisoners of war—
Bibliography.   3. World War, 1939–1945—Personal narratives.   I. Title.
D805.A2S85   1998
940.54'72'0922—dc21   97-47177
                                                                        CIP

CONTENTS

ACKNOWLEDGMENTS

This book represents the hard labor of some talented researchers and writers who contributed to the accounts told here. Special thanks go to Meg Rockwood, who helped Oscar Smith write his original memoir, and to Wilbur Jones, who assisted with the memoir of Hermann Pfrengle and contributed time and research to this book. Thanks also go to Pete House, Hilda Hunter, Gertrude Swedberg, and Martin Wirth, who contributed essential information to help maintain accuracy. The characters of these stories themselves dedicated many laborious hours of interviews, review, and research to make this book a reality, for which they each deserve much appreciation. Finally, special credit goes to my husband, Michael, whose support made all of this possible.

I have to live with myself and so,
I want to be fit for myself to know.
I want to be able as days go by,
    To look myself straight in the eye.
I don't want to stand with the setting sun,
    And hate myself for the things I've done.
I never can hide myself from me,
    I see what others never see,
    I know what others may never know.
I never can fool myself and so,
    Whatever happens I want to be,
    Self respecting and Conscience free.

Prayer Meeting, Stalag IX B,
Bad Orb, March 21, 1945.

INTRODUCTION

W hen German tanks rumbled across Poland's border in September
1939, signaling the beginning of World War II, millions of people
worldwide would not know that their lives would be changed forever.
The impact this war had on humanity is unrivaled in history. To tell the
stories of just a handful of those millions who endured the rigors the
war doled out is to demonstrate just how immense it was—so immense
in fact, that while there are more books accounting this war than any
other, they will record only a small fraction of the stories.

This book was written to chronicle just a few of those lives, from
a unique perspective. The experience of incarceration is brutal and
demoralizing in its own right; it is so common during wartime that
despite more than twenty years of peace, ex-POW organizations are
still thriving in this country.

But the experiences in POW camps vary as much as the personalities
of the people captured. This book attempts to capture a snapshot of four
men and one woman who were held during and following the war for
the real or imagined threat they posed to the other side.

The stories here follow the experiences of a young American soldier
captured by the Japanese in Bataan, a middle-aged British professor
incarcerated by the Japanese in Shanghai, a thirty-year-old American journalist captured by Germans during the infamous Battle of the Bulge,
a German boy captured by the Americans as he tried to flee the war with
his friends, and a German girl arrested by the Russians for alleged spy

activity against them when the Cold War took over where World War II had left off.

The stories speak for themselves and, as the author I hoped to impose neither judgment nor moral. Instead, the reader can determine those as the many similarities and striking contrasts in these five characters come to light. All, I believe, merit both sympathy and admiration, if for no reason other than their ability to survive by using innovation in a world that forbade it.

• • •

Oscar Smith, who joined the military after he finished high school, was captured at the age of twenty. With his friends, who also proved to be at times his worst enemies, he managed to survive what has been described as the most brutal prisoner experience for American military men. He used his talents with radio repair to secure himself a job in the Japanese camps, and then his guile, his recklessness, and his sense of humor to torment his captors. Whether he was running away with the Japanese military truck in the Philippine jungles, selling aspirin to Japanese soldiers stricken with venereal disease (pawning it off as sulfa), or stealing food from sacred Japanese graves, he proved that some prisoners could not be controlled and that no amount of degradation could harness his spirit.

Robert Salmon, a British biochemist teaching at a medical school in Shanghai, was captured and incarcerated in Shanghai. There his enemies were hunger and boredom, and he tackled both with the professorial style he had practiced for twenty years. Unlike the American soldiers, this group of political prisoners was treated with enough civility to create a shocking contrast with the story of Oscar Smith. This compound soon became a civilized community, and Salmon took over the monitoring of nutrition for fellow prisoners. He helped to establish a complex network of adult courses in a prison populated by everything from lawyers and judges to drunken bums.

In Europe, Edward Uzemack was captured in his hiding place in the cellar of a Luxembourg inn. He was taken to a Stalag, where the Americans held there organized themselves and established an escape committee, which dictated when prisoners could "bust out." Uzemack was a reporter, and he soon went to work, in his uniquely personable style, coaxing up contacts and producing a daily newspaper that plotted the course of Patton's First Army as it made its way toward the camp. When the Americans finally arrived to release these men, they found hungry but well-informed prisoners awaiting them.

German born Hermann Pfrengle was sent to war at the age of fifteen and did his best to hold his own with two weeks of training. After their release by the commander, Pfrengle found himself and his friends fleeing the German SS and Russians while hoping for capture by the Americans, rumored to be kinder to their prisoners. At the same time, the boys, all younger than he, depended on him to deliver them to safety. Pfrengle managed a surrender to the Americans, but soon discovered that they were not the generous people he had hoped. In this story he offers American readers a personal and often painful glimpse of the way the Americans treated some of our own prisoners when the war ended. Here starvation was the rule as German provisions dwindled. Pfrengle managed to help his friends by appealing to the sympathy of guards for "KP" duty, where they feasted on potato peelings, and eventually to try to convince his captors to release the boys.

When the war ended, for many Europeans the fallout would be deadly. Helga Wunsch was finishing high school when the Russians learned that some of her school chums were operating a crude spy organization in eastern Germany, now occupied by the vengeful Russians. She found herself implicated and, in a hasty military trial, was sentenced to twenty-five years. She then took an eight-year journey through the concentration camps that had not long before housed Jewish inmates, and eventually to the infamous East German prison at Hoheneck. Wunsch was a survivor who used a needle to squeeze out blood for a letter home and who unraveled her own sweater to reknit it with strands of cloth from her mattress to survive the cold winters. While many of her friends died, Helga lived to be released with the purchase of her freedom by West Germany.

All the characters relocated to the United States following their experiences. Each provided me with his or her account, and I have tried, in turn, to tell the story as they did, maintaining not only the veracity but the point of view that varies so much among them.

When telling a story of those incarcerated during World War II, one almost immediately thinks of the European Jews who lost at least six million of their people through the camps that housed them. Their story, so immense, requires a forum of its own and for that reason is not told in this book. Instead, these accounts represent the history of five people who later expressed varying degrees of bitterness over what happened and perceived a heroic desire to put their experiences behind them. Now they have cooperated in allowing the world a glimpse at how a few people used guile, pride, stubbornness, and every available resource to survive while in "enemy hands."

Despite the wide variations in their stories, a theme among the characters rises to the surface. Each had a talent that he or she brought along, and each used that talent to survive. It is no coincidence that these characters are the ones who lived to tell their stories. Experiences told by survivors tell us not only about the horrors of captivity but also about human nature and what sets the survivors apart from those less fortunate. Much was luck; the rest was stubbornness, craftiness, and just plain intelligence.

Each person left the camps to continue a productive life. Now we may use their stories to understand not only the nature of war and captivity, but the human spirit as well.

PROLOGUE

A fter Japan's attack on Pearl Harbor, Hawaii, on December 7, 1941, America officially joined World War II, sending troops to the Pacific and Europe to protect Allied countries. (This infamous invasion came one day later for those living in the Pacific and its later time zone.) Among those points of interest for the Japanese were the Philippines, a series of islands that included Bataan, an American outpost. About eighty thousand U.S. troops were stationed there as Japan launched its aggression against its Pacific neighbors. First Japan took Singapore, Manila, Wake, and Guam. After fighting off the initial Japanese attacks in Bataan, American troops retreated to their rear battle position running across the peninsula from Bagac to Orion in late January 1942. This move marked the beginning of a two-month-long stalemate, accentuated by disease and malnutrition despite large quantities of ammunition, fuel, and food supplies stockpiled by American forces. American troops were placed on half rations and then third rations. Ammunition, some of it dating from World War I, was in short supply and outmoded.

On March 12, General Douglas MacArthur, whom President Roosevelt had named commander of Allied forces in the Pacific Theater, was taken out by torpedo boat to Australia, flown from his headquarters on Corregidor, and replaced by Lieutenant General Jonathan Wainwright.

By April 7, the reinforced Japanese had penetrated four miles into Allied territory, then claimed victory with the April 9 surrender. More than seventy thousand Filipino and American soldiers were forced to walk the sixty-five-mile distance from Mariveles north to San Fernando, where the Japanese prepared to house them.

It was this parade around the peninsula that became known as the Bataan Death March. Of the ten thousand American servicemen who embarked on the long march, fewer than eight thousand of them survived the jungle trails, only to arrive at a prison camp—Camp O'Donnell. Oscar Smith was one of them.

At the same time, Robert Salmon of Shanghai was under house arrest. Tensions in China were growing as the Japanese took control of the international sector of the port city of Shanghai, which was governed equally by Americans, British, and Japanese. With the attack on Pearl Harbor, the Japanese officially took charge of the international section of the Chinese city and marked all westerners as "the enemy." In January 1943 the Japanese arrested Salmon along with thousands of other civilians, and sent him to one of Japan's many overcrowded camps.

While Salmon and Smith were housed in Asian prisons, journalist Edward Uzemack was covering the war for the *Chicago Times*. It was not until 1944 that he was drafted to join thousands of men to replace troops lost in the heavy fighting in Normandy, France. There Uzemack joined in the infamous Battle of the Bulge in the winter of 1944. By December of that year, six armies had joined with the British for an all-out attack on the German Siegfried Line. It was expected to be another in a series of successful thrusts proving Allied dominance, but instead the Germans retaliated. Under Commander Marshal Rudolph von Rundstedt, the Germans attacked in the Ardennes region of Belgium, forcing their way into the Allied lines. The initial key to the German strategy was to capture the small Belgian town of St. Vith in two days. This town was a major crossroad in the Ardennes and the headquarters for the 106th Infantry Division. The defense of St. Vith for eight days proved to be the eventual catalyst for German failure, but the eight days of fighting resulted in more than fifteen thousand Americans killed, wounded, or captured. To the south, in Luxembourg, the German 2nd Panzer Division was making its drive toward Bastogne by crossing the Clervaux River in the village of Clervaux. During the night and the following day, German tanks rumbled through the villages along the Our River toward Clervaux, past the small inn where Uzemack and his company men were hiding.

By spring of 1945, however, Germany was being pounded by Allied bombers and one after another of its historic cities were being reduced to rubble. German forces fought on to protect the Fatherland, using young soldiers side by side with their elders. Hermann Pfrengle, at the age of fifteen, was among those thrown into Hitler's last-ditch effort to save Germany. By the time Pfrengle was captured in Sudetenland, the United States, France, and Great Britain were storming into Germany, and Russia was taking its own share in the east. More than two million Germans lost their lives during the course of the massive exodus that followed the fall of Germany. Germans were forcibly displaced from their homes, including in Bohemian Sudetenland, Czechoslovakia, where a German family housed Pfrengle and his comrades for the night.

According to German statistics, 17,700,000 German people were displaced, and 1,100,000 died. Pfrengle may have made the right decision in surrendering to Americans. The Czechs immediately after the war set up internment camps for Germans awaiting expulsion from the Sudetenland or deportation to forced labor in the Czech interior during the summer of 1945. Former Jewish inmate H. G. Adler reported afterward that most in the camp were children and juveniles, locked up only because they were Germans. Over eleven million German soldiers were held behind barbed wire from American and Canadian barracks to the slave camps in Siberia and Central Asia.

When the Russians swept across eastern Germany, there was, at first, no talk of imposing a communist government on Soviet-occupied Germany. Soon, however, the KPD (German Communist Party) and the SPD (German Socialist Party) were inaugurated as the new political parties. Western intelligence units like the U.S. Army Counterintelligence Corps turned their focus from the pursuit of Nazi fugitives to covert operations against Soviet intelligence maneuvers in occupied East Germany. Helga Wunsch's classmates joined this American effort to follow the movement of the Soviets. The growing hostility between the communists and the anticommunist Western influence led to thousands of arrests for minor and, in many cases, trumped-up charges. Helga Wunsch was swept up in this massive crackdown on "subversives." By the time she was released, the results of World War II had firmly supplanted themselves in Germany. World War II passed the baton to the Cold War.

PART ONE

Radios in Bataan

*Oscar Smith dedicates this story to his children
Barbara Jean Pearce and William David Smith.*

CHAPTER 1

S mitty looked into the shriveled face of a dead American soldier. With blue eyes open, the face stared blankly at the gray sky, looking peaceful despite the suffering that skin stretched over jutting bones suggested. The only difference between them now, Smitty thought, was that for him the suffering hadn't ended.

Two days ago they could have been friends; today he was carrying the man's body to a mass grave. Smitty, a Japanese POW for three days, had pulled burial detail.

The body was naked and Smitty wanted to protect it from the pelting tropical rain, but there wasn't enough clothing for the prisoners who survived, let alone for the dead. Instead, in an effort toward respect, he trained his eyes upward through needles of rain at the blurring line of litters strung out before him.

Smitty was one of fifty thousand sick and starving American and Filipino prisoners destined for prison camp after the surrender of Bataan. It was the final defeat after four hungry months of fruitless resistance to the Japanese onslaught.

He had been here for three long days, and he wondered how much longer it would be before American troops would land in the Philippines to rescue them.

"Kuds! Kuds!" A Japanese guard barked behind him.

The command seemed to mean everything from "stupid" to "hurry up," and it was accompanied by a blow between Smitty's shoulder blades. The prisoner staggered but held tightly to the bamboo poles he carried over his shoulders to support the rear half of the litter. He gulped in a mouthful of air and rain as the mire beneath his bare feet threatened to slide out from under him.

At the front end of the litter, Smitty's fellow prisoner and ally, Revere Matthias, waited a few seconds until the guard had walked ahead a dozen yards, then cautiously looked back over his shoulder.

"You okay, Smitty?" he asked.

"Yeah. The dirty, slant-eyed bastard!"

It was the first time a Japanese soldier had touched him at Camp O'Donnell. Smitty's short, hunger-thin legs trembled while his red hair prickled against the back of his neck.

Nearly one hundred bodies had been stacked like cordwood outside the prison barracks that morning, destined for a burial ground that amounted to a gully, about three-quarters of a mile from the prison compound, into which water drained from the lower end of a sloping field of coarse, foot-high grass. The prisoners wore an oozing, black path of mud through the field. By tomorrow, it would be a quagmire.

Smitty and Matthias were near the end of the long line. Their faltering steps slowed as the first litter bearers began maneuvering down the slippery sides of the gully. Hardly moving, Smitty was aware again that he was staring into the face of the corpse stretched out before him. Long, blond hair was pasted down over the pale forehead by the rain. The sunken cheeks and bony chin reminded Smitty of the pasteboard skeletons in store windows back home at Halloween.

For an instant, Smitty imagined the corpse's head had turned, just barely enough to be perceptible, but he knew it had to be the rolling motion of the litter.

A moment later it moved again, jerking stiffly in the blanket as the eyelids rolled open.

"My God!" Smitty screamed and dropped his end of the litter, sending the body tumbling face down into the mud. Ahead of them a startled guard whirled and rushed at them as if they had dropped the body intentionally. His right arm flashed out from beneath his dark green poncho, striking Matthias's face before he could turn around to find out what had happened. The tall prisoner lay sprawled in the wet grass beside the mud path.

"He moved!" Smitty's voice was shrill as his quivering hand pointed toward what had been a corpse. "He's still alive."

Matthias struggled to get up, holding his nose as blood trickled out between his fingers. The body let out a whimpering moan and rolled over on its side, revealing a face covered with mud. Then the eyes closed again.

The guard let out a screech and spun away from the live skeleton at his feet. As he lurched back, two other guards came forward and became tangled in the confusion. All three shouted furiously in Japanese.

Other prisoners in the rear, halted by the commotion, put down their blanket litters; a few ventured close to see what was happening. Smitty recognized one of them, an older soldier in his forties, with only a fringe of hair spanning his bald head. He was a medic who helped the few American doctors back at the camp.

Looking at the guards, Smitty hesitated. There they stood in the rain jabbering excitedly. One of them held his bayonet pointed toward the body.

"Look," Smitty said turning to the medic. "We've got to do something. He's still alive, but they're liable to kill him. They don't know what to do."

The medic cast a questioning glance at the Japanese soldiers kneeling beside the now prone figure. He put his ear to the man's chest, listened for a few moments, then looked up. "His heart's still beating, but it's awful weak," he said. "We gotta get him back to one of the doctors right away."

Meanwhile, the guard in charge of the detail had silenced the others and stood watching the medic. He spoke in Japanese, pointing to the dying man and then back toward camp. The medic and his litter partner placed the still-living figure on the blanket and, with one of the guards, headed back along the muddy path to camp.

Smitty still stood in the same spot where he had been when he dropped the litter. As the guards began to reassemble the prisoners, one of them shoved Matthias and him toward the corpse left behind by the two who had returned to camp. A small pool of water had gathered around the body and it splashed as they picked up the litter. They fell into line and again headed toward the burial ground.

They picked their way awkwardly over the naked bodies that had been placed in rows on the ground, looking for a spot to deposit their burden in the flooding ravine. In some places water dammed up an inch or more against the bodies.

"Over here," Matthias instructed, heading for a spot where a slight projection jutted out above the level of the water draining from the field above. They lowered the body to the ground, then turned to begin digging the graves.

Other prisoners already were busy with shovels excavating large, shallow holes and burying the Americans in common, unmarked graves about twenty-by-twenty feet large and no more than four feet deep. Each time a shovelful of earth was dug, the hole would fill almost immediately with water. Soon Smitty couldn't tell where the grave had been.

The guards, posted on the banks above, and soaked with rain, began to fidget. One of them called out the shrill order: "No more dig! No more dig!"

The prisoners stopped their work and looked up. The guard jabbed his right thumb down toward the ground, indicating they were to start placing the bodies in the graves. The prisoners began carrying the bodies to the holes and sinking their dead comrades beneath the water.

First, one body floated to the top of the grave where Smitty and Matthias worked, and then another bobbed to the surface, face upward, its eyes open, staring wildly. A young soldier standing across from Smitty lowered his head and vomited into the open pit.

Over the sounds of the splashing came the irritating singsong of the guards joking atop the bank. One laughed and the rest joined in.

"Dear God in heaven," a voice sobbed among the prisoners, while the men, some crying openly, lifted body after body into the graves.

The prisoners picked up the shovels again and while some held down the bodies with the handle ends, they began covering the graves.

No chaplains were present, so the men were committed to the soggy ground without ceremony. Matthias brushed the perspiration mixed with rain from his eyes. "Somebody ought to say a prayer or something," he offered.

"I guess so," said Smitty looking around at the others. They milled about waiting for a command from the Japanese to return to camp. Some stood with their heads bowed, but Smitty was not sure if they were praying or merely numbed by the horror of their gruesome task.

Smitty lowered his head, too, but no prayers came to his angry mind. "The hell with it," he shuddered.

CHAPTER 2

"A soldier's paradise"—Oscar Aloysius Smith, Jr., had been told when he signed up for service in the Philippines. The prospect of serving in tropical Southeast Asia attracted Smitty far more than a ravaged Europe, where, if the escalating conflicts didn't kill you, the harsh winters might.

Born in Lancaster, Pennsylvania, in 1918, the twenty-two-year-old private completed six weeks of basic training at Fort Slocum, New York, and made his way via the Panama Canal, to Fort McDowell in San Francisco. From there, he shipped out to the Philippines and arrived in February 1941 in Manila, where he was assigned to the 10th Signal Service Company.

When the war broke out on December 8, 1941 (because of the time difference, war was declared on December 7 in the United States), Smitty, along with his company and about eighty thousand of MacArthur's troops, was sent to the Bataan Peninsula on the western side of Manila Bay. Bataan was a stronghold Americans never expected to lose, but come spring of the following year, Smitty surrendered with thousands of other starving, exhausted troops. He then became a part of the Bataan Death March as he and his comrades walked at gunpoint across the peninsula to their new places of imprisonment under the Japanese.

Now, in April, one day after Smitty's labor on burial detail, the rains had passed out to sea overnight. Early morning sunshine poked through the clouds to illuminate the soggy, thatched roofs of the barracks inside the mile-square prison at Camp O'Donnell.

The burial detail already had left the compound on its grim mission and the other prisoners were filing out of the old, unpainted mess hall at the end of the barracks row, carrying their rations of rice. There was little time to eat their meager breakfast before beginning another long day of work assignments.

Smitty, wearing the only clothing the Japanese had permitted him— a pair of khaki pants he had cut off above the knee, sat on the steps of his nearby barracks, his mess kit on his knees. He brushed at swarms of fat, black flies with his left hand while trying to spoon the rice into his mouth with his right. The flies hung in clusters, drawn to the compound by the open-pit latrines that overflowed along the entire length of the compound fence. Within seconds after a meal was served, the flies would begin their assault.

Matthias came out of the mess hall carrying his rice in a tin pan covered by a floppy overseas hat. He wore a loincloth fashioned from the remains of a shirt about his middle; his tall, muscular body was just beginning to show the effects of austere prison life. "Hey, Matthias," Smitty yelled as his companion headed up the muddy street away from the mess hall. Matthias looked back, then turned and came toward him.

Smitty felt a close tie to the big, black-haired soldier; the man's presence always seemed to bolster Smitty's confidence. There was little similarity in their appearances, though both were twenty-two. Smitty, his thin body covered with freckles the color of his red hair, was dwarfed by his six-feet-one-inch companion. But the two friends did share a determination to outlast the Japanese. That determination was not easily come by. Some of the prisoners already were broken in spirit; a few had just given up, sat down, and died.

"How did you get out of burial detail today?" Smitty asked.

Matthias glowered at the mass of flies hanging off his mess tin as he sat down beside Smitty. "I was going to ask you the same thing," he replied. "I guess they need more guys back here to dig latrines."

Matthias swept at the insects with his hat as he ate. "Lousy stuff," he commented to Smitty. "No wonder the Japs are such funny looking bastards if they eat this slop every day."

As Smitty watched his companion battle the flies, Sgt. Wilbur Bunch emerged from the barracks behind them. He was a career soldier with whom Smitty had served briefly in Manila before the war. "Did you two guys get the word?" he asked. "I think you're being transferred out somewhere. There was a slope head in here while you were in the mess hall. He had a paper with your name written on it. There musta' been twelve, maybe fifteen names."

Smitty looked at Matthias, who was busily sloshing water from his canteen into his battered tin dish. "Well, what did it say?" Smitty demanded impatiently. "Where are we going?"

"All I know is you're to report over by the gate right after chow if you can call it that. Hope you get a good deal," he added, offering his hand to the two younger men. They shook and Bunch started off for his work detail. "Oh yeah," he said turning back. "You're supposed to get all your belongings together to take along."

"I got 'em on," Matthias replied looking down at his loincloth. While Matthias finished cleaning his mess kit, Smitty went inside and packed the few belongings he had managed to keep from the looting Japanese guards. There was a bottle of iodine, a small New Testament, a few letters and pictures from home, and a razor. He packed them into his musette bag and stood to leave, then stopped and opened the bag again and took out the pictures. There were a few photos of the girls he knew; on the bottom was a picture of his parents in front of their new home in Harrisburg, Pennsylvania. "To our dear son" read the inscription at the bottom of the photograph. Smitty fought back tears as a sudden wave of homesickness caught him off guard.

"Come on, Smitty," Matthias yelled through the door. "Hirohito's waiting for us." Smitty rubbed the back of his hand across his wet eyes and jammed the pictures back in the bag.

Fourteen prisoners, including Smitty and Matthias, waited inside the gate, each one with his few belongings tucked under his arm. The sky was nearly clear of clouds, and the blue Zambales Mountain range just west of the camp looked cool and inviting.

The men looked one another over and exchanged bits of information about themselves. A short, dark-haired sailor next to Smitty introduced himself as Lyle Hughes, and another said his name was Shay. "Hear any dope on where we're going?" he asked.

Smitty shook his head and professed his ignorance. He paused and glanced around Hughes in the direction of the Japanese quarters at the top of a rise a short distance beyond the prison fence. "I think we're about to find out something, though," he said.

An officer, flanked by two guards, walked briskly to the gate and was let through by a sentry. He crossed the open ground between them and halted in front of the ragged detail of prisoners. The guards stopped just behind him. The Americans bowed as they had been taught to do early in their captivity. He looked down their rank with a cold stare as he inspected each man; when he finished he turned quickly to his left, and the guard standing there stepped back a pace nervously.

There was a staccato burst of instructions in Japanese; the guard translated as best he could. "You go Manila. Work for Japanese Army."

The officer strode up and down in front of the prisoners as he launched into a speech. When he was done, he looked again at the guard.

The reluctant translator appeared to be in over his head, stammering in Japanese and spreading his arms in a gesture of bewilderment.

The officer silenced him with a shout, then turned back to the prisoners. "Americans fix ladio," he snapped. The officer glared at the men, his legs spread in a defiant stance, while the oversized breeches above his leggings reminded Smitty of a pair of floppy elephant ears.

The prisoners exchanged looks. "What the hell is a ladio?" one of them asked.

"Ladio! Ladio!" the officer stamped his foot and screamed. "You fix."

"I think he's talking about a radio," Smitty said.

"Ladio!" said the officer through clenched teeth, who then wheeled and marched off, leaving the two guards to stand watch over the confused prisoners.

"Ain't he a nice son of a bitch?" commented Matthias sourly.

The inept translator smiled at the prisoners, taking the derogatory comment as a compliment. "Nice sonbitch," said the guard bowing deeply at the waist. "Officer-San nice sonbitch."

"And you're a big, fat bastard," Smitty said smiling and bending low, setting off another round of obeisance. The guard beamed with delight. He was still bowing in response to a steady string of insults when a military truck pulled in front of the group. Two guards bounded out and put an end to the ceremonies. They pushed the men into the back of the vehicle and lined them up on benches built into the sides of the stake body truck. When all were settled, the guard seated himself beside the driver, while the other guard sat—his rifle between his knees—with the prisoners.

The seventy-five-kilometer ride to Manila began almost as a pleasure trip for Smitty. The truck bounced along the road, its gears clashing each time it approached one of the frequent hills along the route. Filipinos, mostly women and children and occasionally an old man, waved furtively to the Americans from the side of the road. The somber expressions on the faces of these people told of their misery in captivity. Many of their young men had been captured or killed;

thousands more had melted into the jungles just before the surrender and were living as fugitives.

The truck slowed to a crawl, its engine whining in low gear as it bounced over a bomb-pocked section of road in one of the small villages. Two skinny children followed the vehicle and tossed several large bunches of bananas on its floor.

Matthias, seated last in the rear across from the guard, picked up one bunch and cast a glance at his captor. When he made no sign of objecting, Matthias ripped off a banana and passed the rest down the line. The guard watched with disinterest, then turned his head to stare out at the road again.

Smitty peeled back the skin and deeply inhaled as he caught the sweet, ripe scent. He shivered and took a bite. It was the first food other than rice he had eaten in more than two weeks. He closed his eyes and tilted his head back, chewing slowly to savor the rich flavor.

"Don't save any," said Wells, a tall, blond sailor in his midtwenties who had survived the sinking of the gunboat *Canopus*. "The Japs would only take them away from us anyway."

For the next few miles, banana peels went zipping out through the stake sides; as quickly as a prisoner finished one, he dived into the dwindling bunches to grab another. Smitty bet he could eat two faster than Wells could eat one. He crammed both bananas into his mouth at once, choking and swallowing, but still managing to keep even with the gunner. The banter grew louder, and some of the men laughed for the first time in months. They completely ignored the guard, who by now was nodding and leaning dangerously close to the open rear of the truck.

Hughes was the first to notice. "Hey, look at Humpty-Dumpty back there," he said. The rest turned toward the guard whose chin had fallen against his chest, partially burying his face inside his open tunic. He swayed from side to side, then forward and backward with the motion of the bouncing truck.

"Hope he falls out and cracks his damned, sloped head," Wells said. Suddenly the rear wheel under the guard lurched into a hole; with a yell he fell backward off the bench, his right hand still holding the rifle, his left grabbing desperately at the air.

Matthias leaped from the bench opposite him and caught the guard's groping hand, pulling the top half of his body back inside the vehicle. The guard scrambled to his hands and knees inside the bed of the truck, spouting a string of obscenities in Japanese. He glanced in the direction of the men in the front of the truck, who stared back at him with angry faces. The embarrassed guard turned to Matthias in frustration.

He thrust his bayonet toward the prisoner, barely missing him as Matthias hurled himself backward against the stake body of the truck. The guard felt behind him for the bench as he slowly sat down again, keeping his rifle pointed at Matthias.

The prisoners sat like statues. Smitty's cheeks bulged with banana, but he didn't chew. Finally the guard lowered the rifle across his knees and leaned back against the truck, but his eyes never looked away from Matthias's face. The trip continued in silence.

CHAPTER 3

The truck rolled through the heart of Manila, down the wide pavement of Dewey Boulevard beside the bay, but Smitty couldn't match the city he saw now with the one of his prewar memories. Palm trees lining the road had been smashed, their fronds hanging limp and torn and turning brown. The dock area was pounded to pieces and the upturned hulls of small vessels jutted incongruously out of the oily water in Manila Bay where they had been caught in the first bombing attacks.

Military equipment was strewn everywhere—tanks, field pieces, trucks of all sorts—as well as construction machinery, all of it brought ashore from the huge fleet of Japanese ships moored a half mile out in the bay.

Smitty saw fighter planes and bombers that had been using Dewey Boulevard for a landing strip lined up in rows along one side of the street. Japanese work crews, shouting at one another and scurrying about in hectic disorder, became more numerous as the truck neared the center of the city. Some were busy repairing bomb craters in the streets; others were stringing electrical and communication lines; still others hurried in and out of buildings carrying loot that might be of benefit to the invaders.

The truck often slowed to a crawl to avoid the other Japanese vehicles and work details, but the driver managed to thread the truck through the heavy traffic without stopping, and he accelerated as they left the main part of the city.

Five miles beyond the densely built area of Manila, the truck swung off the main highway and headed for Quezon City, the modern section of the capital. Smitty had been here before and experienced a sense of relief to see that the friendly community and its gleaming white buildings had been spared by the war.

There were few Japanese soldiers in sight. Filipinos waved to the Americans; Smitty felt momentarily removed from the war.

The driver suddenly swerved the truck sharply off the road, nearly jolting the prisoners from their seats, as he halted in front of a small, fenced-in compound containing several barracks and other buildings. Smitty had his back to the structures and when he turned to see where they were, he recognized what formerly had been quarters for a Filipino constabulary unit.

The guard leaped down from the back of the truck and motioned with his rifle for the prisoners to follow. They climbed out and stretched their cramped legs for a few moments until the wide, wooden gate swung open, and a detail of guards appeared to escort them inside. The guards, Smitty noticed, were dressed more smartly than the ones back at Camp O'Donnell, and the compound was clean and neat. The first building inside the gates was a large, one-story warehouse, and the guards lined the Americans in front of it.

"I don't see any other prisoners around," Shay remarked, peering toward the other wooden structures at the rear of the warehouse. "Maybe this won't be too bad."

"There are Japs here, ain't there?" Matthias answered. A minor officer barked out an order in Japanese and though they didn't understand what he said, the prisoners snapped to attention and bowed in his direction. "Someday I'm going to bow to you Japanese bastards just long enough to pick you up, and then I'm gonna knock your lousy brains out," muttered Matthias at the guards as he straightened up.

The other prisoners picked up where they had left off with the translator back at O'Donnell. They disguised their best back-alley language with bland smiles as they heaped curses on their captors.

At the next command, the guards drew to attention and Smitty saw an officer in a white navy uniform approaching. He was taller than any of the other Japanese Smitty had seen and he walked smartly. His lean, tanned face was almost handsome, and he glanced toward the prisoners with strikingly blue eyes.

He halted, spoke to the guards in Japanese, then turned and looked with interest at the prisoners. There was no rancor visible in his scrutiny, just curiosity. He carried a riding crop in his right hand and tapped it against his leg as his gaze went from one prisoner to another.

Refreshed from the ride and with a belly full of bananas, Smitty felt new courage in his unfamiliar surroundings. "If you're looking for your mother, I just saw her back at the kennels," Smitty addressed the officer, bowing low and creasing his mouth with a smile that could have been described as a sneer.

The expression on the officer's face remained indifferent as he surveyed once more down the line of men. Then he slowly walked a few steps toward them. "You should be informed that I speak English perfectly," the officer began, revealing no emotion in his voice.

Smitty felt the blood drain away from his face, taking the smile with it.

"I lived in the United States of America for six years," the officer continued. "And I graduated from Annapolis Naval Academy. I have knowledge of both your language and your ways, so there is very little that you will do here that I will not be aware of."

He tilted his head back and his blue eyes seemed to examine the cloudless arc of sky. When he looked again at the demoralized prisoners, his face was stern and his words clipped. "I would advise you to remember in the future that you are prisoners of war and that your fate is in our hands. If I ever hear another insult from any of you, it will cost you your life."

He stood erect and silent with his eyes seeming to bore holes into the wisecracking American. Smitty's heart thumped in panic, and the wind blew cool on the perspiration covering his body. He shivered.

"All of you have had experience in communications," the officer's voice rang out calmly. "And because our own experts in this field are busy elsewhere at the moment, we have need of you here."

It was the first time any of the men realized they had something in common—a knowledge of radio transmission.

"Your American officers attempted to destroy all of the radio equipment before we liberated the Philippines," the officer said. "And now you will be expected to put it back into working order. You will live and work in the building behind you," he continued, flicking his riding crop in the direction of the warehouse.

"If you do your work well, you will be fed the same rations of food as our personnel receive. If you do not, ..." his voice trailed off, and the Americans mentally filled in the blank that followed.

"You will begin your work immediately," he resumed his instructions. "I am the deputy commandant of this post, and you will be directly responsible to me." He bowed curtly and walked away.

The prisoners, crushed by the sting of his words delivered in their own language, quietly watched the departing figure.

A guard broke the silence by motioning toward the open door of the warehouse. Inside was a large room with concrete walls and floor, lighted by several windows. The room was bare except for a pile of used lumber and a few tools at the far end. "Sleep here," one of the guards said as he pointed to the concrete floor at the rear of the room. Turning, he pointed to the far end. "Work here."

"Aren't there any cots or anything?" one of the Americans asked, pounding his heel on the floor to emphasize its hardness.

The guard looked at him for a moment uncertain of his question, then pointed again to the floor. "Sleep here," he repeated.

"I think he means 'sleep here,'" Matthias said, grinning. The prisoners deposited their few belongings on the floor, then followed two guards to the back of the room where they were immediately put to work building workbenches on which to repair the radio sets. The tools, the wood, even the rusty nails, Smitty guessed, had been provided by the squads of Japanese looters who were stripping Manila bare.

It was late at night when the prisoners finished constructing what they hoped would pass for two large workbenches. They wolfed down their rations of rice from wooden bowls given to each man, and, exhausted, fell asleep quickly on the cold concrete floor, too tired to renew their complaints about the accommodations.

Daybreak had barely arrived when the clashing of gears and the whine of a heavy-duty truck, followed by the hurried, nervous chatter of Japanese voices, shattered the prisoners' sleep. "Holy hell, it sounds like another invasion!" Matthias complained. He then reached back to the shoulder on which he had been sleeping. The others were doing their best to get up, stretching cramped muscles and picking out crumbs of concrete that had become embedded in their skin overnight.

Two guards came through the door, both talking at once and waving for the prisoners to come out of the building. The men rose on shaky legs and followed. Outside was a large truck with three guards lounging in the back among piles of cargo covered with blankets. The soldiers pulled back the blankets and shoved a small dark-gray box faced with dials toward the men, who had gathered near the back of the truck.

Smitty moved in closer and saw the same kind of radio receiver used by the Americans. He peered into the back of the canvas-enclosed truck as Lyle Hughes moved off toward the warehouse with the first set. There were at least fifteen more inside the truck; Smitty picked up the next one and carried it inside.

The receivers were stacked against the wall at the far end of the bigger workbench. Two small boxes containing odd pieces of wire, solder, and several rolls of friction tape were carried in by a guard and placed on the bench.

On the last trip, Smitty waited for Matthias. When he was sure no guards were near, he caught his friend by the arm. "When we pick up the last sets, let's see if we can wrap 'em in some of those blankets in the back of the truck," he suggested softly. "They'd be a lot better to sleep on than the concrete floor."

The blankets had been shoved against the side of the truck, the nearest one about four feet from the tailgate. Without waiting for the remaining radios to be pushed his way, Matthias reached inside and grabbed one, along with the corner of a blanket. He dragged both of them to the tailgate and was wrapping the blanket about the set when a guard crushed his foot down heavily on the prisoner's hand.

Matthias let out a furious shout and thumped the fist of his good hand down so hard on the radio that the case cracked. While the guard stood on the tailgate shouting curses, Smitty walked slowly around to the side of the truck, reached in and pulled out the remaining blankets. He dropped them to the ground, then pushed them with his foot toward the other prisoners. They got the idea, picked up the blankets undetected and carried them inside. The other Japanese guards were in the building looking over the radios, and the lone guard outside was too busy with Matthias to notice.

In the meantime Matthias refused to give up his blanket, still clutching it as he matched oath for oath with his foe in the truck. The guard finally had enough; he swung the butt of his rifle at Matthias's head, but the prisoner ducked the blow. The guard leveled the action end of the rifle at Matthias, and still screaming at the top of his lungs snatched the blanket away. He waved his arms menacingly toward the warehouse for Matthias to get back inside.

Smitty put the last receiver down on the floor and looked up in time to see Matthias charge through the door, cursing and looking about wildly as he held his injured hand.

Frightened more by what Matthias might do than by the Japanese, Smitty grabbed him by the arm. "Come on," Smitty pleaded. "Cut it out or you're gonna get us all killed. Take it easy."

"Easy, hell," snorted Matthias. "All I wanna' do is get hold of that little slanty-eyed son of a bitch. I'll tie his ears around his damned neck."

The guards looked up from where they were inspecting the radios, but made no move to intervene. "Let's see your hand," said Smitty. "Do you think it's broken?"

"Naw, but I didn't even get the lousy blanket."

Smitty smiled. "Never mind," he said, turning toward the workbench. "Look over there." Tucked beneath it were the other blankets; doubled up, there would be enough to go around.

"Damn my Aunt Nellie," Matthias marveled. "And I didn't even see you do it." His lips cracked at the corners in a smile. "I guess it was worth it."

While Smitty calmed Matthias, all the guards except one returned to the truck and drove off. The remaining guard watched as the prisoners began inspecting the radios. The first few they looked at appeared to be damaged beyond repair.

One seemed to have had a grenade explode inside its case. The entire insides of another had been smashed. Resistors, wires, and other parts were ripped from others. The prisoners went over the sets hurriedly, looking for one that might hold promise. "You fix," the guard instructed them, watching as the Americans picked through the pile of sets.

"Hey, this one doesn't look too bad," said Shay. The others crowded around as he plugged the set into a receptacle hanging at the end of a long cord that dangled from the ceiling. He twisted a dial and a voice came from the set, faintly at first, then becoming stronger as he adjusted the dials.

"That's Japanese," Hughes said. "Must be one of the local stations. Wonder how many of the others are okay?"

Smitty shouldered in between Wells and Hughes and grabbed the receiver. "Let me look at it for a minute," he said. He reached into the set, turned his back to the guard, and tore a wire loose. Looking at Matthias, Smitty touched the loose wire to a stationary one. There was a poof and sparks crackled, then silence. Smitty arched an eyebrow. "I betcha' we could fix every one of these radios just like I fixed this one."

"I think we've got a little business going," Hughes announced.

The guard approached; standing on tiptoe, he peered over Smith's shoulder. "You fix?" he asked.

"Sure, Charlie," Matthias replied, looking down at the guard. "We fix real good."

CHAPTER 4

"Hey c'mere you guys, listen what I got!" Wells said without looking up from the receiver set he was working on. The others left their places at the workbenches and surrounded the gunner. He glanced over his shoulder to make sure no guards were in the building, then twisted the dial.

". . . Don't want to set the world on fire, I just wanna' start a flame in your heart . . ." sang out the radio. Shay beamed as he watched the expressions on their faces. The music sounded distant and strained, but there was no mistaking it—it was stateside. "How do ya like it, huh?" he gloated. "KGEI out of San Francisco. Man, listen to those Top Hatters."

Smitty leaned in close as the music touched bittersweet memories— the fragrance of perfume, the touch of a soft cheek. Lost in reverie he almost mistook the long, groaning sigh for his own, but the voice was too deep. Turning, he saw Matthias, his eyes closed in an ecstasy rekindled from the past and his broad mouth smeared into a smile that recalled conquests. His head swayed to the slow tempo.

"Well, for God's sake," Smitty exclaimed. "Will you look at Elsie, the Borden cow?"

The big GI with eyes closed began shuffling circles around the prisoners' work site, while the others scurried out of his errant path. From somewhere in the back of his nose, he hummed his own off-key accompaniment. "Matthias, what the hell's the matter? You got the colic or something?" asked Hughes.

"Me and Natalie used to dance to this . . . Stardust. . . ."

"That's not 'Stardust,' dum-dum," Smitty said. "It's —"

"Stay the hell out of my dreams," interrupted Matthias who proceeded to whirl with his left arm extended elegantly and his right arm encircling an imaginary Natalie. He hummed so loudly he didn't hear the door open and, with his eyes closed, he couldn't see the Japanese naval officer enter. Matthias was out of reach of the others who quickly scrambled back to the radio in a frantic attempt to shut off the music. Someone succeeded, and the set went dead.

"What are you guys doin'?" Matthias demanded. His smile transformed into a frown. "You got something against romance?" Their stares left Matthias's face and slowly drifted over his left shoulder to the officer behind him. "Come on," the prisoner insisted, "Turn that damned thing back on." Matthias soon realized something was amiss; he turned around slowly.

"So you are an entertainer," observed the officer as he scrutinized the dirty soldier. Matthias started to bow, then straightened up stiffly. The officer paced off a slow circle around him before speaking again.

"I allowed you the freedom of no guards in the building in the hopes that you would return my generosity with work," he said. "Instead, I find you holding a party."

Turning to Matthias, he poked him sharply in the ribs with his riding crop. "And this one, a dancer."

His blue eyes roamed down the soldier's chest and bare belly and stopped at the loin cloth. "A very sensuous costume," he remarked. "It reminds me of a female impersonator I saw once in the United States of America. I disliked him intensely." Putting a finger to his chin in thought, the officer looked up at Matthias and asked, "Are you a female impersonator?"

"I . . . uh . . . don't know . . . sir," he stammered throwing a pleading look in the direction of his companions. No one responded.

"Silence!" shouted the officer. His voice had lost its farcical tone. "You have been here for four days, and none of you has repaired a single receiver set. You Americans are not fit to serve the Japanese. You will work all night tonight with no rice rations for twenty-hours, and there will be a guard here to see that there is no more idling."

He spoke to Matthias again: "There is a special job for you. Tonight you will report at the latrines. I will have a guard bring a bucket to you, and you will clean out the latrines down to the bare earth. I guarantee you will not feel like dancing."

Matthias didn't look up as the officer walked out of the building. Smitty was the first to speak. "When are you going to start shaping up?" he asked. "You just fumble and bumble your way through. Man, you just don't think. Then everybody gets in trouble."

Matthias, his head still down, drew pictures with his toes on the concrete floor. "Now come on," Smitty instructed the other prisoners. "Let's get back to work." Matthias didn't move.

"Well, come on, Matthias," urged Smitty. He still didn't move.

"Look," Smitty implored, "If I hurt your feelings . . . "

"Naw, it's not that," said Matthias.

"Well, what's the matter?" Matthias drew pictures on the ground with his toes, looked up and asked: "What's a female . . . uh . . . repersonator?"

"Aw, ya dumb—"

A guard entered and the men headed for the workbenches. "Some day I'll explain it to you," muttered Smitty from beneath a frown. "After you grow up."

The next day was miserable. The sky was shrouded by dull gray clouds that matched the prisoners' spirits, and by noon it was raining torrents. With no rice rations or sleep, the men looked at one another through burning, red eyes; their stomachs rumbled painfully. Nerves were raw and tempers strained. Matthias, badly in need of a bath after his stint the night before in the latrines, had come within a hair of swinging at a guard who had wrinkled his nose distastefully at the odor.

Radio parts lay strewn about the workbenches. Smitty found it hard to remember what belonged in which set; his numbed mind refused to care. A radio suddenly fell to the cement floor and burst open. Jangled nerves vibrated at the loud noise. "Dammit! Watch out!" Hughes shouted, clenching his fist as he stared at the wreckage. No one spoke as Smitty and several others bent down to pick up the pieces.

It was early evening, nearly time to quit, when a truck arrived with a new load of radios. "What the hell! We'll never get outta here," Matthias complained. He was still fuming when three Japanese soldiers entered, each carrying a radio. The sets were in crates and looked new. The guard spoke to one of them, then pointed toward the prisoners. The soldier glanced their way and shook his head negatively. The Americans stood and watched the soldiers, dripping from the rain, carry the receivers in and stack them in a corner; the prisoners realized then that the guard had volunteered them for the unloading of the truck, and the soldier had refused.

"Ain't that something?" Matthias reflected in amazement. "They don't want us to get wet."

"They must be new sets," said Hughes. The soldiers completed the job in a few minutes and drove off.

"Hey, Tojo," Matthias called to the guard. "How about we eat now, huh?" The guard just looked at him. "You know, food," he said, scooping an imaginary spoon toward his open mouth.

The guard looked at his watch, then motioned them toward the door. They took off immediately, cursing and yelling as they shoved and pushed one another to get through the narrow doorway. The cool mud was a balm to their tired, burning feet. They dug their toes into it while the driving rain stung feeling back into aching muscles. Smitty saw Matthias squint and turn his face into the downpour. The drops made flat, hollow sounds as they pelted against his forehead. The rain felt wonderful.

"Come on," someone yelled. "Let's eat." The prisoners sloshed across the parade ground and filed into the mess hall. The first rice in more than a day steamed its way into their stomachs, generating new energy and spirit. It was the same thing they had eaten for every meal since their capture, but tonight it tasted good—the only complaints were over the size of the portions.

Afterward, they walked back slowly through the downpour. Matthias rubbed himself down briskly in the rain to remove the stink of the latrines. Back in the barracks, the men eased their tired bodies down onto the blankets that separated them from the hard floor. Some lay down, closed their eyes, and fell immediately to sleep. Others chatted, relishing the feeling of food in their stomachs.

"If I could have anything I wanted," Smitty mused from the corner where he sat propped against the wall, his skinny arm dangling over a bony knee, "I'd take a great big piece of chocolate cake right now. Real moist with thick, white icing."

"Yeah," Matthias taunted, "and then you grow up and find out about girls." He smiled greedily. "'Course you wouldn't know about things like that, son."

Hughes spoke, ignoring Matthias: "When I get home I figure on opening a little bar, and I'm gonna toast you guys every hour on the hour with a beer. I'll hold the glass way up high, like this," he demonstrated thrusting his arm high over his head. "Then I'll watch the foam run down my arm and think about each one of you pitiful bastards before I drink it."

No one spoke for a few moments. Then Smitty asked the question for everyone. "How long do you think it'll be until we get home?"

Matthias answered first: "Well, I figure it can't be too long now. They won't be able to stand all that awful pressure back in Washington. They'll have to do something soon."

"What pressure?" asked one of the men.

"All them girls back home," reasoned Matthias. His face brightened with a conceited smile. "Why, they were just gettin' used to me and if them pretty little things hear I ain't comin' back right away, well hell, there's no tellin' . . ."

Smitty was serious as he repeated his question. "No kiddin', don't you guys think they should be here soon? Hell, it's been a month now that we've been cooped up here and at O'Donnell. I just don't understand why the United States is waiting so long."

"It's just that the Japs caught everybody by surprise," Wells said. "You know damned well they aren't going to just leave us stranded here. Any day now . . . boom! No Japs. And we go home."

"The best thing we got goin' for us is the guys on Corregidor," Hughes interjected. "I think they can beat the Japs by themselves. But they won't get the chance. We're gonna have planes and boats over here all over the place soon."

"And girls, too," Matthias said, stretching out his long legs.

"Yeah, but I haven't seen any planes or anything yet," Smitty said.

"What the hell—you don't think they're gonna send over one or two do you?" Hughes cut in. "It won't be long. You'll see."

Matthias sat up. "You know," he began, "this time I ain't kiddin'. When our guys get here I'm gonna ask our commanding general for one little favor. I want them to give me that Jap navy officer bastard so I can take him back to Ohio."

He stood up and began talking louder for attention. "I'm gonna go home and build me an outside privy, a five—no a ten-holer. Then I'm gonna chain that son of a bitch down in the bottom of it. Then you know what? I'll advertise in the papers for everybody to come out to my place and crap, free, right on his freakin' head."

Smitty laughed along with the other men. Having Matthias around erased the monotony of prison life, but the fatigue and malaise returned quickly. Smitty walked over to the light switch. "Let's knock if off so this clown can get his beauty rest," he said.

He lay down in the darkness and closed his eyes, warmed by a new sense of hope and exhilarated by a feeling of comradeship with this small group of men. It gave him strength. He wanted them to be his friends, very close friends, long after they departed camp and went home—and that would be very soon.

CHAPTER 5

The men awoke the next morning to a dark sky and a lump of cold rice. But Smitty didn't care. He could get by on rice now that he knew the Americans were coming. His spirits were lifted from the conversation of the night before, and he believed they were on the verge of being rescued. Every day brought them closer. The others felt the same.

The men were at their workbenches before the guard assembled them. Poking about among the sets brought in the previous night confirmed what they thought: they were all new. "What do they expect us to do with these?" the gunner asked. "They weren't even used yet. How can we fix something that's not even busted?"

"Easy," Smitty replied taking one from its crate and carrying it to the workbench. "We bust it."

"Wait a minute," Matthias cried as he put his ham-sized hand over the set before Smitty put his words into action. "We bust the sets, and the Japs bust us. The first part's okay, but the last part, I don't like."

Smitty brushed Matthias's hand away from the radio. "Watch," he instructed. He took good parts from the new set and quickly installed them in an old one. Next he took out the crystal, crushed it in a vise and put it back in the new set along with some old parts lying on the workbench. "Now, neither one's any good," he announced to his companions. "Simple?"

"Holy hell, Smitty," Hughes said. "Matthias is right. If the Japs catch you, they'll murder all of us." Smitty shook his head emphatically. "They aren't gonna catch us. You mix up the parts from the good ones and the bad ones, and they'll all look alike to them. Hell, you know they couldn't tell crap from kidney beans about radios."

The action was made possible by the guards' inattention to the work the prisoners were doing. A growing pile of radios deemed "irreparable" displayed the ironic faith that the Japanese put in the work of their prisoners.

Many of the guards had been chosen to watch prisoners because they were not mentally or physically fit to serve in the Japanese military, and they seemed to lack the intelligence of the Japanese people in general.

With that knowledge, Smitty was sure the guards and the commander would be fooled by his trickery. He studied the faces of his comrades for their support.

"Let's try it," Wells said slowly as he brushed a couple of chips from the smashed crystal under the workbench with his foot. "Anything would be better than repairing these things so the Japs could use them against our guys when they get here."

It was all the encouragement they needed. The prisoners had most of the new radios uncrated by the time the guard arrived. He was short and stocky and uncharacteristically good-natured; he grinned at the prisoners with an air of friendliness and an apparent lack of intelligence. When he smiled, he displayed a huge gap where several teeth were missing. Smitty found him almost likable and miraculously gullible.

"Morning, Tyrone," someone addressed him by the Hollywood name with which they had tagged him. He liked it.

"Ha, ha, yes," he answered, bowing to the prisoners.

The work went well. By midafternoon nearly a dozen of the new sets had been torn down and their parts strewn about the worktables. Smitty had just removed the tubes from a set when the naval officer walked in. The guard snapped off a salute and stepped back out of the way as the officer approached the workbenches. As he fingered through some of the loose parts, the only sound was the tense breathing of the prisoners.

Finally he spoke. "How many have been repaired today?" His voice sounded casual, almost as if he didn't care. There was another silence. Each prisoner hesitated to reply. The officer looked at Matthias who was standing to his left. "You will answer," he commanded. "How many sets have been repaired today?"

Matthias, as was often the case when he was addressed by the officer, was unsure how to respond. "Uh . . . I didn't fix any . . . uh . . . none, sir." He was either too innocent or too dumb to lie, Smitty concluded.

"Why not?" bellowed the officer.

Matthias looked backed into a corner as he struggled for an answer. "It's these here crystals. Uh . . . the ones in them new sets. . . ." The officer's riding crop flicked out; it caught Matthias across the neck and a long, red welt discolored the soldier's deep tan. Matthias bent under the blow but looked up at the officer with unmasked rage and hatred. The officer stepped back several feet.

"Now, what about the crystals in the new sets?" he demanded. Matthias grew sullen, communicating only resentment in his glaring eyes.

Smitty sucked in his breath. "The damned fool," he thought. "He'll strangle the Jap in a minute, and everyone of us will be shot." The riding crop was nearly at the top of its arc again when Smitty interrupted. "This one here will work, sir," he said in a high-pitched voice. "I'm almost finished with it."

Smitty was glad he hadn't tampered with the set yet, and he prayed that it was in as good working order as the other new ones had been. The officer lowered his crop and turned to look at the set Smitty had before him. "Make it play," the officer commanded, and the look in his eyes told Smitty that if it didn't, he would pay for the intrusion.

"It'll be finished in a second," said Smitty. Bracing himself before he put the good tube back in the set, he plugged it in and switched on the dial.

Nothing happened.

He looked at the officer long enough to see the fury in his eyes. Quickly he turned back to the set, shook it and turned the volume up high. At first, a faint, then more discernible, voice spoke in Japanese; it was probably one of the local stations seized in the invasion.

The relief surged through his veins as he took a deep breath.

"Very well," the officer paid a cold compliment to Smitty. "I will take this one with me. And I want to see many more like it."

Smitty turned to unplug the radio. "I'll have it ready in a minute," he said reaching with his pliers into the back of the set. A final adjustment and the set was ready to go. The officer picked it up and walked out, oblivious of Matthias's eyes blazing into his back.

"Man, was that close!" Hughes exclaimed as he flicked perspiration out of his eyes.

Matthias, the purple veins standing out at his temples, walked to the front of the room and back rubbing his neck. As usual, his wrath subsided quickly and he approached Smitty. "Thanks buddy," he said sheepishly. Then he put a huge hand down affectionately and shook Smitty by the back of the neck. "I guess I was wrong about you Pennsylvania Dutchmen bein' dimmer'n mules. That's what they always taught us in school back in Ohio, anyway."

The gunner interrupted: "I hated like hell to see him take that set out of here like that. That's one for the Japs." He looked at the guard who watched, unaware of what was being said.

"Don't worry about it," Smitty advised. "Look here," he said calling several of the prisoners in close. "I just got the idea before the admiral walked off with the set. I pinched the lead-in wires so that they almost broke—not quite, but almost. It'll only be used a few times then gaflooey, no radio. And they can't blame us because it worked when it left here."

Hughes nodded. "You know, Matthias could be right. Maybe you aren't as dumb as everyone says." The gunner glanced across the room again at the guard whose face lighted in a smile. "At least we won't have to worry about that one," he said, "if only that damned officer stays out of here. I don't see why we can't give the Japs what they think is a good radio once in a while and then knock hell out of ten others."

It was agreed. For the next few days no one bothered the prisoners. The officer stayed away and they assumed that regular reports by their affable guard kept him satisfied. The work had become almost a game. When a set occasionally was made to work, the guard's toothless smile would break across his face at the sound. "Work good. Ha ha, yes. Work good," he would say, nodding in approval.

Outside the window, meanwhile, the pile of worthless radios grew into a bountiful harvest of junk. As each set was rendered useless, it was passed on to the guard. He would shake it several times, then nod his head in judgment. "Domi, domi," he would say, pronouncing the set no good. Out the window it went onto the junkpile.

"Dummy, dummy," Matthias liked to mock him.

"Domi, domi. Ha ha, yes."

CHAPTER 6

None of the men had been outside the compound's barbed wire enclosure since they had arrived three weeks before, and Smitty felt uneasy when he and Matthias were summoned one morning for new work detail. They were handed shirts and pants and told to board a truck at the main gate.

A driver Smitty had never seen before and the friendly guard from the radio repair unit came out of the Japanese headquarters building and climbed into the cab. "Hey, Tyrone," Smitty called. "Where we going?"

The guard looked back at them in the rear of the open vehicle and flashed his smile. "Yes. Ha ha." He slammed the door. Smitty and Matthias sat down and looked at one another.

The driver gunned the motor and the truck lurched through the gate, heading toward Manila. Wasting no time, they sped along the highway. Occasionally the driver sounded the horn, scattering Japanese soldiers and Filipinos alike. The two prisoners held tightly to the stake sides to keep from being bounced out onto the road.

The truck skirted most of the city, rarely slowing, then swung off the road and pulled up to a long, low cinderblock warehouse. Armed guards were posted at the two doors that opened out onto a loading platform. The Japanese in the truck jumped down, spoke a few words to the guards, and handed over some papers. The guards read the documents, then opened one of the doors and disappeared inside. The driver climbed back into the truck, swung it around and backed up to the loading dock.

The prisoners, still seated, were summoned by a wave of the hand. They got out and followed Tyrone inside.

Mountains of cardboard cartons lined the walls into the rear of the structure. Filipinos, under supervision of guards, already were stacking some of the cartons by the door. Smitty and Matthias approached the boxes, hoping to gain a better view of the contents.

"Holy hell, Smitty," said a startled Matthias. "Look! The place is loaded with food." The labels were all familiar: Aunt Libby's peas . . . carrots . . . string beans and Stokes' creamed corn. . . .

Smitty guessed that the Japanese must have cleaned out every store in the city and hauled the food here. For the prisoners, subsisting on one bowl of rice a day, it was almost too much to absorb. Smitty and Matthias were dreaming of stately dinners from the stockpiles when a guard rapped his knuckles loudly on one of the cartons. When they turned to him, he pointed to the cartons and then to the truck.

"I guess he doesn't want to get his hands dirty," Matthias said, pulling down a box marked Heinz oven-baked beans. Smitty hauled down another and followed him out to the truck.

"Wonder where our boys went?" Smitty asked.

"You mean Tyrone and his buddy? Up there," Matthias said, nodding toward the street where the two soldiers were walking away from the building. "I think they got something better in mind than doing this."

"Yeah, well I'd rather be here with all the food," Smitty said. "We're not going to get any of it, but it's kinda nice just to see it again."

It was nearly two hours later when they put the last carton on the truck, leaving room barely for themselves for the return trip. They sat on the loading dock to wait for their escorts back to camp; the hot breeze blowing over their sweaty bodies felt cool against their wet clothes.

Smitty had nodded off to sleep when Matthias finally spoke: "Hey, here they come and, holy hell, look."

Smitty snorted awake. He squinted down the street in the direction that Matthias was pointing. At first, it looked like a figure "A" moving toward them with four legs and two heads—then he made out the two soldiers leaning against one another for unsteady support. "Geez, they look like a pair of walking bookends," Matthias exclaimed.

The driver held his right hand clutched tightly over his face to shield his eyes from the blazing sun and left the navigating to his companion; his left arm dangled limply around the neck of Tyrone, who was having trouble keeping in step. "Man, are they ever crocked!" Smitty marveled.

Guards from inside the building came out onto the loading dock to watch; they cheered the pair on and laughed at each wobbly step. The two drunks, oblivious of the spectators, walked an uneven course toward the truck. They didn't stop until the driver's head came in contact with the open door of the vehicle.

The sound startled Tyrone, who glanced at Smitty. The driver's hand had fallen to his side to expose a flushed, perspiring face; he began to crumple, and the surprised guard hugged him close to keep him from falling. They embraced for several moments as the driver snored loudly against the other man's shoulder. The bigger man eventually slipped through the guard's arms and fell to the ground, his back resting against one of the truck's wheels. The Japanese in the background howled with laughter.

"Damned if I'm riding anywhere with one of them driving," Matthias declared. "They can shoot me first."

Smitty looked down at the driver; his legs extended in a V, his arms hung limply, and his head snored into his own shoulder. "Maybe there's another way," Smitty suggested. "You know how to drive one of these things?"

"Now wait a minute! You don't mean that I'm supposed ta' just drive off in this rig, and all these Nips'll just stand there and wave good-bye, do ya'?"

"Well, I guess it's okay if you would rather ride with him," Smitty said, nodding toward the sleeping driver.

"Hell, no, I don't want to ride with him. But they ain't gonna let us just up and drive away, and what about those two?" he asked. "Look at 'em!"

"I think it's worth a try," said Smitty. "We'll just load them in the back and drive off."

Matthias was apprehensive. He could hear the soldiers on the loading platform still laughing and jeering. The drunken guard's eyes were glazed, and he swayed slightly, but stood faithfully by his fallen companion. "I don't know; that's damned risky right in front of them and everything."

"Aw, hell, if you're scared, forget it," said Smitty.

"Okay," Matthias said. "Come on." He collected the dangling arms and legs of the driver and carried him to the back of the truck. Smitty led the other one by the arm. "Man, I wonder what they were drinkin'?" Matthias mused, turning his head as far away as possible from the limp form in his arms. "It smells like vinegar."

"I don't know," Smitty replied. "But whatever it is, I bet there's no more of it left on the island."

The guard reached an arm up around Smitty's shoulders for support. "Ha, ha, (Hic) yes," he said.

The Japanese on the loading dock enjoyed watching Matthias maneuver the insensible driver into a narrow opening between rows of boxes on the truck. There he got stuck. Matthias grabbed him by the tunic and heaved; the driver grunted as his head slid upward over a box of peaches so that his boots just cleared the tailgate. Matthias turned around and reached down to Smitty, bracing the driver to keep him from falling; together they lifted the drunken guard aboard.

"Now's when we find out if we can hack it," Smitty said.

Matthias jumped to the ground, pretending to ignore the soldiers behind them. "Let's go," he urged.

They walked slowly around to the front of the truck and climbed in. Matthias, for the first time, looked for the keys; they were awaiting him in the ignition where the driver had left them.

"We'd better get out of here quick," Smitty said anxiously. Matthias pushed down the clutch, flipped on the switch and ground his other foot into the starter. The engine roared to a start as he thrust the gearshift into position. As soon as Matthias let the clutch out, the truck lurched backward and smacked into the platform with a jarring thud.

"My God, you got it in reverse," Smitty shouted.

Matthias slapped the gear back into neutral, then down again. When he put his foot on the accelerator, the vehicle moved out toward the street. Smitty waited for rifle bullets—they never came. After the truck had put a full block between them and the warehouse, he looked back— no one was in pursuit.

"I thought you knew how to drive one of these things," he fumed.

Matthias didn't answer. They rode in silence for about a mile through the outskirts of the city without seeing any soldiers. Smitty finally spoke again. "I wonder what kind of reception we'll get back at the camp when we roll in with two drunk Japs in the back."

Matthias spun his head to look at Smitty in disbelief. "Are you nuts? We ain't goin' back to camp. Man, we're free."

"What the hell are you talking about? This whole place is occupied by Japs," Smitty shot back. "What are you gonna do? Drive this thing across the ocean?"

"See them mountains?" Matthias said, pointing toward the distant horizon. "Zambales. That's where we're goin'! We're gonna get lost in them jungles up there and they'll never find us. And we got enough food in the back of this here rig to last us a couple of years."

Smitty didn't answer. It was a temptation, yet he was afraid; he almost felt like a deserter. "What about the other guys still back in camp?" he asked.

"Well, . . ." Matthias seemed puzzled for a moment. "Hell." He drove on silently.

"And what about these two guys in the back?" Smitty continued. "What would we do with them?"

Matthias just stared at him, and Smitty knew the answer.

"You can't do this, Matthias," Smitty argued. "Dammit, use your head. First of all, we'll never make it all the way to the mountains without getting stopped, and besides, look, it isn't worth it. The war's bound to be over real soon. Our guys will be landing here any day and they'll need help. And where are you gonna be? Sittin' up in the mountains eating canned asparagus?"

"Yeah, well it sure beats rice," he countered.

"Come on, let's start back before we get caught."

"Nope and I'm gettin' damned tired of listenin' to you, so just stow it, huh?"

The miles ticked away; Smitty grew more and more uneasy. Any minute, he thought, they'd be picked up by a patrol.

Miraculously, they had passed only a few soldiers, who had paid scant attention to the military vehicle with the bright rising sun insignia painted on the sides. Smitty had run out of arguments. Anything else he said would only deepen Matthias's stubborn determination.

As the truck passed into a dense jungle area, Matthias scanned the sides of the road. He finally swung the truck into a narrow road leading off the highway and pulled to a stop when he was sure they were hidden from view. Shutting off the engine, he draped his arms over the steering wheel and peered at Smitty. "This is it, buddy boy, our new home. This is where we're gonna live for a while," he smiled.

"Yeah, some living," Smitty said acidly.

"The Japs will never find us here," Matthias assured him.

"How long do you think it'll be until they find this truck? Then they'll rip this whole place apart to find us. If we had made it to the mountains, we might have had a chance. But they'll find us here sure as hell. I'm going back to Quezon. Nobody could live in this mess."

Matthias cocked one eyebrow as he gazed into the impenetrable tangle of vines and wild palmettos. Snarled together beneath the trees, heavy grass and bamboo thickets grew riotously. "I'm going," Matthias announced and opened the truck door, hanging one foot out. "Oh, here, I'll show you how to jockey this thing." He climbed back in and Smitty watched dejectedly as he went through the gears, explaining how to double-clutch and when to shift going up and down hills.

"Got it?" he asked.

"Yeah, I guess so."

"I'll leave those winos in the back for you. If you show up without them you'll be up to your backside in trouble. And I'm gonna' take a couple of them boxes of food along."

He climbed out, went around to the back of the truck and took down two cartons marked Spam. Smitty slid over into the driver's seat and watched. He fought down a desire to leave the truck and join his friend. But he couldn't. It wasn't fear; he just knew the war would last only several more weeks—a month maybe—and he had to be there when it was over.

Matthias, carrying a case of Spam under each arm, walked back to the driver's side of the truck. "Sure you won't come with me?"

Smitty couldn't answer. He shook his head.

"I'll miss you old buddy."

Smitty refired the truck engine and managed to get the vehicle turned around, stalling it only twice. He blinked hard as he steered along the narrow trail toward the highway. "Hey, Smitty, wait!" Matthias called out suddenly.

Smitty slammed on the brakes, stalling the truck. Looking back, he saw Matthias running down the trail toward him, still clutching the Spam under his arms. Reaching the truck, the big GI put a foot up on the running board so he could balance one of the cartons, freeing his hand to open the door. "You're right," Matthias hollered as he sat. "They would kill the others, and probably you. We're in a firing squad."

"Here, take these," he said, shoving the boxes at Smitty. "You open the meat, and I'll drive."

At camp that evening the other prisoners were reluctant to believe the story but enjoyed it wholeheartedly. "The funniest thing of all," Smitty told his grinning audience, "was when we tried to sober up those two Japs. We knew we couldn't come driving into camp with them drunk in the back, so we found a stream. But Matthias here holds each one by the neck under water and he won't let go."

"Yeah," Matthias added, "but when they came up they were sober."

"I don't know, though, Smitty," Gunner Wells remarked. "I think you made a hell of a mistake bringing this clunk along back. We could have been rid of him by now." Matthias sneered, but he was enjoying the role.

"And when the Americans get here," Hughes said, "we'd all be going home, and Matthias would never know the war was over. He could be a sort of caveman. Hell, he even looks like one anyway. Ever notice how his eyes are too far apart—"

Matthias lunged over Smitty who was lying on his blanket and grabbed Hughes by the leg. "Ya bigmouth bastard—"

"Ahee!" shouted a guard who entered through the gloom at the far end of the building. The men scrambled quickly to their feet. The guard approached until he was illuminated by the dim bulb that hung over their heads. His hands on his hips, he motioned for another figure to emerge from the darkness. The men strained to see as the newcomer shuffled a few steps closer to the light. He too was a prisoner and wore a dirty, gray T-shirt and tattered khaki trousers that exposed long, bony legs, matching an emaciated body. He looked too young to belong there.

He introduced himself: "Hello, I'm Vince Grayson." Smitty thought there was something refined about his voice and face.

"You from Camp O'Donnell?" Hughes asked.

"Yes. They told me I was to be assigned to radio repair work. Is that what you do?"

"Yeah, kinda," Matthias replied. Then he laughed. "Only we kinda fix 'em in a different—"

"Knock it off," said Smitty, jabbing him with an elbow. The men on the floor were relaxed once again.

"Look, come on over and sit down," Shay invited him. "You can share this rag with me." He moved over to make room on his blanket. The newcomer stepped over the tangle of legs and sat beside Shay in the middle of the group.

"I guess it's still pretty rough at O'Donnell, huh?" Hughes asked.

"It's awfully overcrowded and most everyone is sick," the newcomer said. "Several American doctors are doing wonders with the little they have, but a lot of the men are dying. They've cut back on the food quite a bit, too."

"Well, this ain't exactly the Rudolf Astoria," Matthias said, "But it's better than O'Donnell." He reached beneath his blanket and pulled out an opened can of Spam. He fished out a piece with his fingers. "Here, try some of this."

The soldier thanked Matthias and bit off a small mouthful. He smiled for the first time, his even white teeth setting off his fine facial features.

"Where in the world did you get this? " he asked. "I'm sure the Japs don't give it to you."

"Don't ask, please," Wells pleaded. "We just went through all that the last hour, and we don't want to hear it again."

Grayson smiled and finished the Spam. The prisoners introduced themselves and learned that he lived on Long Island and had one more year to complete at New York University when he was drafted. He had arrived in the Philippines two days before the attack.

"One thing," Hughes informed him, "this is no country club, but they let you alone most of the time. It's a hell of a much better place to finish out the war than O'Donnell."

"Finish the war out?" The soldier stared at Hughes in astonishment.

"Sure," Hughes said confidently. "They'll be bringing more men over here than you ever saw to reinforce Corregidor. The Nips'll never know what hit 'em."

"Wait," Grayson interrupted. "None of you know, do you?"

"Know what? What are you talking about?" Hughes asked.

"Corregidor. It's been surrendered," Grayson answered.

A somber silence filled the room as the prisoners absorbed the news. Smitty spoke first. "How the hell do you know that?"

He didn't wait for an answer. Anger flared crimson in his cheeks.

"I've heard more damned rumors—the Japs are going to do this, the Japs are going to do that—but none of them are ever true. Somebody tells you something and you believe it, and then you go around telling—"

"Hold it, Smitty," Hughes said, grabbing him by the shoulder. "Take it easy." He turned to look at Grayson. "Now how do you know Corregidor surrendered?" he demanded.

Grayson was almost apologetic as he answered. "I was on Corregidor. There were so many men lost. We tried to hold out, but we ran out of everything. It was no use. No help ever came. We surrendered three days ago."

Smitty's gaze blurred as it slipped slowly off the soldier's face and onto the dirty, brown blanket under him. He lay down and turned his face to the wall. The room was quiet as someone turned off the light. It had been their last hope. Now they knew no one was coming to rescue them.

It was a long time before anyone fell asleep.

CHAPTER 7

S mitty hated his new assignment: cleaning the commanding officer's bathhouse and preparing his tub. The tub was a filthy, repellent mess, and it made him wish they had never run out of captured American radios.

The first time he saw it, he had to fight the impulse to retch. It was a huge, wooden thing, at least four feet deep, ten feet long, and five feet wide. The water came nearly to the top, and it was covered with thick strings of gray scum. How could a man be so slovenly.

The inside of the one-story wooden building was squalid. Wet cigarette butts and discarded pieces of pale, yellow soap littered the concrete floor. But worst was the fetid odor. Smitty decided that the tub would have to be emptied then scoured.

He leaned over one end and searched for a plug to drain the water; it was like trying to find the bottom of a swamp. Smitty backed away, took a deep breath and turning his face to the side, plunged a bare arm deep into the murk. Extending his fingers, he reached deeper—as far as he could stretch without dunking his face in the water. Still, he couldn't reach bottom.

"Sons of bitches!" he swore as he hauled out his arm and wiped at the muck that covered it. Taking off the loincloth he had made from a towel, he eased himself onto the broad rim of the tub and considered the foul-smelling water. Staccato orders in Japanese startled him. Whirling about, Smitty almost fell.

A guard charged at him, stopping just short of the tub. He raised his rifle butt threateningly, and, with rapid gestures, pumped a finger up and down over the general location of the stopper. Smitty hesitated, then crouched lower, extending his right arm until the rancid water stroked his chin. He cocked his head back and gained several more inches' reach. The stopper still eluded him.

He had to get the tub drained before the guard went berserk. "Bastards," he muttered through his teeth, then slipped his legs into the grime. The water came halfway up his chest, and the wet wood on the bottom felt slimy beneath his feet. He held his arms up and out of the water. Moving about slowly, he searched with his toes for the plug.

Wrong end. He turned carefully and, fixing his gaze on a towel one of the Japanese had left hanging on a nail in the wall, he made his way to the opposite end. His foot slid over the stopper; he tried unsuccessfully to hook his big toe into the ring. Maybe from a different angle. This time the ring moved, but he couldn't fit his toe into it. Everything was too slippery.

The guard screamed at him. Smitty looked across the length of a bayonet-tipped rifle into eyes ugly with hate. He took a quick breath, closed his eyes and ducked under. His fingers found the slippery ring and he pulled. It lifted right out. He thrust his head to the surface, gasping for air, gagging and retching.

The guard was laughing. Smitty climbed over the side and ran outside, into the air. He breathed deeply through his mouth to fight down the sickness. It passed, but he couldn't escape the smell. It permeated him.

A verbal fusillade summoned Smitty back inside. The laughing guard walked to the far end of the room, took a wooden pole from the corner and held it out toward Smitty. Smitty eyed the six-feet long, splintered stick with a hook on one end of it. A hook. The thought jolted him; the hook and the pole were used to pull out the plug. The guard broke into loud, mocking laughter when he saw that Smitty had caught on.

When the guard had grown tired of the game and left, Smitty went outside again and tried to clean himself off with palm leaves. He took some of his anger out on his skin as he rubbed briskly. The wetness went away, but the smell remained.

He put on his loincloth and began cleaning the tub. He scrubbed vigorously with a stiff brush until splinters stood out like bristles on the sides. There were benches built into the inner walls of the tub for several bathers to loll on; and when he finished scrubbing, he plopped down on one, exhausted.

Precious daydreams, his only real possessions, enveloped him. Home was in this haze and he heard "Harbor Lights." The music came from the dance band he had played with back home. Matthias was on the stage, but he didn't belong there. He wasn't in the band. Nor was there a bassoon, but one was playing. Now it was talking. Shouting. In Japanese.

Smitty woke up. The bassoon was just outside the door. His heart hammered as he leaped from the tub and ran to the doorway. Matthias was bent over, retrieving a load of kindling he had dropped. The ugly, little guard castigated him and kicked furiously at the scattered pieces of wood. Smitty watched in admiration as Matthias, showing his disdain for the guard, slowly and deliberately picked up the fallen pieces. Matthias then turned his back on the guard and strode off toward the kitchen with the load of wood.

The guard then spotted Smitty in the doorway and picking up an ax he had dropped, beckoned Smitty to follow him into the woods at the rear of the compound to chop wood. The ax was dull and Smitty hacked away, concentrating on smaller, dead limbs that yielded more easily than the bigger logs—it was tiring work. Whenever he paused, the guard would shout out his dissatisfaction and jab toward him with his bayonet.

Pretending to ignore the wild antics, Smitty maintained his chopping, but he was scared. The vicious soldier was about Smitty's height, but much huskier. The pupils of his bulging eyes were unfocused and his thick lips hung apart, the lower one cradling his exposed tongue.

Smitty carried load after load of wood to an outside alcove of the bathhouse where an old-fashioned, potbelly stove was used to heat water for the tub. When the guard thought the supply of wood was sufficient, he left Smitty alone to start the fire and stoke it.

The water hissed and gurgled as it cooked in the coils running through the top of the heater. There was ample time before the main contingent of Japanese returned for the evening, but Smitty was eager to finish the job. Perspiration and a film of stinking slime streamed down his body, tickling and itching wherever it ran.

Jamming the last chunks of wood into the firebox, Smitty watched the flames lap out for air through the cracks in the dilapidated stove. Inside the bathhouse, he grabbed the faucet and yelled in pain as the red-hot metal seared his thumb and forefinger. Protecting his hand with a towel, he released the water into the tub. As it gushed against the wooden bottom and began building up the sides, he leaned in close to let the steam rise over his body. It was hot, but it felt clean and the wet wood smelled sweet and musky. When the tub was half full, he turned on the cold water to bring the temperature down to a comfortable level. He was surprised at how quickly the tub filled.

Turning off the faucets, he straightened up and watched as the last of the trickling drops sent delicate rings spiraling toward the sides of the tub. He could see the plug clearly at the bottom of the crystal water.

Running his hand through his thick, red hair to stop the itching from the streaming perspiration, he silently cursed the Japanese for their luxury. How long it had been since he had been in a bathtub, and now here was the biggest one he had ever seen.

He climbed in.

The warmth enveloped him. He eased onto one of the benches and slid low enough in the water so that his shoulders, aching from swinging the ax, were covered. With the back of his head resting against the side of the tub, he felt the exhaustion seeping from his body. He closed his eyes; a bird sang outside. It was the first time he noticed the song of a bird since becoming a prisoner.

The sound of the approaching Japanese voices, many voices, roused him. He sloshed over the side of the tub, sending waves splashing onto the floor. The soldiers were back. Grabbing the towel off the nail, he rubbed himself hurriedly and left.

The other prisoners were gone by the time Smitty reached the mess hall, so he took his ration outside to eat it. A feathery breeze brushed lightly over his clean body as he plopped on the ground beneath a stunted palm tree. He leisurely spooned his rice and watched as the soldiers completed their day's chores. Looking up from the bottom of his cleanly scooped bowl he was surprised to see the commanding officer come out of the bathhouse. Having finished his bath while Smitty was in the mess hall, he ambled across the parade ground toward his quarters.

The thought of having to clean the tub again tomorrow—and God knows how many days afterward—disgusted Smitty. One thing consoled him: it couldn't be as dirty tomorrow as it was today.

Smitty noticed three other officers entering the bathhouse. He waited a few minutes. When they didn't emerge, he walked toward the building. They were in the tub laughing and splashing. He went back to his tree and sat down to watch. The officers came out about ten minutes later and two more went in. When they came out, others were lined up. Finally, the last officer came out and five enlisted men entered.

My God, Smitty thought, the whole outfit's taking baths in the same water. He was counting by this time . . . 24 . . . 25 . . . No wonder it was like a pigsty in the morning. . . . 37 . . . 38 . . . 39 . . . And they seemed to delight in the chance to bathe even in someone else's filth. They came out laughing and joking . . . 48 . . . 49 . . . 50. Fifty men altogether.

Disgusted at the squalid episode, Smitty headed back toward his barrack. Scummy water would await him, but at least he knew where the pole with the hook was.

When Smitty entered the barrack, the other prisoners were grumbling about their new assignments. "Hell, I cut enough wood to win the damned war for someone," Matthias complained. "That whole lousy kitchen is stacked full. And do ya' know why?" He snorted but didn't wait for an answer. "So they can cook that stinkin', rotten rice."

Grayson was lying on the half of the blanket he shared with Shay. He didn't look well. "What's the matter, Vince?" Smitty asked. "You sick?"

Rolling over, Grayson raised his thin, white face off his arm and answered: "I'll be all right. They had me digging slit trenches all day, and I guess that with all that heat I just got a bit sick."

"What you need is a good bath," Smitty said. Grayson looked at him oddly.

"Why don't you order us one, huh?" Matthias spoke from under his heavy-browed frown. "And while we're waitin' you can have room service bring us a couple of broads."

Smitty headed off the rest of the wisecracks. "If you guys'll just shut up and listen, I just might decide to do something good for you."

He described everything in detail—the stove, the giant tub and, above all, the beautiful water, clean and warm. "Now, I think I can probably work it so that all of you guys can get a chance in the tub. The rest of you finish your work before I do, so I can give you the sign if it's okay. No kidding, it feels great."

"Sure," Matthias said, "we just all go marchin' over there like a big parade, right through the center of camp."

"You can't all come over at once, hell no. Just a couple at a time each day," Smitty explained. "That way, everybody will get at least one bath a week."

Matthias liked the idea. He volunteered to be first the next day. "Okay," Smitty agreed, "but bring Grayson here along. Maybe it will make him feel better."

The next day, Smitty encountered the same filthy mess he had endured the day before. But this time he was prepared; the first thing he sought was the pole with the hook on it. The drain gurgled as the suction formed a whirl on top of the water above the pipe. The same noisome odor assaulted him as he watched the water run out, leaving its curdled deposits clinging to the sides of the tub.

As Smith scrubbed, the guard was less attentive than he had been on the previous day, but he was at him constantly as he cut the firewood. He screamed at Smitty, taunted him, threatened him. At times he would give a loud grunt, then thrust the bayonet toward his prisoner. Smitty dropped the ax and jumped back again and again. Sometimes the guard would laugh; other times he would become infuriated. Smitty wondered what protection the ax would be against the bayonet and rifle if the guard really attacked.

By the time the wood was stacked by the stove, the tension between the two men was unbearable. Smitty could feel himself trembling, certain the guard was crazy. It was not until after Smitty had stoked the stove and its sides glowed red that the guard finally left him. He started to worry about bringing Matthias and Grayson into the bathhouse. If the guard caught them, death awaited all three of them.

He watched the prisoners leave the mess hall and go into the barracks; then he filled the tub. Every few minutes he scanned the camp. Matthias and Grayson lounged outside their doorway. He checked again—still no guards. He apprehensively nodded the all clear signal to Matthias and Grayson.

The two prisoners sauntered across the parade ground toward the bathhouse. Smitty began to get nervous. It was taking them an eternity. "Come on!" he called in a loud whisper when they were close enough to hear. He herded them through the door.

Matthias was first to spot the tub. "Wow! Ain't that somethin'?"

Smitty tried to hurry them. "Peel off your stuff and . . . " Matthias was already in the center of the tub, leaping about wildly and yelling. He hadn't bothered to remove his loincloth.

"Shut the hell up, you ape!" Smitty warned. "You wanna ruin everything?" Matthias quieted down and floated on top of the water, while Grayson removed his shorts. "Go ahead and get in, Vince," Smitty said as he stood watch at the doorway. Grayson climbed over the side and sat on one of the benches. He put his head back and relaxed in the water's comforting warmth. Matthias, still frisky, ducked his head under, then did a handstand on the bottom. He came down with a belly-whopping splash, nearly knocking Grayson off the bench.

"Hey Grayson," Matthias said, wiping the water from his eyes. "I'll bet you never went skinny-dippin' before, huh?"

"We used to go in without trunks every Wednesday night at the Y," Grayson replied, sitting straight on the bench in preparation for Matthias's next water assault.

"The Y? You mean you belonged to one of them things? Hell, back in Ohio we always went down to the creek. There was a real nice place there, grass along the edge and everything. We called it BAB—bare-assed beach. Girls went there, too. Beats any YMCA."

Grayson smiled and settled low in the tub again, closing his eyes. They remained in the water about ten minutes until Smitty announced it was time to go. "Take another minute, and then you better scram," he urged. Hearing running water, he jerked around quickly. Grayson was out of the tub, putting his shorts back on. Standing on the side of the tub, bent over so that his back nearly scraped the ceiling, was Matthias, urinating into the water. "My God, Matthias," Smitty yelled at him. "What the hell are you doing?"

"We always did this when we were done swimmin' in the old BAB and it never hurt none, so I guess it ain't gonna hurt them Japs none either," he explained.

Smitty puzzled for a second, and coming up with no arguments against it, joined in.

CHAPTER 8

S mitty swung the ax hard against the base of the kamagong tree. It made a dull thud and fell away, barely leaving a mark on the black trunk.

"Damn it to hell," he muttered to himself. He realized he had made a mistake; the tree was too big and the ax too blunt. He walked a few steps away in search of a more suitable target, one that would yield to the nicked blade. The guard screamed for him to return and pointed to the tiny incision in the tree trunk. He wanted that one.

Disgusted, Smitty walked back slowly and bent to get another grip on the ax. Before he could raise it, a rifle butt dug its metallic plate into his shoulder. "Okay, okay," he shot back at the guard, whirling about to face him. It was the first time he had talked back. The guard cocked a meaty fist, and his raspy voice snarled out an order.

Smitty deflated his rising anger with a snort of contempt and hefted the ax again, slamming it fiercely against the tree. A tiny notch appeared a few inches above the other one. It was no use. He picked up the ax and turned to the guard, running his finger along the blade to show the ragged, pitted edge.

"Look. Can't you understand? It's just too dull. If I had something to sharpen—"

The punch clipped him above the ear. The ax fell from his hand as he reeled backward, striking his head on the tree. He staggered forward a step with his chin on his chest, then fell to the sandy soil on his face. When he didn't move, the guard stomped a heavy shoe down on his leg.

Smitty rolled over slowly and opened his eyes. He was looking through a long tunnel; at the end of it, he could distinguish the foggy outline of the guard. Blackness rimmed the picture; and, although the guard's lips moved and his jaw muscles contracted, all Smitty could hear was a loud whistling inside his head.

The guard kicked him again. Smitty struggled to his knees and waited there for the next kick. It landed on his hip. The stabbing pain ripped loose a violent burst of fury. Sobbing through clenched teeth, he staggered to his feet, then bent over unsteadily to pick up the ax in front of him. Turning his back, he just walked away.

The guard stopped shouting. He watched Smitty in bewilderment until the thin, tottering figure disappeared into the woods. He made no move to go after him.

Smitty slogged on, the whistle echoing in his head. He eventually realized that he was on the path back to the bathhouse, and the perception of what he had done sent a shiver down his spine. He looked over his shoulder, but no one was in sight. He remembered he still needed one more load of wood to add to what he had already collected. Lying along the edge of the path were small limbs that needed little chopping. Spikes of pain seared his muscles with each feeble stroke of the ax. Half a load would have to do; he gathered up the wood and left.

When he reached the bathhouse, he hurriedly tossed kindling into the stove, lighted a fire, and lay down on the ground. He felt dizzy and sick to his stomach. The belligerent guard had probably picked on him ever since he was assigned to the bathhouse detail, because he was the smallest of the prisoners. Recalling the attack made Smitty mad again. Everything hurt and was beginning to get stiff, but he forced himself to get up.

As he stoked the fire in the stove, his anger mounted. "Son of a bitch Japs!" he said under his breath. He jammed in more wood. Tongues of fire spit out through the joints in the rusty old stovepipe. More wood. The water hissed and gurgled in the coils. The fire penetrated the pipe and lapped at the wooden roof of the bathhouse.

The heat was intense. Shielding his face with his arm, he tossed the last chunks of wood on top of the stove; they ignited almost instantaneously. The roof was now on fire and the whole length of the wall next to the stove was smoking. The flames quickly engulfed the entire building just as the soldiers entered the gate in a fleet of trucks. Hoping to hide his angry acts, he ran to the front of the bathhouse and screamed, "Fire! Fire!"

The last of the trucks were easing through the gate when the flames blazed above the roof. The soldiers leaped out of the vehicles and headed toward the burning building. Smitty knew he had to make some pretense of fighting the fire; he turned on the hot water faucet, again burning his hand. Steam hissed from the spigot until the water flooded into the tub.

Thick clouds of steam added to the heat from the fire as Smitty grabbed a bucket, filled it quickly, and heaved it toward the open doorway. The scalding water splashed chest high across the tunics of the first two Japanese entering the bathhouse. "Oh my God!" Smitty said in a hoarse whisper as he cringed. There was no time for reprisals. Others shoved inside, yelling loudly as they pushed against the two scalded men trying desperately to get back out.

Soldiers continued to swarm in and out of the building. In the midst of the turmoil, the water ran over the sides of the tub, creating a new crisis. The soldiers howled in pain and stomped out a frenzied dance as the steamy water surged over their feet. Smitty, wedged into a corner near the doorway, dropped the bucket and squeezed between the jostling bodies to get outside before the water reached his own bare feet. If not for his pain, it would have been almost funny.

The other prisoners had been watching from outside their barracks. Several of them hurried over to Smitty. "Holy hell, Smitty. What happened?" Matthias asked.

Smitty gazed into the fire as he answered. "I'm having a cookout. Wanna come?"

Matthias laughed. "Yeah, that's pretty good. We'll have Japs on a rotisserie."

Shay was annoyed. "Don't you ever stop clowning, Matthias? That could mean real trouble for Smitty." He watched the fire for a few moments before he spoke again. "Did you set the fire on purpose?" he asked. Smitty just looked at him. Shay nodded his head. "I thought so."

Suddenly shouting erupted and soldiers rushed from the building. Seconds later the roof collapsed in a shower of sparks, and flames devoured it. Grayson looked at Smitty in the flare of orange light. "What happened to your head?" he asked. Smitty put a hand up to the purplish knot that protruded through the short hair above his right ear. The lump hurt. So did everything else. "I mouthed off to the guard, and he took a swat at me," Smitty replied.

Grayson reached out and took hold of Smitty's head for a closer look, then quickly withdrew his hand. "The back of your head is cut open," he said, looking at the drying blood on his fingers.

"Yeah, I think his fist came out that side," Smitty said. He tried to laugh, but it didn't come off.

"Come on back to the barracks, and I'll try to clean that up for you," Grayson offered. They walked back slowly. The concrete floor hurt the bruised muscles where the guard had kicked him, but Smitty was grateful for the chance to lie down. A wet cloth eased the throbbing in his head, and the whistling sound gradually subsided. As Smitty sketched for him what had taken place, Grayson cleaned the caked blood and dirt from the back of Smitty's scalp. "What do you think might happen now?" Grayson asked.

"Who knows? The Japs aren't going to be too happy about losing that crummy bathtub. I guess if they have a firing squad, I'll probably be out in front of it tomorrow."

Grayson smiled. "I doubt if it will be that bad. But they might decide to give you some kind of punishment."

"What the hell kind of punishment could be worse than having to work with that crazy guard? That bastard's like a yellow King Kong in uniform," said Smitty. Fatigue finally overcame the dull pain and strain of jangled nerves, and Smitty talked himself to sleep.

Limping to the mess hall in the morning, Smitty looked at the pile of ashes that had been the bathhouse. The two charred faucets jutted out over the debris from water pipes; the stove lay on its side, partly covered by pieces of blackened timbers from the roof. "Nice job, Smitty," Matthias complimented. "Wanna try for the Jap barracks tonight?"

Smitty smiled but he was in no mood for joking. They went inside the mess hall and took their rice to the far end of a long dining table. Smitty had missed his meal the night before and realized for the first time how hungry he was when steam from the rice reached his nostrils. He finished quickly, ahead of the others. Grayson offered him his own ration, but Smitty declined.

When they were done, they walked slowly back to the barrack. No one said a word, but Smitty knew they were all worrying about what had happened the night before. Smitty sat on his blanket and began rubbing the back of his neck where the headache seemed to originate. The whistling sound, at least, had disappeared overnight, but he ached all over and his arms and legs were stiff.

Smitty was the first to see the guard come through the door. His heart thumped out a fast warning, and the throbbing hurt his head. The soldier stopped in front of the prisoners, some of them sprawled on the floor, others lounging against the wall, and motioned them outside. "Cut wood. Cut wood," he said, walking to the back of the room.

As the prisoners left the barrack, a surge of relief flushed the worry from Smitty's mind. The guard hadn't singled out anyone for punishment. It was just another work detail, and he was included. Even with his aching muscles, it was a welcome assignment. He winced as he raised himself off the floor and headed outside.

Busy with his thoughts, Smitty didn't notice the guard's outstretched arm until the hand against his chest jolted him to a stop. The soldier shook his head no and gently pushed Smitty back inside. Next he took Grayson and Matthias by the arm and shoved them toward the back of the room with Smitty, paying no attention to the surprised look on their faces. Then he left with the others.

"Now what the hell. . . ." Matthias wondered aloud, as he watched the guard disappear through the door.

"I should have known that was too good," Smitty said bitterly. He would have welcomed the opportunity to cut wood with the others, no matter how much it would hurt. "This'll probably be the end of me."

"Yeah, but why would they want all three of us?" Matthias asked.

"They probably need two pallbearers," answered Smitty.

"I wonder if they found out I pissed in their bathtub?" frowned Matthias. Smitty just looked at him, but Grayson laughed.

"Well who knows, they mighta," Matthias said defensively. "Hell if you two guys are gonna be in trouble, I wanna go too. They could have a damned rough time with the three of us."

"It's okay, Matthias," Smitty shut him off. "Forget it."

About a half hour later an officer entered. He walked directly to the small cabinet at the far side of their living area. He tugged open the door and pulled out towels, mess kits, razors, several Bibles, and some clothing. He dropped them on the floor, then spread them out with the toe of his shoe to get a better look.

The prisoners watched him—puzzled. He couldn't have wanted anything of theirs; there was nothing of any real value. Finished with his examination, the officer grunted and looked at the prisoners. "Pack your things," he instructed them with an irritated wave of his hand. The startled prisoners hesitated. "Pack your things!" This time his voice had more authority.

He watched them scramble about on their hands and knees, picking up their belongings and wrapping them hurriedly in a towel or an old shirt or whatever they could collect. Smitty had managed to hold on to his small cloth bag; it took him but a minute to scrape everything inside.

When they were finished, Grayson began putting the other items back inside the cabinet. The officer reached down and pushed him away, almost knocking him over. Grayson looked up in surprise. The officer shook his head no. "Wait," he instructed them and walked out of the building.

As soon as he was gone Matthias spoke. "My God, I bet they're going to shoot all three of us."

"I'd hardly think so," said Grayson. "They wouldn't bother having us pack our things if they were going to do that."

"Yeah? Trouble is you're too damned easy going," said Matthias excitedly. "You don't know what they might do. But damned if they're gonna shoot me without a helluva fight. Now listen, I got an idea. Most of the Japs already left for the day, see, so when we go outside we jump the others. There aren't too many—"

"Revere, you know we can't do that," Grayson broke in. "They'd shoot us before we could get anywhere near them."

"Okay, I got a better idea. Soon as that Jap comes back inside, I'm gonna jump him. I can get his gun away and we'll use him for a . . . you know . . . a . . . uh . . ."

"A hostage?"

"Yeah. We'll put that gun right at his dumb, freakin' head and march right out of here. No, we'll get a truck and take him along. We can head for the mountains or the jungle. They won't do nothin' long as we got the Jap with us," he looked at Smitty. "Only this time we ain't comin' back."

Smitty protested: "Matthias, you're nuts. You can't—"

"The hell I can't. Just watch."

He walked to the door and stood just inside, out of sight of anyone who would enter. "You guys don't need to help. Just stay there so whoever comes in will see you and won't look back here at me."

"Aw hell, Matthias . . . " A sound outside interrupted Smitty.

"Shut up!" Matthias commanded and flattened himself against the wall. Smitty and Grayson stood helplessly in the middle of the large room, not wanting to see anyone enter. The figure barely cleared the doorway when Matthias sprang. They thudded on the floor, with Matthias on top.

There was a scream. "Stop it! For God's sake, stop it!" Matthias jumped to his feet and looked down on the floor at Wells.

"What are you doin' here?" Matthias asked awkwardly.

Wells looked up. Blood smeared under his nose where his face had struck the concrete floor. "What am I doing here?" countered Wells. "What the hell are you doing here, ya stupid ape?" Matthias reached down hesitantly to help him up.

Wells shook him off. "Get the hell away from me!" He got to his feet. He was breathing hard from fright and his voice was hoarse. "What are you tryin' to do, kill me?" he asked, looking at Smitty and Grayson, who still stood rooted to the middle of the floor. "What's the matter with this nut?"

His question broke the spell and Grayson hurried over to Wells. "We tried to talk him out of it," Grayson explained, "but he wanted to jump the officer and use him as a hostage to get free. He wouldn't listen to us."

"Let him go ahead," Wells said, "And I hope they shoot him."

Matthias collected himself and fumbled clumsily with his hands in an effort to apologize. "Geez, I'm sorry, honest. But listen, now that you're here, I know we can make it. All you have to do—"

"Nuts! With a capital K!" Wells shouted back at Matthias.

Grayson was shaking Matthias by the shoulder.

"Come on," Matthias pleaded. "It's gonna be easy."

"Revere!" Grayson shook him harder. Matthias stopped talking and looked at him. "What?"

"You can forget the whole thing now."

"Why, I'm tellin' ya—"

"Look behind you."

Matthias spun around toward the doorway. "Son of a bitch," he hissed after his vanishing scheme. Three guards had their rifles pointed at the prisoners, and the officer standing in the middle looked annoyed. "We go now," he growled.

CHAPTER 9

"I just don't understand why you would tell that officer we were sent here as truck drivers," Grayson said. He looked with disapproval at Smitty, who was stretched out on one of the four bare, filthy cots that filled the small thatch hut to which they had been assigned. "You should have said something to us first."

"Look," Smitty's voice was full of assurance as he pulled himself up on the edge of the cot, "you have to admit that when we left Quezon City you thought we were gonna have our heads chopped off, too, right?"

He spread his hands and shrugged. "So, I got an idea when I saw they were bringing us back here to O'Donnell, and we would wind up with a good deal. Now what are you mad about?"

"Smitty, I'm not mad. It's just that I can't drive a truck," he said. "What happens in the morning when they tell me to take one of the trucks somewhere?"

Smitty walked over to Grayson, flopped down and slung an arm around his shoulder. "Come on, Vince, now don't worry, huh? Matthias here can teach you how to drive. It's no sweat, right Matthias?" There was no reply. "Hey, can't you answer?" Smitty called, squinting into the evening gloom toward Matthias, who was leaning out the window on the opposite side of the room.

"Hold it down," Matthias urged, waving his hand behind him for silence. "I'm watchin' something."

Smitty hurried over and crowded in beside him at the oblong opening in the grass wall. "What's going on?" Their hut was the last one at the edge of Camp O'Donnell. A stretch of bare, rock-hard ground separated them from the fence fifty yards away through which a side gate led to the area where the trucks were kept. To the rear was a small grove of coconut trees, rising out of a hollow where the wire fence meshed together to form a corner of the prison.

"Over in them trees there. See?" Matthias said as he pointed to a path for Smitty's eyes to follow in the twilight. Smitty could make out four— no, six—figures. They were bowing toward the trees.

"What are they doing?" Smitty asked, not noticing when there was no reply. "Hey, it looks like they're putting something down on the ground." The figures bowed again, then melted into a single shapeless shadow as they walked back together in the direction of the hut. Smitty and Matthias stepped back from the window and watched until they passed. It was a detail of guards.

Smitty waited a few moments, then poked his head out to make certain they had gone. "Wonder what that was all about? I know damned well they left something out there."

Matthias shrugged. "Let's go see."

Grayson, who had remained on his cot, rose quickly and intercepted them at the doorway. "Now look here, you guys, we just got out of one scrape. Don't go looking for more trouble," he said. He put a hand on Matthias's shoulder and added: "You know we're not supposed to go outside after dark." Matthias pulled away and ducked through the doorway.

"It's okay, Vince, we're not going to get caught," Smitty assured him. "Come on, go along," he tossed the invitation back over his shoulder as he followed after Matthias. When Smitty looked back again, Grayson, with a skeptical shake of the head, was following them.

Outside, the last patch of twilight spread into night, as a pumpkin-colored moon silhouetted the roofs of the prison barracks behind them. Matthias listened, then whispered, "I don't hear nothin'. Come on." He headed across the open ground for the grove of trees. The earth was silent beneath their bare feet until Smitty crunched down on a dried palm frond at the end of the clearing.

"Holy hell, keep it quiet!" Matthias hissed, stopping so suddenly that Smitty and Grayson, following in tandem, collided with him. "Watch where you're goin'!" he growled, pushing them away. "What's the matter with you guys? Can't you see?"

"No," Smitty replied. "Can you?"

Matthias had a way of never acknowledging his own blunders. "Now they were right over in here," he said, starting into the grove.

Smitty and Grayson stayed well behind him. They had gone only about ten yards when Matthias called back a warning: "There's some kind of lumps in the ground here. Look out you don't fall over 'em."

Smitty plunged ahead in the darkness until he felt a sudden, small rise beneath his foot. Another step and he almost tumbled off the other side. Stooping down, he groped with his hands until he felt the mound of earth, about three feet wide and a foot high.

"Holy hell!" Matthias's voice bellowed out just ahead.

Smitty leaped to his feet. "What's the matter?" he called anxiously.

"Son of a bitch!"

Smitty scrambled toward him in the darkness. "Matthias! What did you do?" Smitty reached out and grabbed Matthias by the arm. "Don't come any closer! Stay there! I think I stepped in a latrine. Son of a bitch!" Matthias pawed furiously at the ground to wipe his bare foot.

"There aren't any latrines out here," Smitty said. "Besides, you could smell them if there were." He let go of Matthias and dropped to his knees. The moon's orange blush was dissolving into pale silver as it climbed higher above the camp; by its dim light Smitty could make out a round shape on the ground at the end of one of the mounds. He bent closer, running his fingers along the edge of the object, then quickly plunged his hand into the center of it.

"Oh man, this is better than gold," he said, jumping up holding what appeared to be a large pan. "Look what you stepped in. It's rice!" He held the pan up so that its contents showed faintly white against the moon.

"Holy hell!" Matthias said. "Now why would anyone wanna put rice out here? Hey," he interrupted himself, "I bet those Japs stole it and hid it here, then they're gonna come back later and get it."

"No, I think I know why," said Grayson, who was busy examining the little knoll where the pan of rice had been found. "These mounds must be graves of Japanese soldiers, and the rice was put here as an offering to their spirits."

"Oh my God," Matthias said softly, a shiver running through his voice, "a graveyard."

"What's the matter?" Smitty teased. "You afraid?"

"Naw, I guess not," Matthias replied. "Hell, they're only Japs."

By this time, six of the mounds were visible in the moonlight, and Grayson was walking among them, probing about with his hands. "They're graves all right," he announced. "There's some kind of board at the head of each one, and they've put bowls of rice at the other end."

"Well, come on," Smitty invited, "let's eat." He was about to dump the rice that he held when Matthias made a grab at the bowl.

"What the hell ya doin'?" he demanded. "Gimme that."

"You don't want it," Smitty answered, still clutching the bowl. "This is the one you stepped in, remember?"

"The hell I don't," Matthias snapped, yanking it away from Smitty. Plopping down astride one of the graves, he began shoveling the rice in his mouth with his fingers.

Grayson picked up one of the broad leaves scattered about on the ground and began rolling the rice inside it. "Listen," he said, "we can't stay here, we'll get caught. Wrap it up like this, and we'll take it back with us."

The light from the moon made the job easier as Smitty and Grayson gathered up the bowls hurriedly, careful to replace each one where it had been. Getting up, Matthias took two of the pods the others had rolled, wiped his mouth on the back of his hand and led the way back to the hut. Not a grain of rice was spilled.

The absence of light was no drawback to the hungry prisoners. They spread out their prizes on the floor and divided them up. "You already had one out there in the cemetery, Matthias, so you only get one more," Smitty decreed, sliding a gummy leaf-platter toward him. "Vince and I divvy up the other four."

"Come on now, that ain't fair," Matthias argued. "Hell, half that stuff stuck to my foot when I stepped in it. Besides, a little runt like you don't need as much."

Smitty already had split up the rest of the rice and, ignoring the complaints, fished his spoon from his belongings and began to wolf down the gooey mound he had hoisted onto his lap. When no one paid any attention to his grumbling, Matthias unfurled his leaf, picked it up at both ends watermelon-style and buried his face in it. "Hmmmmmmmm, that's not too bad," he said, gulping down the remains of a giant mouthful. "But you know, it tastes better if ya' step in it first."

Grayson sat quietly on his cot during the exchange, eating slowly, almost daintily. He was starting his second helping as the other two finished. Smitty used the edge of his spoon to scrape the leaf of its last particles of rice, while Matthias licked his clean.

"Holy hell, Smitty," Matthias goaded him, "talk about me, you hogged down two of them things in the same time I ate one. You're gonna' have a lump in your belly like a pregnant goat." Smitty didn't answer. He lay back on his cot and hoped a burp would loose itself to ease the gurgling inside his stomach. It felt like bubbles boiling up and bursting in a hot tar pot. •

Matthias had switched his attention to the other prisoner. "See, Grayson, you stick with me and Smitty and we'll getch'ya through this damned war."

Grayson chuckled, "I don't think I'll be going anywhere for a while. Besides, anyone who can come up with this much food in the middle of a Japanese prison camp is worth sticking with."

"Yeah. Now what we need is a big slug a' beer," Matthias fancied. "You know, to kinda swish all that rice around inside. Geez, I can just feel it—"

"Hey, Matthias, knock it off will you?" Smitty called weakly from his dark corner.

"Aw come on, Smitty, you can sleep later," replied Matthias. "Hell, tonight we're celebrating." He leaned in Smitty's direction. "Hey, you got any rice left you don't want?" There was no reply. "Hey, Smitty," he persisted, reaching across to him. "Wake up!" He shook the still form roughly. "You got any rice—"

"Don't!" shouted Smitty suddenly, and he leaped up and ran across the room, bumping cots out of his path. He lowered his head out the window and vomited his rice.

"Geez, I'm sorry, Smitty," Matthias apologized. "I didn't know you were sick."

Grayson helped him back to his bed. "You'd better lie down and try to get to sleep. You'll feel better in the morning." "Oh God," Smitty groaned. "My stomach feels like it's all pasted together." Matthias and Grayson sat silently, until they were certain from Smitty's even breathing that he was asleep. Matthias spent the rest of the evening explaining truck driving to Grayson.

CHAPTER 10

Smitty awoke in the morning sticky and wet with perspiration. He remained motionless with his head in his hands for a few minutes, listening to Matthias snore as he waited for the dizziness to subside. Unnoticed, a guard suddenly banged a rifle butt on the floor inside the doorway, rousing the prisoners. Smitty bolted upright, then sank back on the edge of his bed again as new waves of sickness swelled and tossed inside him.

Yawning loudly, Matthias stood up, stretched, then looked down at Smitty through a sleepy mist. "Come on," he urged, "get up. You'll be better when you get some hot rice in your belly."

"Rice," moaned Smitty feebly, as he lay down again.

"You know you can't stay here," Grayson reminded him. "And they won't let you report in sick with just an upset stomach." He waited for a reaction from Smitty, but there was none. "Come on, you might as well go along with us to the mess hall. Matthias can eat your rice, and maybe you'll feel better when you're up and around for a while."

As Smitty walked unsteadily to the mess hall, the ground seemed to slope away from him like the floor of a fun house. He sat down between Matthias and Grayson, but the odors and the sight of the rice gave him a muddy feeling in his stomach. He had to turn his eyes away as Matthias finished his own rice and began bolting down Smitty's serving. All he wanted was to get out of there. Matthias scratched at the bowl with his spoon to get the last remnants from along the sides.

"Come on," Smitty pleaded, "I can't take any more of this place."

Matthias hung back for one more scrape and a lick at his spoon, then hurried to catch up to Smitty and Grayson, who already were walking toward the door. Smitty felt better as soon as he stepped outside in the bright sunlight. They walked to the side gate, which was opened by a guard who accompanied them to the trucks.

Matthias headed straight for the nearest one. He opened the door on the driver's side and called to Grayson. "Climb in behind the wheel and I'll show you how to jockey one of these things," he said. Grayson looked at the guard, who was not paying attention. He got in as Matthias began his instructions, "Now, remember the stuff I told you last night? And always double-clutch, remember? Once to get it outta' gear and then you do it again before you push it into another one. Okay?" Grayson tried it several times, gingerly at first, then more firmly as he gained confidence.

Smitty stood on the running board beside Matthias. His assurance of the night before suffered with his queasy stomach. He was beginning to have doubts about the whole business. Watching Grayson slip through the gears, pumping the clutch, he felt a pang of regret for the trouble he was getting his companion into. And another thought disturbed him: He didn't know much more about driving a truck than Grayson did.

The noisy approach of three soldiers through the gate broke up the driving lesson. The prisoners climbed down from the truck and stood by watching. The soldiers were in good humor, laughing loudly and slapping one another on the back. They stopped at the line of trucks, exchanged a few remarks, then each one headed for a different vehicle, still chortling. A young soldier, his uniform smartly pressed and his cap listing jauntily, walked to the first truck, tossed an order back in their direction, and motioned for a driver.

"You'd better go first," Smitty told Matthias. "You're the best driver."

"Yeah, okay," Matthias said looking at Grayson. "Don't forget now—double-clutch, got it? Double-clutch." As he turned to leave, he slapped Smitty with an open hand. "That goes for you too, buddy."

Smitty's stomach tilted sideways with a sickening lurch. He swallowed down his gorge. "Big dumb bastard!" he muttered after Matthias. It made him feel a little better. Matthias had opened the door of the lead truck, and Grayson already was seated in the next one. Smitty began walking toward the end of the line where a scrubby soldier, as short as Smitty and just as thin, stood waiting. Smitty got in and started the engine as the Japanese man crawled up beside him on the seat.

The motor sputtered, then eased into a steady throb as Smitty watched Matthias pull out toward the road. A blue cloud of exhaust burst from the truck ahead of him. As he waited, he could hear its motor racing above the clatter of his own engine, but Grayson's truck remained motionless. The little soldier beside him reached across Smitty and sounded the horn impatiently.

Smitty didn't like the look of annoyance on the face of the guard seated to his right. "I'll go give him a hand," he offered, pointing to himself and then to the other vehicle. When there was no sign of objection, Smitty climbed out and ran to the side of Grayson's truck. Grayson was white with desperation as the guard beside him cursed in his ear. The engine roared, coughed, and threatened to wind down, then came to life again as the clutch luckily caught. Grayson stroked the gear back into neutral with a grinding noise and opened the door. "Smitty, I don't know what's the matter with this thing. It just won't go," he said.

"Do you have it in gear?" Smitty asked, ignoring the guard's oaths.

"Yes, I had it in low. Look." He pressed the clutch in once more and lodged the stick into position. As he let the clutch out, the motor whined again, then died before he could catch it. "See? I can't make it move!" His voice trembled with agitation.

Smitty jumped on the running board and looked inside. He reached a hand in beneath Grayson's legs. "Here, you forgot to take off the brake," he said, releasing it. "You'd better get going."

Grayson grimaced. "Lord," he moaned, as the guard swore at him again, then settled back against the seat. Grayson kicked the starter and the engine came back to life. "Thanks, Smitty," Grayson said. "I'll remember next time."

Smitty entered his own truck and looked at the guard, sitting impassively. Together they watched the truck ahead of them bump and jerk over the grassy field toward the road, where Matthias and his passenger were waiting.

The sight calmed Smitty's stomach for the moment. Keeping his eyes on the truck and praying that Grayson would do nothing else wrong, Smitty slammed his own rig into gear and hit the accelerator. The truck lunged into motion—reverse motion. The guard's head made a clanking sound as it hit the dashboard; he grabbed at the panel with both hands to keep from falling off the seat.

"Oh my God!" The words rasped across Smitty's dry throat. (A picture of Matthias backing into the loading dock flashed through his mind.) He reached out to help the guard, then pulled back as the soldier's head jerked off the instrument panel. The startled soldier ignored Smitty, straightened himself, and folded his arms with newfound dignity.

Smitty, awestruck, eyed the scarlet lump ballooning over his passenger's left eyebrow. A curt nod of the guard's head unfroze Smitty's mind. Reluctantly, he turned his gaze away from the soldier's face, started the stalled truck and pursued Matthias and Grayson.

As the small convoy headed for Manila, Smitty worked up the nerve to glance over at his seatmate. The guard smiled from under the knot that was turning the color of a purple plum. The smile unnerved Smitty. No Japanese had smiled at him since the amiable guard Tyrone haphazardly watched over the radio repair work at Quezon City.

CHAPTER 11

As the truck rolled to a stop in Capas, Smitty saw the women right away, seven of them. They were sitting on the steps leading up to the thatch house, the only building on the short, dead-end street. Lounging against the rickety, wooden hand railing that hemmed in the set of steps, they reminded Smitty of dolls arranged haphazardly on shelves. He nosed his truck in behind the other two trucks as they slowed to a stop. The girls stood in greeting, their scarlet smiles revealing white teeth.

The guard was out of the truck before it stopped rolling, leaving his rifle propped against the dashboard. Without taking his eyes off the girls, Smitty reached down and yanked on the emergency brake, forgetting the ache in his arms from loading the trucks with rice back at Manila.

The women, in their early twenties, were Filipino prostitutes. It was a perfect set-up, Smitty figured, living here in Capas—they could be near the Japanese soldiers stationed at O'Donnell. Their faded, loose-fitting dresses, magnified the blaze of rouge and lipstick. None of them was very pretty, Smitty decided.

Laughing and taunting the soldiers, the girls bunched up at the foot of the steps while they haggled with the Japanese over price. Smitty's roving gaze stopped on a girl who stood with her back to him. The broad curve of her hip jutted out to support a small brown hand. One leg was thrust in front of her, stretching the lower half of her garment taut across the back to clearly define the roundness of her behind.

A shiver rippled down his spine, as the guard, who had ridden with him, moved over to the girl. Smitty stewed. He wanted to look away, but he couldn't.

The guard smiled, and Smitty hated him and that damned plum that stuck out on his forehead. Smitty overheated. "How the hell could they have anything to do with the Japanese?" he wondered. "Bitches!"

The girl stood slightly back from the others, her face turned away from the jealous American watching through the smeared truck windshield. She wasn't bad to look at, Smitty suddenly admitted to himself. Without the paint, she could be quite attractive.

Matthias's tall frame loomed up unexpectedly to block his view before Smitty even realized he had left his truck. The greeting Matthias received was genuine. The girls, taken by his size and dark, good looks, pressed around him, giggling and chattering admiringly. Smitty had an uneasy feeling that Matthias should have remained in the truck. Draping his arms in a sweeping embrace of the four girls who remained outside, Matthias cocked his head to look back over his shoulder toward Smitty. With a wide grin, he nodded for Smitty to join him.

Smitty wanted to get away—he loathed the idea of any woman offering herself to the Japanese. Then he saw her again. She was looking right at him, smiling. Flecks of blue indigo glinted against the sunlight in the straight, black hair that fell across her shoulders. Her nose, too small for the rest of her broad face, hinted at a delicateness that found no continuity in the rest of her features.

"Come on," Matthias called to him. "We ain't gonna be here forever!"

A flush of annoyance, or embarrassment—Smitty wasn't sure which—stirred inside him as he opened the door of the truck and climbed out. He walked slowly toward Matthias and the girls. "Hey, Smitty," Matthias gushed, "I want ya to meet some friends of mine." He stepped a pace away from the girls, surveying them admiringly. "These here little gals just naturally took a shine to old Revere, and any friends of mine are friends of theirs."

Smitty looked at the girls close-up. How many Japanese had the women bedded in the months since the invasion? "I think we ought to get back in the trucks," he advised, looking only at Matthias. "If those Japs catch us out here, there'll be hell to pay."

Matthias brushed away the warning with a wave of his arm. "Naw, we just got here. Now, don't worry, huh?" He drew one of the girls to his side. She giggled, opening cracks in her cosmetic mask, as she removed Matthias's hand from her behind and pulled it up around her waist.

"See," Matthias said smugly, "Now how can I just up and leave when they're dependin' on me?"

"For what?" asked Smitty wryly.

"Now you just go over there and get Grayson and I'll show you. This here's our war too, and we're gonna win a piece of it right now from the Japs."

Smitty stared at him in amazement. "You mean that you're going to. . . . You're crazy as hell."

"Yeah, so were Adam and Eve, but if it wasn't for them, you wouldn't be here. Now go on, go get Grayson." He dismissed Smitty as he turned his attention back to the girls.

Smitty snorted in disgust and stalked off toward the truck. Grayson slumped behind the wheel, his eyes gravely studying Smitty's face as he approached. "You'd better come on over with us, Vince," Smitty said through the open window. "I think we're safe for a little while yet."

Grayson didn't move. "I'd rather not, Smitty. You go ahead; I'll wait here."

Smitty's voice grew agitated. "Look, that crazy Matthias is all humped up like a bull and we gotta get him away from there. Now, come on!"

Grayson opened the door and dangled his long legs out onto the running board. "I'm sorry, Smitty. I thought maybe you. . . . Well, anyway, I'm sorry."

"Yeah, okay, but come on." Smitty was irritated, but it was mostly with himself.

Matthias greeted them with a big smile as they approached. "Listen," he began. "Me and her are goin' over in the truck for a while." He winked. "You guys go ahead and do whatever you want to, but give me a whistle if ya see any of them Japs come out, you hear?"

Smitty's impatience churned into exasperation. "Matthias, you're nuts! Hell, the. . . . " His voice trailed off as he looked in astonishment at the transformation in the girl's expression. No longer smiling, she pulled free from Matthias, her eyes filled with horror. Her pinched and haggard face looked as though she had been sick for a long time.

"Americans very fine. We love Americans, hate Japanese." Perplexed, Smitty looked at the other girls. They weren't smiling either. "We cannot make love to you," she continued.

"Aw, come on, don't let that bother you," Matthias said, grabbing for her again. His smile couldn't hide his confusion.

"Shut up, will ya' Matthias, and let her talk," Smitty snapped. He looked at the girl who had just spoken. "How come if you hate the Japs, you . . . well . . . take them in there?" he blustered, nodding toward the house.

"We fight the Japanese only way we can," she said. Smitty saw a flicker of anger in her eyes. "Japanese kill many in our families—our mothers and fathers, our brothers. Doris," she continued, placing her hand on the arm of the girl who had caused Smitty his dilemma, "her husband die fighting Japanese."

Smitty looked at the girl again, this time just at her face. She was married; she was widowed. The other feelings inside him evaporated, replaced momentarily by sympathy, but that sentiment quickly disappeared, too. "Well look . . . if . . . uh . . ." Smitty groped for the words. "Dammit, I just don't get it," he blurted, lifting his palms up in bewilderment. "Why would you have anything like this to do with the Japs then?"

"I tell you, this how we fight Japanese," she said, looking Smitty directly in the eye. "We have gonorrhea."

The group fell silent as a muted grunt from inside the house punctuated her announcement. "Holy Jesus!" Matthias's voice broke on the words. His tanned face was several shades paler. Smitty looked at Doris. She had turned her back and stood staring into the grove of trees behind the house.

"You shouldn't feel sorry," the girl resumed. She smiled at them vivaciously. "We keep Japanese soldiers on the run."

No one laughed. Grayson alone showed composure as he walked closer. "Wouldn't you be better off running away some place, losing yourselves in one of the bigger cities? Anything to get away from this?"

"No, we do what we want to do. Soldiers can get shot for having disease. We give it to them."

Smitty was dumbfounded. Where was the warmth and tenderness that in his mind had always been the mark of a woman?

Grayson spoke again, but it was a helpless gesture: "I wish there were something we could do—"

"No," she interrupted him. "We do something for you." She turned to one of the other girls and spoke in an island dialect. The prisoners watched the girl disappear into the trees and brush at the rear of the house. Within moments, she reappeared, her hands hiding something behind her back. When she was sure the Japanese still were inside, she hurried forward and thrust a small, white cloth sack toward the prisoners.

"You take it," she instructed Smitty. "Maybe you can use it."

Smitty opened the bag. Inside were small boxes of aspirin, jars of guava jelly, and several sticks of sugarcane. He looked up questioningly.

"We get things from Japanese," the girl said. "You keep these, but don't let Japanese see them. We have more. We use them for people of village. Many children get hungry, sick. Now go before Japanese come back."

Smitty handed the sack to Matthias. "Here, hide 'em in the truck someplace until we get back to O'Donnell." As Matthias hurried off, Smitty turned back to the girls and said: "Thanks, and . . . uh . . . good luck." He was embarrassed by the inadequacy of his remark. Grayson shook hands with the girls, but said nothing, then turned and walked back to the truck.

Matthias returned from his errand and pushed into the midst of the girls. "I put 'em under the seat," he told Smitty. "We can get 'em out while they're unloadin' the trucks." He put his huge arms around two of the girls and squeezed. "I'll be back honey," he addressed both of them with high confidence. He gave each of them a pat and headed back to the trucks. "Come on, Smitty," he called. "Let's get goin'."

Smitty glanced at Doris, who was standing nearest him. "God bless you," she said. Smitty no longer saw a face splashed with vivid color. All he saw were her eyes and the warmth and tenderness in them.

CHAPTER 12

The makeshift hospital was filled. Arms and legs hung out of every narrow bunk; Smitty and Matthias had to pick their way around the overflow of patients who had been assigned to open spaces on the floor. Not as many prisoners were dying as when Smitty had been here before, but still there was a lot of dengue fever, pellagra, severe dysentery, malaria, and beriberi. "Where's the doc?" Smitty asked a medic bent over one of the patient's bunks.

"Dunno," the medic answered blankly. "You'll have to look around." Smitty moved on through the rows of bunks toward the back of the converted barracks. Flies buzzed, and the air stank of sweat, excrement, and urine.

"Sure don't smell much like a hospital," Matthias observed.

"Well, what are you gonna do without medicine or enough help?" Smitty retorted.

At the back of the room Smitty swung around a corner and came upon a tall, lean man crouched over a bunk, his sparse black hair pasted fast to his balding head by perspiration. A stethoscope stretched from his ears to the chest of a bloated beriberi victim. "You the doctor?" Smitty asked.

"Yes, but you'll have to wait," the man answered without looking up. Smitty glanced down at the patient. His naked body was horribly puffed up, and his contoured face was the color of a turnip. As Smitty and Matthias watched, the doctor switched the position of the stethoscope several times. Finally, the doctor stood up and removed the stethoscope from his ears. "He's dead," he announced matter-of-factly. He looked at the two prisoners. "Now which one of you is sick, or are you both?"

"Oh, we're not sick, Doc," Smitty explained. "See, we're truck drivers here, and, well . . . we got some stuff we thought you might use here at the hospital."

"Yes, I'll bet you do," said the doctor testily. "Well, what is it?"

"Well," Smitty began, "we have a whole bunch of guava jelly and some aspirin." He reached under the waistband of his ragged trousers and pulled out the sugarcane. "And we thought some of the guys here could chew on this sugarcane. I know you don't get any sugar."

The doctor's eyes narrowed, tightening the wrinkles on his high forehead, as he studied their faces. Smitty began to feel uncomfortable. "Okay," the doctor asked. "How much do you want?"

"Huh?" Matthias broke the awkward silence.

"Look, I'm busy as hell here," the doctor complained. "Now if you'll just tell me how much you want, we can get this done with."

Smitty was the first to overcome his shock. "We don't want anything—we're trying to give it to you." Anger began to push aside his surprise. "Holy hell. We're Americans too, you know. You don't think we're gonna try to sell the stuff to you for these guys when they're sick, do you?"

The doctor squinted at them again, this time quizzically. "You mean you want to just give us these things—no deals, no whiskey, no cigarettes?"

"Yeah, yeah, that's what we've been saying," Smitty simmered. "We picked them up yesterday."

"Yeh," Matthias cut in, "these here girls—"

"We got them from some Filipinos," Smitty interrupted him. "We have twenty jars of guava jelly and about a dozen tins of aspirin. If you need them, you can have them."

"We have aspirin, but I suppose we can always use more," the doctor replied. The harshness was gone from his voice. His face, lined with fatigue, softened as he spoke. He was about fifty, Smitty figured, and would look pretty imposing dressed in a white uniform and seated behind the desk in a physician's office. "The guava jelly, though, would be quite helpful," the doctor continued, "both for the diet and the morale."

"Okay, we'll bring it up to you this afternoon," Smitty said. "Matthias here has the aspirin. Where do you want it?"

"Over here," the doctor said, walking toward the far side of the room where an old cabinet stood upright in the corner. He stopped in front of it. "Listen," he said gently, "I'm sorry that I was rough on you. We've had a steady stream of truck drivers in here. It seems they have access to all sorts of things, but most of them want to be paid or make trades— cigarettes, medicinal alcohol, all sorts of things." His mouth folded at the corners in a dry grin. "I'm sorry I misjudged you two."

"That's okay, sir," Smitty said. "And if we get anything else we think you can use, we'll bring it to you."

Matthias pulled ten of the small tins of aspirin from beneath his shirt and laid them on the tabletop that fronted the wooden medicine cabinet. In the middle of the tabletop lay two small, white pills in the lid from a glass medicine container. Matthias picked them up. "Here's a couple of pills layin' out, Doc. They look like aspirin too."

The doctor frowned as he took them from Matthias. "Damn! I keep telling these medics not to leave medicine lying around. But they get busy, and half of them are as sick as the patients we're treating, and they just forget."

He started to put the pills back in the container, then held them out for Smitty and Matthias to examine. "See these? That little ridge running through the center? They're sulfa, the most precious medicine we have, and there's damned little of it. I doubt that you'll ever run across any, but if you do, grab it up. We need it desperately."

"Sure thing, sir," Smitty responded. "Well, we have to go. We'll bring in the jelly later." The doctor accompanied them toward the front of the hospital. Smitty saw the shadow on the floor before he saw the Japanese soldier who made it.

"Uh oh," the doctor muttered as the soldier came through the doorway, "I think I know what he wants. Stay here with me until I get rid of him."

The soldier approached to within a few feet of them and stopped. The frozen features of his sullen face and the cold arrogance in his eyes were clear indications of his contempt for the Americans. "Kusuri to tchiusha agette kudasai," he ordered.

"I can't give you sulfa pills and injections," the doctor replied, shaking his head firmly.

"Chimpu byocki," the Japanese snapped.

The doctor looked at Smitty and Matthias. "He says he has gonorrhea."

He turned to the soldier and shook his head again. "No, I can't give you any. See your own doctors."

The soldier growled out his demands louder than before. Patients disturbed by the noise turned restlessly in their bunks. Rebuffed, the soldier spat on the floor and walked out. The doctor sighed. "They aren't supposed to come in here, but the Japanese army code is strict as hell about venereal disease. If they're caught, they're sent to prison and broken in rank. Sometimes, they're beaten."

"Yeah, well, we'll be seeing you later, Doc," Smitty said, heading for the door.

"What the hell's the hurry?" Matthias asked, trailing Smitty out the door down the steps.

"There he goes," Smitty said, pointing to the soldier who had just left the hospital. He was several buildings away, walking with one of the guards. "We gotta catch him."

"We gotta what?"

"We have to catch that Jap. Come on before he gets out of the compound." The two prisoners chased the Japanese soldiers, the skeptical Mathias lagging behind. When the friends caught up to the pair, the man afflicted with gonorrhea glared at them contemptuously. Smitty stood his ground and bowed to the pair. "Sayonara," said Smitty, but there was no answer. "We have medicine for you," he said, smiling as he spoke.

Smitty looked at the other Japanese. "You speak English?" he asked. The soldier nodded his head yes. "Well, tell him we have the medicine, the sulfa he wants."

The guard translated for his companion, and Smitty saw a glimmer of interest in the infected soldier's eyes. After a quick consultation in Japanese, the guard turned to Smitty with a smile. "Give us," he said, stretching out his hand.

"No," Smitty said wagging his head as he in turn held out his hand. "Cigarettes."

There was another huddle in Japanese. "You have for both of us?" asked the guard, holding up two fingers.

Smitty pretended to consider it. When he answered after a few moments, he held up four fingers. "Four packs of cigarettes."

"Okay," the guard agreed. "We got cigarettes," he said, turning to his companion.

"No, wait!" Smitty cried. "Tonight, our nipa hut." He pointed to the end of the row of buildings where their hut stood off by itself. The soldier with the nasty disposition was eyeing him suspiciously. Smitty squeezed his arms tightly to his side to fight off a shudder.

"Okay," consented the guard. Smitty bowed and walked away. As soon as they were beyond range of the Japanese, Matthias began his tirade.

"Smitty, what the hell are you doin'? How the hell are you gonna' get any pills? You know the Doc ain't gonna' give ya' none. Besides, if that son of a bitch got the crud, let the bastard rot away. What do you wanna' help him for?"

"I don't," Smitty replied. "Let's go. We have to get back to help Grayson unload his truck when he gets in from Manila."

That afternoon Matthias and Grayson observed Smitty at work. In the waning light he carefully grooved the aspirin with a fork tine. When he was finished, the tiny white pill looked exactly like the sulfa tablet he had seen at the hospital.

"There you go," he announced proudly, blowing the chalky dust from the pill and holding it up for the others to see. "Guaranteed to get rid of the clap." He returned it to the aspirin tin, took out another one, and began working on it.

"Smitty, you're either a genius or a damned nut," Matthias said. "Now you wanna play doctor. Hell, I think every damned Jap here has it. When they hear you got pills, they'll be after you. Then whaddaya gonna' do?"

Smitty kept working as he spoke. "We got two boxes of aspirin we kept for ourselves. That's twenty-four pills. And now that we get out in the trucks, we can get more." He finished the second pill and put both of them under the blanket on his bunk. The aspirin tin with the remaining ten tablets was returned to its hiding place behind one of the thin, upright timbers supporting the wall of the hut.

"I hope they get here soon," Matthias grumbled. "I wanna get some of that rice in the Jap graveyard. I'm hungry as hell." Nearly an hour later the Japanese arrived. Darkness cloaked the prisoner area, but by the dim glow of the light in the hut, Smitty could tell the soldiers were drunk. One smiled; the one who had spoken to the doctor stood just inside the doorway, slightly off balance, glowering at the Americans—his face mean, his mouth curled into a snarl. "Pill," he growled in a guttural tone, holding out his hand.

Smitty extended his own hand. "Cigarettes," he demanded in return. The smiling soldier stepped forward on wobbly legs and handed two packs of cigarettes to him. Sitting up on his cot, Smitty reached behind him and removed one of the grooved aspirin from under his blanket. "Here," he offered it to the soldier, who grabbed it gleefully.

"One more," the soldier said, waiting with his hand outstretched.

"Two more packs of cigarettes," Smitty answered. The soldier shook his head. "No. More pill."

Smitty waited defiantly. The other soldier came at him with a throaty growl. A badly aimed fist grazed Smitty's shoulder; the blow spun him off his cot. "Pill!" the soldier shouted down at him. Smitty could smell the alcohol. He was scared, but he couldn't back down now. "Two more packs of cigarettes," he said, looking up at the soldier and waiting for the second blow. It never came. Muttering to himself the soldier fished about beneath his tunic until he pulled out the cigarettes. He threw them in Smitty's face and they scattered across the floor under Grayson's bunk.

Smitty sat up, reached under his blanket and took out the other aspirin. The Japanese snatched it from his hand and tossed it toward his mouth— he missed. It hit the floor and broke in two. The soldier kicked Smitty's legs out of the way and retrieved both halves of the tablet; he shoved them between his lips with his huge palm. Looking for more pills, he ripped the blanket off Smitty's bed. Finding none, he picked up the flimsy bunk, turned it upside down and shook it, looking at the floor to see if anything fell out. Angered by his futile search for more medicine, he threw the cot down on top of Smitty and made his way to the door. The other soldier, looking down at Smitty bowed. "Thank you," he said and followed his companion.

"Well, Smitty," Grayson said, "I hope that puts you out of the drug business." Smitty didn't answer. He was busy retrieving the cigarettes from under Grayson's bed. Matthias went over and righted Smitty's bunk.

"I just can't understand you, Smitty," Grayson continued. "In fact, both of you."

"I didn't have nothin' to do with this," Matthias said indignantly.

"No, not this time, but you usually do. Really, now, why do you take so many chances? This whole thing was crazy."

"Here, Vince, have a Green Death," Smitty said, offering him a cigarette. The tobacco was encased in a heavy, brown wrapper, tipped with green.

"No thanks. I don't smoke," he said.

"Well, I sure do, and I haven't had one for a couple of months. Here, have one," he instructed Matthias, pulling a cigarette from the pack and tossing it at him. Matthias dangled it between his lips, sat down on his bunk and looked at Smitty.

"Ya know it's dark outside, and we can't go out no more tonight," he said. "At least not out to the center of the camp, where the barracks are."

"So who wants to go out?" asked Smitty.

"So ya shoulda' traded another aspirin for a pack of matches," said Matthias.

Smitty stopped his arm in midair with a cigarette halfway up to his mouth. "I'll be a dirty. . . ." he said throwing the cigarette to the floor where it bounced and rolled through a crack in the uneven planks. He looked at Matthias angrily. "Why didn't you think of that before—while they were here?"

"You're the big wheeler-dealer," Matthias answered. "Why didn't you?"

Smitty didn't reply. He sank down on the corner of his bunk and stared at the pack of cigarettes lying beside him on the bed.

"Well, I'm goin' out for some of that rice before the Jap ghosts eat it all," Matthias announced, getting up. "You guys goin'?" Grayson got up to go with him.

"I'll wait," Smitty said disgustedly—without looking up.

Matthias looked back as he was going out the door. "I'll bring ya a couple of sticks to rub together." The cigarette pack bounced off the back of his head and landed somewhere in the darkness.

CHAPTER 13

L ined up, the nervous prisoners fidgeted in the heat of the early morning sun. It was probably the first time anyone had escaped O'Donnell and though Smitty was glad someone had made it, he knew the rest of them would suffer as a result. The entire prisoner population, with the exception of the hospitalized, were lined up facing the fence under the eyes of the guards.

"Wonder how long we're gonna have to stand here?" Matthias grumbled in an undertone. "I'm gettin' hungrier than hell for some breakfast. This damned heat's enough to melt the ass off the devil," he added.

Smitty didn't turn his head as he answered in a whisper, "I don't know, but you had better shut up. The Japs are mad as hell." They remained at attention for another fifteen minutes, tormented alternately by the swarms of hungry, biting flies and each new bead of perspiration that ran an itchy course down their skin. Occasionally, another prisoner, dehydrated by the fierce sun, would sag to the ground to lie unattended at the feet of the other men.

Smitty instinctively jerked his head up as a voice blared out in metallic tones from the loudspeaker atop the pole in front of them. "This is the camp commander. You have been called out this morning because one of your countrymen has escaped. When you came here, you were told that if you cooperated with us you would receive fair treatment. Now, because one man disobeyed and some of you may have helped him, there must be punishment for everyone. Beginning today, you will all be on half rations for a week."

The harsh echo of the metallic voice passed hollowly over the barracks' rooftops behind them. Matthias growled out loud this time, "He can stick his lousy rice and his loudspeaker up—"

"Also, when you arrived here you were informed that you would be put into ten-man squads and that if one man tried to escape he would endanger the lives of the other nine. Let this be a lesson to you." There was a sharp click—the squealing sound that purveyed the voice died abruptly.

Almost immediately the main gate swung open about twenty-five yards from where Smitty stood; two guards herded a group of Americans outside. Nine men carried shovels. Panic gripped Smitty as he studied their faces—none was familiar.

The prisoners stood helplessly in a huddle until prodding bayonets forced them to spread out. A guard issued an order and motioned for them to begin digging. The progress was slow as the spades scraped at the hard, dry ground. Demanding more speed, the guards hustled up and down behind the line of prisoners, jabbing at them with bayonets and rifle butts.

A soldier at the end of the line suddenly cried out as a bayonet caught him in the back of the thigh. His back arched as he clutched at his leg, blood flowing over his hands and between his fingers. He fell, shrieking, his thin body rolling back and forth in the dirt. The guard shouted at him to get up, but he couldn't. The prisoner raised one arm in an effort to protect his head, but the rifle butt smashed right past it and crushed his temple. He rolled over on his back and lay perfectly still.

"Oh my God! Oh my God!" Smitty heard Grayson whimper next to him.

A soldier from somewhere behind Smitty quickly looked toward the fence, then raised his fist at it frantically. "You dirty son of a bitch!" he screamed. "You dirty son—" the rest of the curse dried in his throat as a shot rang out and the soldier reeled backward, falling face down in the dust he had kicked up. Smitty looked away quickly as the dry earth blotted the dark stain that oozed from beneath the body. He kept his head turned as he heard the click of the guard's rifle bolt as it rammed another shell into the chamber. The scraping of the prisoners' shovels resumed.

"That lousy little yella' bastard!" Matthias ground out the words. "I'll never forget that son of a bitch. I'm gonna kill him!" His voice grated through a throat full of hate. "Someday, I'll get him, and I'll kill him with my bare hands. So help me God!"

Smitty kept his eyes fixed on the ground, not really seeing anything. He didn't look up again until the digging had stopped. Blinking to clear his vision, he saw the eight prisoners standing in front of the holes they had dug. The ninth man still lay beside the few shovelfuls of earth he had spaded before being bayoneted.

As Smitty watched, the gate opened again and seven more guards left the compound. They lined up, one behind each prisoner. Smitty's eyes ran up and down the row of American faces. One caught his attention, that of a young, blond soldier, square-shouldered and almost healthy-looking despite his imprisonment. He looked as though he should have been back home practicing with the high-school football team.

Further down the line, Smitty's gaze stopped on a shorter, older man. His bony arms and legs extended from beneath a ragged T-shirt and shorts. His balding head was raised so that his eyes stared over the compound into the endless haze of heat that simmered under the cloudless blue sky. He must have been about the same age as his father, thought Smitty, as a shudder started at the top of a deep breath and died somewhere in the emptiness inside him.

"No! Don't! You can't kill me! Please, don't!" The young, blond prisoner at the end was being forced to kneel in front of the hole he had dug. He fought hard to keep his feet against the efforts of the two guards who had seized him. Finally, one kneed him in the groin; when he fell, he stayed down.

The other seven prisoners stood submissively, resigned and waiting. He heard Grayson whimpering in a coarse voice beside him. Turning his head at a slight angle, Smitty glanced at the tall soldier. His eyes were squinted tightly shut, but his lips moved. He was praying. ". . . gently. Please, dear Father, let them die gently."

Smitty's attention was riveted on Grayson's contorted face when the rifles roared in unison. The thundering noise snapped his head forward spontaneously, in time to see the bodies falling as the Japanese lowered their weapons. Some tumbled into the freshly dug holes; the guard shoved in those that didn't with their boots. A slight breeze swirled brown dust in front of Smitty, but it couldn't blow away the sickness that filled him. The guards inside the compound remained still for a long time, allowing the lesson to sink in, then noisily began regrouping the men for the day's work details.

Smitty noticed that his hand trembled as he wiped away the sweat from his face. "I don't want nothin' to eat," Matthias announced and began walking slowly toward the far end of the camp and the gate that led to the motor pool. Smitty and Grayson followed. Most of the prisoners headed the opposite way, either to the mess hall or to work assignments that took them away from the south fence.

As they neared the truck area, Matthias, who was walking in the middle, suddenly stopped and thrust out his arms to stop the other two.

"Hey! What the hell is that?"

Smitty turned in the direction Matthias was looking. A bare, scrawny leg projected from behind a clump of scrubby brush against the fence. Grayson got there first and kicked down the weeds with his bare foot. Smitty could see it was a prisoner faceup on the ground, the fingers of his one hand clutching the lower strands of fence-wire.

Shadowy hollows ringed the closed eyes in the bony skull; the body above and below the tattered shorts was an emaciated sack of skin that meagerly covered his ribs and joints. Grayson quickly bent over the still body and pressed his ear against the man's chest. "Is he dead?" Matthias asked.

Grayson waited until he was certain, then straightened up. "I'm afraid he is." He gazed down at the dead man's face. "Wonder who he is?"

"Here come some more guys," Matthias said. "We're gonna get in trouble if the Japs catch all of us hanging around here."

"Well, we can't just go off and leave him here," Grayson said. "Stick around for a minute."

Four other prisoners whom Smitty didn't recognize pressed around them. "What happened?" one of them asked.

"We found him here," Grayson replied. "We don't know who he is."

"That looks like Old Man Hoffman," one of the newcomers said. He pushed between the others to get a better look. "Yeah," he confirmed, "that's Hoffman. He was in the barracks next to ours. He's the one the Japs thought escaped. Hell, he couldn't escape. He's been real sick for a week, out of his head with fever. Was he shot?"

"It doesn't look like it," Grayson said, examining the body again. "There don't seem to be any bullet wounds."

"If he had the fever like you said," Smitty reasoned, "then I'll bet he just wandered out here in the middle of the night and died."

"Those dirty bastards!" Matthias fumed. "They killed ten other guys then just for the hell of it."

Just then a guard approached. The Japanese was only twenty yards away, heading toward them. It was too late to leave. Keeping a short distance between himself and the prisoners, he took in the situation quickly, then waved his rifle toward them.

"Who kill?"

"No one," Grayson said, shaking his head firmly. "He just wandered out here and died. He was sick, and he died. Do you understand?"

The guard looked at Grayson suspiciously. "You kill?" he repeated.

"No, I didn't kill. I just told you he was sick. Understand? Sick. And he died. This is the man you thought escaped."

The soldier lowered his rifle and looked at the prisoners with a new apprehension. Enough of the explanation had registered to make him aware that this was something serious. But his expression indicated he didn't know what to do about it.

Looking about, he spotted an officer at some distance on the other side of the fence and called to him. The prisoners stood silently, watching as the officer strolled to the gate and walked back the length of the fence to them.

Listening intently to the guard, the officer studied the faces of the men, then examined the corpse. He spoke briefly and motioned his head toward the prisoners. Smitty began to wish they had never noticed the body. At an order, the guard marched the seven men back to the main gate and herded them toward the Japanese quarters.

Walking up the hill and into the center of the grouping of buildings that housed their captors, Smitty tried to avoid the scorn in the glances of the Japanese they passed. He had become inured to it, but here the concentration of hatred was too great to ignore.

As they approached the headquarters building, two guards walked down the steps toward them. Smitty recognized the one who had gunned down the prisoner inside the camp during the execution. Matthias spotted him too. "There's that trigger-happy son of a bitch," he murmured. "I'm tellin' ya, someday I'm gonna kill that little bastard."

Smitty studied the guard's features. They were typical of the Japanese faces he had seen during the last five months—cold and sullen, rigidly impassive. His face looked as though someone had seized him by the top of his flat head and the underside of his jaw and exerted tremendous pressure. As they passed within a few feet of one another, Smitty had a momentary sense of panic—as though he were in the presence of something abominably evil. It chilled his insides, though his skin felt greasy with sweat. How could they tolerate one another.

The officer walked ahead of them into the main building, where they were made to stand just inside the entrance. He knocked on a door that led off the long hallway, then paused until he heard a terse order from within before entering. The narrow corridor where the prisoners waited was oppressively hot. Leaning against the wall, Smitty watched the grime on the floor turn to mud as it mixed with the puddles of perspiration made by the prisoners.

His back was beginning to ache from standing so long when the officer reappeared and ushered them into the office. The lean, short man who sat facing them pushed back against the wooden swivel chair, causing it to squeak, and let his gaze wander over them casually. The large desk in front of him, badly scarred like the rest of the small room, detracted even more from his size, but there was authority in the tan, quiet face fringed by the short, gray hair.

His eyes concentrated on Grayson, the tallest of the prisoners. "My lieutenant informed me that you came upon the dead body of one of the inmates of the camp. This is very unfortunate. Apparently he became ill and died. Had we known he was ill, we would have seen that he had treatment."

Smitty recognized the voice immediately. But speaking now without the vibrating blare of the loudspeaker, the camp commander's tones sounded flat and less frightening.

"Sir," Grayson replied, "this was the man you thought had escaped—Hoffman, I believe, was his name." He looked at the other prisoners for confirmation, then continued. "Your guards shot ten other men because of this mistake. Hoffman was in camp all the time."

The commander leaned forward and folded his arms on the nearly chest-high desk. His thick eyebrows arched in a false pretense of indulgence, but his voice this time hinted at sternness. "You are mistaken. The man you found was not Sergeant Hoffman. We already have identified the body. Sergeant Hoffman escaped during the night."

Smitty knew he had to be lying; there hadn't been time to make any identification.

"No sir," Grayson insisted. "These men knew Sergeant Hoffman. They say he was the man found lying beside the fence. The guards didn't really look, or they would have found him."

Smitty's uneasiness flushed toward the surface of his sweat-soaked skin. Grayson always had been the levelheaded one in the bunch, but now Smitty sensed a stubbornness that was unusual in the lanky soldier, and it scared him. The commander narrowed his eyes, the lines around his mouth displaying his fury.

"I remind you, I am in complete charge here and it is my official finding that Sergeant Hoffman escaped. I will hear no more. You have made a mistake that reflects my reputation."

"With all due respect, sir. . . . " Grayson began.

Smitty's heart sank.

"Silence!" The commander slammed the palm of his hand down on the desk with a crash and rose to his full five-feet-five height, knocking the chair over behind him. "You Americans all are an insolent bunch of pigs who never learned your place. I will see to it that you are transferred to a camp where you will find out the meaning of the word respect!"

The instructions to the officer who had brought them there were brief; he hurried them out of the office quickly, apparently just as eager as the prisoners to get out of range of the commander's voice.

"What the hell you tryin' to do, Grayson?" Matthias growled as they marched under guard toward the compound. "Get us all killed? That was real smart."

Grayson didn't reply. Smitty looked at him—his face, drained of color, was calm. Something admirable had been done, though Smitty couldn't figure out why the young man had done it. The guy had guts; there was something downright secure in being around him. "Stick around, Grayson," he said. "Maybe Matthias and I can use you."

It was June 1942—three long and arduous years before Smitty would be a free man.

CHAPTER 14

In the following weeks the three friends noticed their comrades disappearing. Without warning, one group of ten after another was called from the barracks and unceremoniously boarded onto trucks, not to be seen again. Hundreds of prisoners were dying of starvation and disease and Smitty guessed the truth—the Japanese could no longer sustain the camp with its thousands of prisoners. Eventually they would all be dispersed.

There was no opportunity for goodbyes. When the guards called Smitty's name he stepped into line with dozens of prisoners, leaving his closest friends behind. The truck he climbed onto took him to his eventual detail on an airfield at Los Penos not far from Manila.

Over the next days he wondered if he would be reunited with his friends. "Any word on Matthias or Grayson?" he asked the men around him, but each question yielded a shrug or a shake of the head, "No, nothing."

He still had years ahead of him under Japanese control, but without Grayson and Matthias the ordeal became even more oppressive.

Still, Smitty and his fellow prisoners made every attempt to foil the Japanese war effort. While working on the airfield landing strip where smooth, even terrain was of the utmost importance, Smitty and his crew tampered with surveying posts, forcing the Japanese engineers to be called back at least three times.

The American and Filipino prisoners were often in danger of dying not only at the hands of their capricious captors, but also from exposure to friendly fire from the frequent Allied bombing raids at the airfield, which began in September 1944.

Allied bombings prevented Smitty's work detail from ever completing the airstrip. In October 1944, he boarded a prison ship at Manila and sailed to Hong Kong, where, for two weeks, the boat sustained continuous bombardment by the British air force. The boat finally reached port in Japan, where the prisoners were put to work in the Osaka Steel Mills. Out of the fourteen POW ships that departed the Philippines for Japanese destinations, only four arrived safely with about sixteen hundred surviving prisoners per ship's hold.

Once Allied bombing raids had destroyed the steel mills, Smitty was sent on a work detail to Maibara, where the men were to dike up a lake, the bottom of which would then be used as a rice paddy.

On August 11, 1945, the prisoners realized that something was happening because their guards simply vanished. Free men at last, it had been forty-one months since their capture at Bataan.

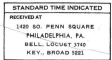

STANDARD TIME INDICATED
RECEIVED AT
1420 SO. PENN SQUARE
PHILADELPHIA, PA.
BELL, LOCUST 3740
KEY., BROAD 5221
TELEPHONE YOUR TELEGRAMS
TO POSTAL TELEGRAPH

Postal Telegraph

Mackay Radio
All America Cables
Commercial Cables
Canadian Pacific Telegraphs

THIS IS A FULL RATE TELEGRAM, CABLE-GRAM OR RADIOGRAM UNLESS OTHERWISE INDICATED BY SYMBOL IN THE PREAMBLE OR IN THE ADDRESS OF THE MESSAGE. SYMBOLS DESIGNATING SERVICE SELECTED ARE OUTLINED IN THE COMPANY'S TARIFFS ON HAND AT EACH OFFICE AND ON FILE WITH

JUN 25 12 03

BUY UNITED STATES WAR SAVINGS BONDS STAMPS

P.WB267   LA543W (TWO 39 GOVT=PXXWMU WASINGTON DC 25 1054P

MRS MABEL M SMITH=

2105 WEST ERIE AVE(PHILA PENN)=

REPORT JUST RECEIVED THROUGH THE INTERNATIONAL RED CROSS STATES
THAT YOUR SON PRIVATE FIRST CLASS OSCAR A SMITH JR IS A PRISONER
OF WAR OF THE JAPANESE GOVERNMENT IN THE PHILIPPINE ISLANDS
LETTER OF INFORMATION FOLLOWS FROM PROVOST MARSHAL GENERAL=
ULIO THE ADJ GENL.

Telegram sent to Oscar Smith's mother following his capture by the Japanese.

MILITARY COMMANDS

Command	Translation
Attention	Kiotske
Fall in	Atsumare
Fall out	Wakare
Forward march	Mai e susume
Halt	Tomare
Double time march	Kakeashi susume
Salute (Military Bow)	Kei rei
"Two" (after salute)	Naore
Eyes right	Kashira migi
Eyes left	Kashira hidari
Eyes center	Kashira naka
Front	Naore
Right face	Migimuke migi
Left face	Hidarimuke hidari
About face	Maware migi

This sheet of command translations was issued to Oscar Smith after his capture in Bataan.

HEADQUARTERS PHILIPPINE DEPARTMENT
FORT SANTIAGO, MANILA, P.I. No. 89

June 3, 1941
Date

The bearer, Oscar A. Smith, Jr.,

Pvt., SC ,

whose photograph and signature appear
hereon, is authorized to enter Fort Santiago.

By command of Major General GRUNERT:

Signature

B. T. CARVER,
Major,
Assistant Adjutant General.

This security pass allowed Oscar Smith limited movement as a prisoner at Fort Santiago.

Oscar Smith today.

Helga Wunsch poses with her friend Inge before their arrest.

Hoheneck Castle, where Helga Wunsch and other political prisoners were held throughout the Cold War.

Helga Wunsch after her release from prison.

Classmates from Frankfurt an der Oder still hold annual reunions in western Germany. Several have written books on their experiences in prison.

Ellis Tucker relaxing at the Salmon summer home about ten years after their release from Japanese internment. Robert Salmon, his wife, and his daughter are pictured in the background.

Salmon and Tucker at the graduation of Salmon's daughter, Gertrude.

Chicago Times *journalist Ed Uzemack greets foreign dignitaries at the Chicago airport.*

Prisoners of Stalag IXA celebrate their liberation as they pose with the camp newspaper. Holding the newspaper are John Dunn (with hat and glasses) and Ed Uzemack (tall and hatless). To Uzemack's right stands Denny Murray.

Ed Uzemack and his wife Patricia at his son's Arizona farm.

Nineteen-year-old Hermann Pfrengle posed in this 1949 portrait with his parents and his four-year-old brother.

At age twenty-three, Hermann Pfrengle is pictured, center, with U.S. Army liaison officer Lt. Col. Paul Kinneson and a U.S. Air Force liaison on the right at a German NATO liaison center.

Hermann Pfrengle in front of the White House during Christmas 1994. He lost his leg in an 1989 skiing accident.

PART TWO

Pootung:The School Behind Barbed Wire

CHAPTER 1

R obert Salmon passed a tangle of Chinese rickshaws and the hostile
Japanese sentries milling around them as he hurried down the narrow
Shanghai street. He swung his tennis racket beside him as he furtively
glanced at the uniformed men. Since the Japanese invasion four years
earlier, the Chinese-Japanese war was closing in, and even a short walk in
this portal city on the mouth of the Yangtze River was becoming an ordeal.

It was December 8, 1941, and it seemed as if there was an extra
tension in the cool evening air. Salmon could hear arguing in both
Mandarin and Japanese as Chinese farmers tried to pass through the
road monitored by heavily armed soldiers. He had grown accustomed
to these arguments, even occasional gunfire since the occupation of the
Japanese here. He was surrounded by the chaos of war wherever he
went in Shanghai, and even St. John's University was no longer a safe
haven. But this night something felt different—more foreboding.

As a biochemistry professor at the school, Salmon had watched the
tranquillity of this international zone in Shanghai erode under Japanese
domination. As he passed between buildings through crowds of both
Chinese and uniformed men, he ignored the cold stares of the Japanese
soldiers—so different from the smiles he had enjoyed from the Chinese
over the past ten years.

Salmon was a small Englishman whose thick mustache had been more
in fashion twenty years earlier. Wearing a white tennis shirt and trousers,
he stood out in the Chinese metropolis and regretted his singularity this
night as he felt the eyes of soldiers on him before they barked a warning in

Japanese, By chance a Chinese beggar passing by along the gutter diverted their attention. As the war surged, destitute Chinese had been making their way from the countryside into Shanghai despite the danger that the Japanese occupation presented.

The beggar, a ragged man with a limping lope and nervous eyes, froze when one soldier stopped in front of him; he waited silently as the soldier appraised him. Salmon hurried on, glad to have the opportunity to leave but hoping the best for the wretched Chinese man. He had made a point of maintaining normalcy amid the war's tension and tonight, as he did each week, he made his way along the narrow rickshaw-crowded roads to join in a tennis match with his close friends: Hughes, a British professor of German; Ellis Tucker, a lanky and good-natured high-school math teacher from Virginia; and Bishop Curtis, the head of the university's Episcopal Church. He cut toward a row of small homes adjacent to Jessfield Park and climbed up the stairway, nodding a greeting to the Chinese servant standing by. Inside his friends were already assembled.

The four walked jovially out of the language professor's home, their tennis rackets in hand, laughing as they compared serving styles. A tennis court awaited them on the other side of St. John's campus, where they all gathered for a match at least once a week. Tucker led the way, and when he suddenly stopped, the others at first protested, then fell silent as their eyes trained in on the obstacle ahead of them. A Japanese sentry at the gate of the campus waved his gun at the group and snarled unintelligibly. Salmon realized that this time there was no one to distract the enemy. Stepping forward, the Englishman tried to explain the purpose of their visit by pointing at his racket and toward the tennis courts in the distance; and in response the sentry menacingly raised his rifle. The four friends recoiled.

"Let's go," Tucker whispered, and the group slowly turned their backs on the guard and his weapon, walking back to the house in silence. When Salmon risked a glance over his shoulder, the sentry appeared to be gone.

• • •

It was no longer the Shanghai he had come to live in nearly twenty years ago with his new bride Laliah. He had come as an educational missionary in his twenties, intent upon improving life in China by teaching biochemistry to medical students. Putting those skills to work at the Hangchow Christian College in Zakow, Chekiang, where Westerners taught Chinese students, couldn't be more removed from what Salmon had been accustomed to in England.

Salmon was born in 1900, the first son of a landed-gentry family living in Chester, Cheshire County. Because his mother died in childbirth, he was raised by an austerely religious grandmother. Gertrude, known locally as "the Old Woman," trained him that suffering and hard work rather than the luxuries of the upper class were the fodder for success. Salmon believed her. He was born with a crippling clubfoot, that curled awkwardly inward. His grandmother spent the first years of his life roughly massaging his foot with her strong hands. Despite the excruciating pain, the young boy learned to exercise the foot in hopes of walking like a normal little boy.

By the age of three he was doing just that, and his grandmother reminded him often that it was her labor and his pain that brought him to his feet. It was a lesson hard learned, and one the rest of the family viewed with skepticism.

"I don't think she's good for that boy," many family members could be heard commenting; but they couldn't argue with his healthy stride, and few wanted to cross the domineering woman.

In China Salmon often found himself thinking of his obdurate grandmother Gertrude. Without her intervention in his upbringing, he never could have managed the rigors of life in China. After his first wife died of meningitis in 1930, he moved to Shanghai to teach at St. John's University, and there he met Frances, an outspoken American physician and former farm girl from South Dakota. They married in 1932 and had two daughters, Gertrude and Hilda.

The Japanese presence around his young family was unsettling from the start. The mail he sent to England was closely censored, and the Japanese kept tight rein over the international concession Municipal Council, made up of Americans, British, and Japanese. The Council presided over the international settlement, a large section of Shanghai, where non-Chinese lived, worked, and raised families.

In September 1939 the Japanese began tightening their grip on Shanghai. At first the puppet police appeared only in the lanes and alleyways off the main roads, but week by week Salmon saw them come out into the open, and often he would tighten his grip on the tiny hands of his daughters as he walked them along the city streets to visit friends. Soon there were eight or more Japanese sentries posted at each of the principal crossroads, while one of their number directed the traffic at these intersections.

Gambling dens and nightclubs sprouted throughout the city, many controlled by the Japanese who also regulated the roads leading into Shanghai. The Japanese funneled farmers and merchants bringing food and fuel by rickshaw onto a single road to tax them, a practice which led to skyrocketing costs for basic necessities in Shanghai. Wandering Chinese bandits took advantage of the confusion the occupation brought with it to enter houses and rob and extort money from local victims. One such victim was a friend of Salmon's, who said he had been robbed twice. When the second band of robbers arrived at his house, the friend said the previous thieves had taken everything. The infuriated second group held the man's wife over a fire, burning her abdomen before they were convinced there was nothing of value to take from the house.

Fire victims came in regularly to St. Luke's Hospital, an institution connected to St. John's University, where Salmon and his wife taught. The Chinese favored flames as a form of torture, but the numbers of burning cases swelled with the Japanese occupation. Salmon learned to be circumspect, because Japanese spies, using the names of other nationalities, had infiltrated the university to root out those who openly disapproved of the occupation.

At the same time, the Japanese were hoping to finally take control of the international settlement by manipulating the Shanghai municipal elections. If they earned enough votes to take the majority of the council, they would control a major section of Shanghai. There were five British candidates and two Americans. The Japanese, who tried to persuade the Jewish refugees living in Hongkew to vote only for the Japanese candidates, kidnapped and beat a Czech woman who tried to persuade the refugees to vote for British candidates. Salmon learned of the unpublicized deed through the active rumor network. Eventually only two Japanese were elected to the council, but Salmon saw trouble ahead. Fear of assassination forced the councilman in charge of education of the Chinese in the international quarter out of the city, and the teachers he left were poised to follow if the Japanese should decide that the schooling had to stop.

In April 1940 Salmon planted lettuce in his back garden while his two daughters watched. Wiping rich Chinese soil from his hands, he pondered that his family might never taste the results of his gardening. As the hills boasted their annual spring green, the temperature rose to 86 degrees, and rumors of a guerrilla presence in a town near Shanghai reached the Japanese. They bombed the village, killing men, women, and children. Meanwhile, Salmon taught anti-gas measures in the case of emergency to a first-aid class. He tried to maintain a peacetime routine, hoping even in a time of killing that new students could learn to save lives.

On Thursday afternoons he taught the least popular subject—gastric analysis. On one of those Thursday evenings, November 16, 1940, the Council of Advice, with support of the group's bishop, decided that the

American Church Mission's women with children should evacuate China on the *USS Washington*, which was sailing in five days. Frances Salmon had five days to pack, buy tickets, and prepare the children to leave. The men, in the meantime, would keep the school running.

Salmon helped his wife pack and took his daughters around the limited sections of their neighborhood where Westerners could still walk, free from interception by Japanese soldiers. Gertrude was seven and Hilda was three; and he was relieved to be sending them to the safety of San Francisco, yet he was unsure just how soon they would be able to come back. Stoic optimism was his mainstay when talking with his wife, predicting she and the girls could return soon.

"It won't be long," she agreed, "until we're reunited either here or on another continent."

To Salmon, the uneasy neutrality of the British and Americans seemed less likely with each day. He watched his family join about one thousand other evacuees from China, then was left with the lonely task of maintaining the school with a skeletal, all-male staff. The Japanese were hostile to the education of the Chinese and were strenuously trying to shut down the schools. Since several had closed in town, St. John's faced record enrollment at the same time that many of the staff had left with the evacuees.

As a single man, Salmon occupied a bedroom and the dining room of campus residence number 4. With the absence of wives and children, the smaller group consolidated their space, and Chinese families moved in to fill the vacuum, in an effort to make the university seem as Chinese as possible. The growing animosity between the Japanese and the American and British Allies was swelling to dangerous proportions for the faculty.

Most of the Salmon family's servants had left except for a Chinese woman, the children's amah, who still cooked Salmon his meals. Several of these servants, including one Frances had hired to do knitting, needed any kind of work they could find. The couple had agreed to pay them for various tasks rather than hand out charity, but now Salmon was without funds to support a crew of Chinese servants. Most returned to their homes in the country to try to make a living on the paltry crops they raised on small plots of land.

The few Western men left behind in Shanghai kept each other occupied with tennis and volleyball. Their discussion groups centered on the latest news as well as topics they taught in school, but their thoughts were always on the war.

CHAPTER 2

A fter the incident at the tennis court, Salmon's group returned to the Hughes's house for a sobering evening talking about the future of the war and that of Shanghai. At 10:00 P.M. they said their good-byes, leaving their worries for the next day, and Salmon made his way in complete darkness along the short walk from his friend's house to his unlocked home. He carried his unused tennis racket, wondering what other activities the Japanese would no longer allow.

Several hours later the sound of the ringing telephone pierced his uneasy sleep. As he groped his way down the stairs in the dark to answer, he steeled himself for bad news. "Hello?" he spoke into the phone.

"Dr. Salmon? It's Dr. McCracken," the voice said. Salmon knew McCracken as a physician at St. Luke's Hospital where his wife had worked. "Japan has attacked Pearl Harbor; the United States has declared war." he said.

"Pearl Harbor, are you sure?" He rubbed his eyes in the dark, considering the ramifications.

"That's not all," McCracken continued, his voice tense. "They've also sunk the British gunboat, the *Peterel*, in the Whangpoo River and the American one has been captured. The Japanese right now are entering the American Consulate."

The war had come to Shanghai, and Salmon and his Western friends were inexorably caught in the middle of it. He could imagine what this would mean for him; if he could continue his work, he would be doing it as the enemy in a hostile country. If he wanted to go to America to his family, he might not be allowed to leave.

"What do you need me to do?" he asked.

"We need someone at the Red Cross Hospital across Jessfield Park," McCracken said. "There are American nurses there who were recalled from Manila. Someone should stay with them in case anything happens."

Salmon hung up the phone and returned upstairs to dress hurriedly, then called the amah to tell her where he was going. She too knew of the declaration of war between the Allies and the Japanese and, as he gave her his instructions, he saw new creases form between her eyes. She nodded without comment; like many in Shanghai she was not surprised by the Pearl Harbor attack or the results of it in China.

Salmon hurried out the door and onto the front step where he heard the roar of light aircraft as he looked up in the gray light of dawn. A plane rumbled over dropping thousands of leaflets. As they fluttered to the ground, he grabbed one; it was written in Mandarin and English and announced that a state of war now existed between Japan and America. After the announcement there followed a warning to remain calm and a promise that the Japanese would "maintain order."

Heading for the hospital, the war announcement in his pocket, Salmon watched the sun rise on another day, a day that changed life forever for the members of the foreign quarter of Shanghai. As light rose, so did a beautiful rainbow sporting deep shades of red. He recalled the old saying: red sky in the morning, sailor's warning.

CHAPTER 3

Salmon spent the day following the news of the Pearl Harbor attack in a fourth-floor apartment of St. Luke's Hospital with three anxious American nurses. Japanese soldiers came and went to foreign business places stealing safes, while bands of Japanese civilians went to foreigners' residences to inventory their possessions.

The Japanese did not arrive that day at St. Luke's, and the English biochemist sat at a card table, politely drinking coffee as the group played a series of tense card games. No one tried to predict what would happen next.

The next day he learned how much his life had changed. The Japanese were quick to "restore order" among foreigners in Shanghai; Salmon joined hundreds of Americans and British waiting in queues to be registered and to receive identification cards and red armbands identifying them as the despised foes of the Japanese. The Westerners, now official enemies, gathered glumly before an office run by an understaffed group of Japanese where they were instructed to turn in anything containing a lens, namely, cameras, telescopes, binoculars.

Salmon worried about the supplies both at the university and at the hospital, which could be used by the Japanese in their war effort. St. Luke's Hospital was the original Shanghai municipal building, and the Japanese had made it clear they would like to take it over. Until now, they had been held back by a lease the Western community had on it, but leases were of little use at this point. The hospital was growing more crowded weekly as starvation and its related diseases struck those living in town and many from outside its borders. Families brought in those they thought could still be saved, and with them came more disease.

Salmon strapped his new armband over the sleeve of his jacket, wondering about Shanghai's future. He wanted to write to his wife and grandmother about all that was happening, but the mail had stopped weeks ago. When he returned home on a streetcar, the new red armband in place over his sleeve, the Chinese conductor gave him a reassuring look. "Now we know who are our friends," the man said, pointing at the armband. He and Salmon exchanged a smile before the Englishman hurried to his seat. The Japanese had hoped to shame those in the armbands as conspicuous enemies, but the Chinese had suffered enough in their own involvement with Japanese occupation to feel that any enemy of the Japanese was a friend of theirs.

With his new ID card and armband, Salmon was not finished waiting in lines, and he next queued up in front of the Hong Kong Bank of Shanghai where his money had been deposited. Here, the Japanese allowed him to withdraw the minimum needed for his survival. Because he had already depleted his funds, he soon drained his account completely. While standing in line he noticed the removal of the two bronze lions at the entrance of the bank. The lions, for the Japanese, represented British imperialism; for the Chinese, however, the removal of the lions had a depressing effect. Several Chinese friends passed and looked at the spot where the lions had been, shaking their heads sadly. Many Shanghai Chinese had formed a superstitious attachment to the statues, some often rubbing their personal belongings against the lions' paws for good luck. It seemed there was little good luck left for the Chinese. "That's a bad omen," they told the Englishman.

Within the week the Japanese had seized the university and confiscated the *National Geographic* magazines for their information about the Pacific. Though the Western faculty was put on house arrest, they were still free to continue teaching, and Salmon did just that for increasingly larger groups of students. School was in session three weeks after the invasion of Pearl Harbor when the American and British professors gathered for Christmas. For all of them it was a somber celebration, despite every effort to adhere to tradition. These few remaining faculty, missing their families and unsure of their future, attended services in the cathedral, and on the church lawn they sang carols around the Christmas tree, their voices rising to be heard only by the Japanese sentries patrolling nearby.

Salmon joined the other foreigners for dinner at a doctor's new house by the middle school. Again the group sang carols after dinner, but there was no opening of presents. As the evening grew late, they filed back to their homes; Salmon undressed in the dark, setting his armband on the bureau for the next day before he climbed into bed.

CHAPTER 4

The next week the school closed its doors under the heavy pressure of the Japanese. With the loss, Salmon and his colleagues saw their supplies and support from the outside world cut off. The hospital's closure soon followed the school's.

On January 4, 1942, medical students scurried through the building to rescue equipment and supplies as they evacuated the buildings. Salmon found that rescuing the equipment was easy, relocating it was more difficult. Transportation was nonexistent and even if it hadn't been, Japanese sentries at a railway bridge across the creek would have confiscated any goods the students smuggled out.

Instead, students carried their supplies from St. Luke's onto the nearby St. John's campus. Salmon was amazed to find the equipment in perfect condition. "It's remarkable that this delicate equipment would fare so well," he commented as he looked over analytical balances and hazardous matter such as liquid bromide and fuming acids.

Not everything, however, could be saved. Two Soochow tubs full of human brains from hundreds of autopsies never made it to the college laboratories. The coolies refused to touch the formaldehyde-filled tubs. To ensure the presence of the brains did not fuel the Japanese propaganda machine against the West, Salmon decided to destroy them himself. That night, wearing dark clothing, he set out with a shovel and pitchfork. With a cloud cover shielding the bright moonlight, he dug a large hole on the grounds of the academy, resting only long enough to rub his arms and search the dark for reassurance that no one was there. When the hole was large enough, he steeled himself and went to work tossing brains into the makeshift grave with a pitchfork. As a chemist he dispassionately considered human remains, but as the pitchfork penetrated the brains that once held the thoughts of hundreds of adults, he felt nausea rising inside him. He quickly stole one last glance around him before filling in the hole with a shudder of disgust.

Although the quarters were more cramped, the medical school still managed to stay open, holding classes at St. John's campus. There was record enrollment, because other Chinese medical schools, including the Peking Union Medical College, were closed. Salmon came into his classes that winter to face a sea of inquisitive faces, many standing in the back of the crammed rooms.

Salmon discovered excellent students, as well as some who used the political situation to intimidate professors into passing them. Meanwhile, more of his personal friends left, including Dr. McCracken from St. Luke's Hospital, who was repatriated with the elderly and the sick. Salmon walked to the hospital to say good-bye to his departing friends, and afterward he felt the loneliness of being among only a handful of foreigners remaining. The contrast struck him with harsh resonance— only a year ago the area had been teeming with missionaries from throughout Britain and America and his daughters had been playing with playmates on streets named after English places and people.

As Salmon walked toward his home alone, he was stopped while passing the Italian Consulate. He was surprised when the Italian sentry there asked him in broken English to stop and talk. Despite the fact that Salmon wore the bright crimson armband of the enemy, the Italian asked him about his life in England and about his family. He talked about his own travels in Europe. The man was so lonely, Salmon thought, that he was willing to talk to any fellow European just to pass the time.

• • •

By fall of 1942 food had become scarce, and rice was such an expensive and rare commodity in Shanghai that smugglers began sneaking it into the city from farms. It was dangerous work, since smugglers had to pass the Japanese lines to bring the rice in; if caught, they were usually tortured and killed.

Salmon, who lived on the Soochow creek, witnessed the most common punishment—a smuggler would be driven out in the deep mud when the tide was out; the victim would then get stuck and, as the tide returned, drown. Salmon was revisited for more than a week by the bloated body of a smuggler that floated back and forth with the flowing and ebbing tide by the Walkers' house.

Even while the Chinese farmers were smuggling rice, the Japanese were looting rice, flour, beans, and metal and bringing them back to the docks of Shanghai to be shipped out in barges. Often these barges, waiting to be filled, would anchor near Salmon's house.

In November 1942 Salmon was not surprised when the Japanese began the miserable practice of picking up what they called "wanted persons" without warning. Bishop Curtis was among those to disappear through these seizures. Salmon knew most were spirited away in the middle of the night, often in nothing but their nightclothes, and were held incommunicado and without food for days.

The resulting negative publicity from the arrests caused the Japanese to build internment camps to house the prisoners. Salmon heard and saw nothing of his friend Bishop Curtis and feared he would be next.

At about five o'clock on a Saturday afternoon, January 23, the phone rang; when Salmon answered, he heard the message he had been expecting. It was a member of the British Residents Association, and he announced perfunctorily that Salmon should report for internment the following Sunday.

"You can pack a bed and roll of bedding as well as one trunk of clothing," the anonymous voice told him, delivering the news for the Japanese. Salmon noticed his hands trembling as he hung up the phone. Staring out the window, he called a friend to learn that two Americans had received the same phone call.

He spent the next week sorting through his possessions, deciding what he could live without. Necessities were his old iron bed and mattress, warm blankets, sheets, a mosquito net and poles. He prepared a strong cup and plate, the least breakable of his possessions, a few bars of soap, some insecticide, a thermos flask, knife, fork, and spoon; he also packed a razor blade, sharpener, and some rolls of toilet paper. There was room left in his bag for only a small item, and he scanned through his large book collection trying to decide what would be most useful for him in the camp. Selecting two chemistry books and, using careful sorting and the force of all his weight, shut the chest tightly.

Salmon then tackled the depressing work of preparing others for his absence. He explained to Mrs. Tseng, the replacement teacher in his physiological chemistry class for medical students, where she could find the carefully hoarded stocks of chemicals and equipment she would need; he gave his scientific journals and books to the head of the chemistry department. But he didn't allow himself time to worry about his future or wonder what lay ahead—instead he filled his days with the tasks of preparing to relocate and tried not to think of his family awaiting him in America.

CHAPTER 5

Early on Sunday morning, Salmon awoke to a sad gathering of his remaining close friends, there to wish him well. They were mostly the Chinese gardeners of St. John's whom Salmon had worked with for so long, as well as Tucker and Hughes. No one could guess where he would be taken or what his fate would be, but they looked at him with teary eyes. Their fear for his future worried him. Amah called a rickshaw, and he climbed in, saying a final good- bye. With his chin up, he headed for the Cathedral Boys School in Shanghai, which was the prisoner assembly center.

When he arrived at the school he was joined by dozens like him, giving information about their families, properties, and financial liabilities while the Japanese offered no information in return. He saw a few friends from the hospital and the school, but all stared about them in confusion and apprehension. "Any idea where we're going?" he asked a few friends but the answer was always the shake of a head.

He lined up with the others, his bags at his sides, and waited with his trunk for his turn with a pair of grim-faced Japanese behind a card table. They took names on a clipboard and checked off names in several folders. Salmon stood before them and exchanged a look with one who appeared to be an officer.

"Name?" the man asked.

"Salmon, Robert Salmon."

The Japanese man seated beside the officer flipped through the pages and ran a finger inexplicably down a list of names beginning with the letter "F." Finally Salmon intervened. "That's Salmon, spelled with an 'S.'"

The officer looked at him impatiently and held out his hand. "Where are your papers?" Salmon handed over the papers he had registered when the Japanese took over after Pearl Harbor. Quickly they matched his name with the one on the internment list, and he was waved aside to let the next man forward.

As he finished with the Japanese, he stood waiting in the school yard and was surprised to hear the strains of music wafting toward him in the early-morning chill. It seemed incongruous to hear music at the beginning of his captivity under the Japanese, and he searched around him until he realized it was organ music coming from the cathedral for the Sunday morning service. Listening closely, he knew he would hear nothing like it for a long time, and softly he hummed along.

By noon the quota was complete. The Japanese stood, clapping hands together and ordering the men to move toward the street. There several more soldiers met them as escorts, and Salmon picked up his bags for what appeared to be his journey away from freedom.

Led by Japanese guards, he began a march, with about two hundred others, down Kukiang Road to the Bund, the main thoroughfare fronting the river, led by Japanese guards. Each had to carry his own baggage— the beds were to be shipped to them. Standing no more than five feet six inches and delicately built, Salmon struggled with his over-packed suitcases and kit bag.

Rather than leave Shanghai in the anonymity of trucks, the Westerners walked down the center of the city for all to see. Chinese, on their way to and from shops and homes, stopped to watch the somber procession that interrupted their otherwise quiet Sunday morning. The trek was intended to humiliate the new internees, but thanks to the Chinese it didn't turn out that way.

Those caught by surprise by the parade offered smiles and words of support to the British, Americans, and Dutch who passed. But as they continued, Salmon noticed larger crowds still, as people lined the sides of the street waiting for their arrival. It was Chinese friends of the internees who had come to wish them well.

As they began to cheer and shout approval, Salmon and the man beside him exchanged smiles. This was not what either they or the Japanese guards had expected. Their escorts stared straight ahead while shouting at the internees to move at a faster clip.

Salmon watched in amazement as hundreds of Chinese waved, not caring whether they knew him personally or not. He also recognized some smiling faces along the route. One of the university caretakers even stepped off the curb and joined him, reaching for his suitcase. Salmon glanced around him, then handed his friend the lighter of the two cases. The Chinese worker, whom he had known for years, smiled, nodded, and continued walking with him at his side, giving him the chance to shake some circulation back into his hand. They walked this way for several blocks in an almost celebratory mood.

They abruptly stopped when a shouting Japanese guard rushed toward them, his bayonet aimed in their direction. Salmon grabbed the case and his friend hurried away, chased several feet onto the side of the road before the guard rejoined the march. But the English prisoner fixed his eyes forward, adjusted his grip on the suitcases, and continued on, his energy restored.

CHAPTER 6

On the Bund the group stopped, put down their bags, and rubbed their tired hands. "Now what?" someone muttered behind Salmon. In large groups they began boarding a lighter that was towed across the Whangpoo River by a steam tug. He climbed off with his coprisoners at a jetty and saw he was near the gateways of the giant British-American Tobacco Company.

From there a narrow railway ran about a half mile to an old factory of the same company that had been abandoned since 1937. Salmon had never been to the factory and had no idea of his destination until now. But there was no time to consider what might be inside as the guards shouted at them to move faster toward their new home.

It looked, from the outside, like a giant tomb with various relics that once served as buildings, roads, and storage units—reminders of the activity that had once gone on there. Crowds of men lined up in front of the decrepit factory, muttering among themselves as the Japanese kept them standing in place.

Salmon's new captors were men who looked too old to be soldiers. He probably had seen them before around the city of Shanghai, but he didn't recognize any of them. The internees fell unusually silent, watching the building and their new "hosts" with the knowledge that they might be in this place for many months. None could have imagined that it would be two and a half years.

When the Japanese seemed satisfied that the prisoners could continue, they waved them forward along an abandoned rail line toward the building.

Salmon lugged his baggage with weary arms and shoulders and was conducted with his fellow internees into one of the large, vacant buildings of the factory. As he entered he passed through the gates of a high brick wall—topped with barbed wire.

Two large buildings of three stories each stood before them. One of these was flanked by two two-story buildings and connected with them by enclosed corridors on the second-floor level. Beside these structures stood a detached building, which had been the boiler house and power plant. The Japanese had removed the boilers and replaced them with a series of Chinese-style brick cooking stoves with large iron cooking pots.

The Japanese had also installed washbowls and toilets in two of the buildings. The large water tank perched on the highest building, which had been the reservoir for an elaborate automatic fire sprinkler system, was still in place, but rendered useless by the removal of the main feed pipe from the tank. This would be their new home, known as Pootung Camp.

As the internees approached the buildings, Salmon glanced down into freshly built trenches and guessed these were the new sewer system. He then passed through a double doorway and saw crowds of his contemporaries waiting in a large, open room. He stood with the others, many sitting on their suitcases, pulling handkerchiefs from their pockets to wipe sweat off their faces and necks. It was a cool day, but the exertion of the trip had been harder on some than others. Several of the older men, some overweight and out of condition, slumped red-faced and exhausted.

By about two o'clock the group was completely assembled in what was to be the mess hall. The room's few windows allowed dust-filtered light to streak white along the factory walls, illuminating what appeared to have once been a room for manufacturing. Now it was filled with eighteen or twenty large tables lined with benches on each side.

Some men complained and muttered among themselves while Salmon stood silently, reviewing the area and considering what life would be like there. Everyone fell silent when the guards stepped aside to allow an officer inside.

The Japanese commandant, who stood before the weary group, paused momentarily as he looked them over, then began to speak. "Welcome everyone—to Pootung," he began, "I trust you had a pleasant journey here." No one responded, although a few men raised their eyebrows or cast a glance at their companions. "You will find communication with me to be no problem," he continued, "I was a consular official in Seattle and am very comfortable with the English language."

He walked along a line of the front row of internees as he spoke. "And now I will be overseeing the functions here at this encampment." He paused, and all was silent as he turned to make another path in front of them. "You are here as guests of his Imperial Highness, the Emperor of Japan." The man was short but carried himself with a confidence that seemed to elevate his stature. He wore a starched uniform with formality, his arms clasped behind his back as if they were sewn there. He looked to be about forty years old.

The commandant paced as he explained that the prisoners would be representing three nationalities and would be allowed to elect their own representatives: one British, one American, and one Dutch. Those representatives would be responsible for everyone's behavior and would report directly to him. "If you try to escape, of course," he said, "you will be shot to death." His eyes suddenly crinkled in a smile. "I urge you now to cherish your happy home."

His swift departure was followed by a flash of sunlight through the mess hall doors before they fell shut with a slam.

The Japanese guards then assigned rooms, with a dozen or more men in each of the fifteen available rooms. The men were assigned randomly, and Salmon found his name put on a list of strangers for one of the rooms in the larger building.

As the prisoners waited, they heard the clamor of pots and pans and smelled the unmistakable scent of rice wafting from the kitchen. Chinese cooks prepared a meal of rice and stew for the men before they were ushered to their rooms. The Chinese had been employed by the British Residents Association, but they and their cooking would last only about a week. After that, the inmates would have to take over.

After the meal, Salmon and his new neighbors were put to work cleaning their rooms with brooms, mops, and pails provided by their guards. Salmon's room was a dreary place, with littered and stained floors and windowless walls, and it looked as if it hadn't been cleaned since the factory was built. Just outside the room, however, along a stairway leading to their floor, was a narrow window overlooking the harbor. From there the internees could see the beautiful day and calm waters. Salmon would have liked to stop and stare out the window, but a guard chased him on.

Scrubbing the floors was a grueling chore that required hours on his hands and knees, soaking his thick, woolen trousers. The oak floors were stained black in spots with tobacco and molasses, and Salmon spent the next several days staring at the filthy floor, scrubbing with a hand mop and occasionally rising straight on his knees to rest his back. At such times he would look up to see that he was under the constant, watchful eyes of the guards. They would regard him suspiciously until he returned to his chore, trying to work his way down to bare wood.

After the first day's work, Salmon and the other internees were shepherded to the front of the buildings, where they wearily gathered to find several truckloads of baggage waiting. They sorted through the items with confusion about their ownership, because Salmon knew he and his closest companions had carried everything they had into the camp.

After they had dragged the luggage off the trucks, the Japanese told them to distribute it to the rooms that were vacant; they were about to be joined by more Westerners. Salmon then realized now just how many people the factory would soon be housing. Several weeks later the additional group straggled in through the gates, bringing the population of the "happy home" to 1,100.

It was then that Salmon saw the arrival of the remainder of his friends from St. John's, including Ellis Tucker, Hughes, and, surprisingly, Bishop Curtis, who had been shuffled from one waiting station to another in Shanghai. Tucker arrived with his wide shoulders slumped forward and his hair pressed wet with perspiration against his scalp. Curtis had the same look of exhaustion, sitting as soon as the group came to a halt in the front yard.

Several hundred men milled around the area with the confusion Salmon had felt himself only two weeks before. This time the guards quickly organized them and sent them to the mess hall for their greeting from the commandant.

As soon as the mess hall doors were reopened, the new internees stumbled into the light with dazed expressions. Among them was a cross section of all kinds of humanity: engineers of all types, tea tasters, bankers, ship stewards, stokers, wireless operators, merchants, lawyers, clergymen, policemen, pharmacists, electricians, sanitary inspectors, teachers, doctors, beachcombers, drug addicts, gunmen, and just plain bums.

They were housed in rooms according to whether they were American, British, or Dutch. Salmon slept in one of the British rooms with a business executive named Beale bunking beside him. Next to Beale was a pharmacist of the Shanghai Municipal Council. At the foot of his bed was Wultz, a stoker off a British ship; at the foot of Beale's bed was Winstanley, a professional tea taster.

To the right of Salmon was Roper, the official hangman of the Shanghai Municipal Gaol and an ex-Coldstream Guardsman who stood six feet eight inches. Salmon first heard Roper's name in disbelief but was not inclined to make jokes when Roper stood to his full height.

The room also held a British Army man, a ship's captain, a Scottish marine engineer, and an insurance man. The main owner of publishers Kelly and Walsh slept beside three oil engineers of the Anglo-Persian Oil Company.

There were also two British steamer captains, a refrigeration engineer of the United Fruit Company, a waterworks engineer, several bankers, an Orthodox Jewish trader who was a descendant of Rabbi Hillel, an Adenese Arab manufacturer, and a Seychellese adventurer.

The individuals in this unlikely grouping turned to each other for a variety of personal problems like old family members. No one asked to be moved, and each was happy with his location. Salmon began to enjoy his own neighbors, Beale and Roper, and they spent unending hours telling each other stories of their lives in China as they languished through the dull first weeks of captivity.

The camp was soon filled to capacity, with each internee allowed floor space of six-by-eight feet. Troubles related to the overcrowding came upon them almost overnight. The sewage system, which was too small for the growing population, stopped up entirely, and the raw sewage began running along the open trenches instead of through the pipes. The problem raised steam and a sickening stench—thankfully January's cold weather spared them an infestation of flies.

Standing before the sewage with a handkerchief over his face, Salmon contemplated the problem before Hughes arrived to introduce him to a friend. The man who shook his hand said he was a sewage engineer. They soon located another such engineer in the camp and the two got to work designing a larger system that would send the sewage outside of the camp.

With the help of Salmon, Tucker, and Hughes, the engineers went to work laying new sewer lines and connecting them to an outside sewer. Salmon rolled up his sleeves and began digging new trenches for the pipes with a broken-handled shovel he had scavenged in the factory yard.

They had been at work for several hours before the guards came to talk to them. "What you do?"

When they were unable to explain in English and hand gestures, the guards nodded, frowned, and walked away. An hour later the camp commandant appeared to watch them with his hands clasped behind his back. He gestured to Salmon, who scrambled out of the ditch and stood to face him, his hands thick with dirt from using the broken-handled shovel, cups, and bowls to dig.

"So you are becoming industrious here, I see," the commandant said. The man was about Salmon's age and was of equal height. He wore a narrow mustache and short cropped hair and spoke American-style English with the slightest Japanese accent. The prisoner only nodded, looking around him at the men who had all stopped their work to watch.

"It is good that you have taken this upon yourselves. Maybe I can make it easier for you." Salmon stared at him skeptically, and the man turned on his heel and walked away. By the end of the day, several tools including shovels were dumped by the ditch, and the biochemist wondered if this was the beginning of a tolerable relationship with his captor.

CHAPTER 7

A rriving with the last group of internees was a young American whose despondency went unnoticed in all the confusion. He always kept himself separate from the other men; Salmon occasionally saw him standing in the hallway near one of the few windows, staring at his feet rather than the view. When anyone approached him, he shook his head and walked away.

"What's wrong with him?" Salmon finally asked an American friend who only shrugged.

"Misses his wife."

Salmon and most of the camp's population were in the same situation, so he put the comment out of mind. Like so many facets of life at the camp, the men accepted it as something they could not control. The American told a few friends that he had left his Russian wife outside the camp and was worried about her. Russians had maintained a good relationship with the Japanese and were being permitted to stay in China.

But the man's quiet presence came to a dramatic end when Salmon, sitting with his bunkmates over cards, heard hysterical shouting in the hallway. Roper was first to the door, with Salmon close behind, and they followed the noise to one of the American rooms where the blood told them the story. The depressed man had slashed his own throat.

The man's horrified friends went to the guards to report the death, and soon the commandant was there, shaking his head uneasily as the guards wrapped the bloodied body and carried it away. It was the first death in the camp, and the commandant prided himself in having a "happy home" that was livable. It did not bode well for the Japanese in charge if news of the death reached the public.

"This man committed suicide," he said repeatedly, as if anyone was planning to contradict him by saying the guards had committed murder. "This is a place where people will live happily together. No more will die," he predicted, then walked away to say the same thing to the entire camp over the loudspeaker. But the internees had other troubles to consider, and the suicide was soon forgotten as a new internee filled the bunk space of the dead American.

Salmon focused his attention on more immediate concerns. Eating his evening meal in the mess hall, he questioned the cook doling food onto plates. Why were the rations growing smaller? "It's not that we don't have the rice," the cook responded, "but we're running out of coal for the cookhouse. I'm trying to go easy because the more I cook the sooner we run out entirely. Anyone care for raw rice?"

"Well, I've dealt with the commandant before; maybe it would be best to pay him a visit," Salmon offered.

Hughes and Tucker, standing beside him, laughed and patted him on the back. "He seemed right impressed with Salmon when he was digging trenches." The cook agreed, and the next morning the two men walked to the commandant's office where they explained the problem.

The next day the Japanese sent Salmon and a dozen men of his choosing to some neighboring factories with baskets and shovels to collect more coal. It was his first trip out of the compound in three weeks, and he relished the freedom of the walk, swinging his basket and shovel as they trudged along. The small crew headed for a Chinese factory, where they waited outside while the guard explained to several employees that the prisoners had arrived for coal. Two men in charge of the factory watched from the doorway, shaking their heads and cursing visibly. No one dared intervene, and the prisoners left with high-quality coal, the likes of which they hadn't seen since the war began.

When the large chunks of coal arrived at the camp, it was up to the prisoners to bring them to a usable size for the cooks. The work relied on volunteers, and Salmon, Hughes, Curtis, and Tucker pounded down the rocks of coal, soon becoming coated with coal dust themselves. Others joined them as they took turns resting. After several hours, Salmon noticed that he and the other members of the group pounding out coal were the same men who had helped dig the sewage trenches and carry coal from the Chinese factory. Other internees wandered by with their hands in their pockets, watching only out of the corners of their eyes.

"Anyone care to lend a hand?" Tucker shouted to a group as he wiped black grease from his forehead. They hurried on, muttering about tasks they said they had to do. After that, most of the internees stayed away entirely, playing cards or getting sleep.

Salmon labeled them the "bums"—those who didn't work before they came to the camp and still didn't work here, allowing others to keep the camp functioning for them. Most of the work, he noticed, was done by the clergy and missionaries led by Bishop Curtis. He, Tucker, and Hughes soon came to resent the camp's slackers.

On one coal run an engineer sidled up to Salmon as he loaded the black rocks into his basket. "Those pipe wrenches could be a big help back at the camp," he said. "See if you can find room for these under the coal in your basket."

That night the same engineer began the arduous task of dismantling the obsolete sprinkler system room by room and hiding the pipe he collected by sinking it into a deep pool of water, which had once served as the sump for the cooling water of the power plant. He had an ambitious idea. Salmon watched him at work, finally asking, "You're not building a showering system are you?"

"You bet I am," he said. "And I can do it, too. We're already half way there with this sprinkler system."

No one had cleaned himself properly since arrival at the camp the month before. This invited the greatest scourge in the camp—the insects that thrived on unwashed skin and spread from man to man in the tight quarters. Some prisoners had brought lice and bedbugs with them, and it wasn't long before nearly all the residents found the bugs crawling on their clothing, scalps, and even faces. The Japanese offered no baths or showers; the tiny washbowls in the washrooms were hardly big enough for them to wash their faces let alone their whole bodies.

Salmon met with the commandant the next day to persuade him to approve this plan. "None of the men have bathed in weeks," he told the Japanese officer after entering his office. "We would like to have showers so that we can not only maintain hygiene but good health as well."

The commandant raised his eyebrows; for the first time Salmon thought he saw anger simmering in the man's dark eyes. "We don't have the equipment or the men to assemble something like that. I think you have forgotten yourself. You are, like all the men here, a guest of the Emperor, and you are not in a position to demand showers."

"Oh, on the contrary," Salmon hurried to respond, "we don't want you to build it; we will build it ourselves. As a matter of fact, we can do it quite easily."

"With what materials?" the commandant asked, his face smiling its skepticism.

"The materials are already in place," the prisoner generalized, hoping to avoid any further questions. The commandant stood and waved Salmon out of the room, ending the conversation and sending the internee to his cohorts in triumph. He didn't like the commandant, but he considered him fair. The men agreed to start work on building the showering system behind the mess hall.

An American engineer scrounged up four old oil drums, which they cleaned out and set in brickwork with tall iron chimneys; each then formed a hot water boiler. The iron piping from the dismantled sprinkler system was then connected into a small room behind the kitchen where six hot showers were rigged up. Again inequality reigned among the prisoners: most washed themselves quickly with the soothing, hot water; some lingered under the steady stream until the hot water ran out; and still others refused to bathe without threats from their roommates. Salmon was often the coaxer in his own room, while Roper was the one to step in for more direct persuasion. He was occasionally seen dragging an unwashed resident to the shower, the victim whimperingly agreeable to bathing.

It was after such a spectacle that Salmon made a suggestion. "Maybe we should organize this process," he commented as the echoes of their arguing roommate could be heard down the hall. "If everyone had an assigned shower time we could avoid all the arguments."

He and a group of like-minded internees collected brass tallies, abandoned by the tobacco company, with serial numbers stamped on them. Salmon assigned a number to each member of the camp and, with that number, each was given a specific bathing time. All internees were then assigned to one ten-minute bath per week.

By that time, only one inmate had to be forced to take advantage of this privilege. He was an American, called Wallace, with a mysterious background and no working skills. The unshaven, overweight man peered through thick glasses at the internees from his bed. His roommates complained that his smell made sleep impossible, and even during the day there was no respite because he rarely left his room. He never spoke of having worked, offering murky explanations for why he was in Shanghai. Wallace stayed to himself and preferred not only to shirk tasks around the compound but to avoid the new showers as well.

Salmon went to the stubborn and unpopular internee to explain the showering system, but the American scoffed at the idea. "What is this, a country club? Who am I trying to impress? I like the way I smell, and I'm staying this way." Salmon stared at Wallace, who was sitting on his bunk pointedly raising a Chinese newspaper as if to read.

"Well this won't be the last of it," Salmon warned him as he left. When bath time came, a posse, led by Roper the executioner, arrived at the ne'er-do-well's door and accompanied him to the showers. Roper stood by to ensure that he stayed under the water ten minutes and put some soap to work as well. Wallace returned to his room wet, clean, and angry while his bunkmates cheered and clapped. The next week the same posse arrived and went through the same routine. Within a month Wallace was bathing on his own. With the showering schedule in place, the insect population began to dwindle. The brass tallies worked so well the men then put them to work as ration passes at meal times—they entitled their owners to one ration and a quart thermos of boiling water a day for making tea.

• • •

By now all camp functions were undertaken by the internees. The camp leaders assigned everyone a job. Tucker nominated Salmon as camp leader, but the English prisoner refused.

"I'll do anything to help out, but the last thing I want to do is try running this nuthouse." Despite that, residents came to the biochemist to resolve arguments, to get medical advice, or to request an appeal to the commandant. After all, the commandant himself had come to know Salmon personally.

In the meantime, Salmon's efforts to organize the motley population were showing some results. There were gangs for the cookhouse, for preparing vegetables, for cutting up meat, for serving the food, for cleaning the mess hall, and for cleaning the latrines. The older men were given jobs such as collecting, checking, and returning the tallies after meals as well as keeping bath lists.

Whether they liked it or not, the residents were turning the compound into their own tolerable town, though it was far from being a "happy home."

CHAPTER 8

Boredom overwhelmed the 1,100 men in the abandoned tobacco factory. The Japanese did not ask much of their internees, except that they not escape or die, but they also offered them nothing to do with their time. Idle time at first was a blessing. Salmon visited with his old friends, Hughes, Tucker, and Curtis and shared stories with Roper and Beale; he walked around the building premises, read through the few books he had, and then read them again. He wrote letters to his wife and daughters that would never be mailed and prolonged mealtimes by picking up each kernel of rice between his chop sticks to practice his dexterity.

He spent a half hour watching the waters of the Yangtze River below the building, the same waters he had crossed to come to the compound two months before. He then walked down the stairs, up again, and stood at the window for another half hour. He chatted with friends, with colleagues, with anyone who would stop to talk to him. He soon knew everyone's story and had heard enough about everyone's views on politics and the war. He discussed religion with Bishop Curtis and said he might consider being ordained after the war.

The many card games grew dull, with nothing to bet except cigarettes—an uncommon commodity. Some of the men were cheaters, some were poor losers; everyone soon knew whom to play with and whom to avoid. Fights broke out among the players so often that no one glanced in their direction when they shouted or even knocked over the cards and table.

At first, Salmon found the dull times broken up by tasks needed to improve the camp. Then those tasks tapered off, and he was left each morning facing a long day in captivity with absolutely nothing to do. With sewer and water systems working, tasks assigned and kitchen fires stoked, the American, British, and Dutch prisoners found themselves desperately bored.

The men knew everyone in their rooms nearly as well as those in their own families. Salmon spent most of his time in conversation, but was growing tired of the same discussions of food, families, and speculations on when they would be released. He began to dread spending each day with the same people with nothing to do. Those around him were having even more trouble with the unending days of idleness. Many were unsociable or shared nothing in common with other prisoners; many were becoming increasingly unpopular as they failed to do their share of the work.

Salmon reminded Tucker of the days before the war when the men, without their families, passed time by discussing a topic at least one of them specialized in. "Remember how much we learned at those meetings?" he said. "My classes were never more crowded than they were during wartime; it's as if everyone is starving for something new and challenging to think about," he said.

"We have more than a thousand people here," Tucker commented. "Why couldn't we start a school? We could offer classes in just about anything, couldn't we? You name a subject, I'll bet someone in the camp knows something about it." They liked the idea and tried it on Hughes, who was a German teacher. They then went to friends who were not part of the college system.

"A university? I had my chance to go to school a long time ago," a longshoreman commented. "What would I do with math or science now?"

"I don't know that you would have to take the three R's," Salmon said with a dry smile. "You could study anything you want." He glanced around him at the varied faces of those sitting on their bunks listening to the conversation. "Anyone who has a skill could teach it. Even if you think you've learned everything you need in life, at least it would pass the time."

They met with the commandant next. The American-educated man looked Salmon and Tucker over and then stared out the window for several seconds. "Just what do you plan to teach in this university?"

"Anything and everything that would interest people. We figured we'd put together a curriculum based on what people are willing to teach and find out how many students we might have out there."

"I would have to see that curriculum and the schedules," the man responded, and they nodded in agreement. "And history should be early history. By that I mean anything before 1895." Again the men nodded, understanding his point—Japan had launched its aggression against China in 1895.

With renewed enthusiasm, Salmon then went to work posting notices that a school was being organized—in hopes of generating interest both from potential students and teachers. The response was fast; within a few days, about 300 of the 1,100 men had signed up either to teach or study in a class, or both. Courses included math, chemistry, twenty-one different languages, diesel engines, botany, American and European history, and accounting. Unrestrained by the high costs of running universities, this school-in-captivity offered classes as long as two or more students showed an interest. Salmon was staggered by how swiftly the classes formed.

At 9:15 A.M. two students came to him asking for a class on classic Arabic; by 12:30 P.M. he had located a professor from Milan University who had studied the language in Cairo, and classic Arabic was added to the curriculum. The next morning the first class was held. Many of the classes were offered by experienced professors, since twenty-five of the faculty of Soochow University, Shanghai University, St. John's University, and Hangchow Christian College were interned there. Salmon enrolled in a heavy load of courses but was most impressed with the classes offered outside the academic circles. He learned electrical theory from an electrical engineer and navigation from a New Zealand ship's captain. A flour mill engineer offered a popular class in botany.

A total of 151 classes were offered. Classes were held in the afternoons and evenings and did not excuse anyone from camp duties. The students had to use their imaginations, however, to find writing supplies. Salmon used the toilet paper he had brought with him, unrolling his notes like an old fashioned scroll, while Tucker pealed labels off cans and made a writing pad with a stack of them.

The Englishman discovered that he was not the only prisoner who had carried several books with him to the camp; the variety of volumes matched the diversity of interests among the internees. He and his friends formed a library, consisting of books available to others to read but only at the bedside of the book's owner. The library by this time consisted of about six hundred books. The Japanese commandant watched the progression of this adult school with interest. At first skeptical, he became a supporter of the school, finding that, if nothing else, the classes helped improve morale and discipline, which made his own job easier.

One morning a guard ordered Salmon to the commandant's office. He dejectedly walked the stairs in front of the guard. Several of the history classes had been skirting the Japanese aggression in the Far East, and the English prisoner wondered if a spy had turned him in. When he knocked at the office door he heard the commandant call him in. He opened the door until it jammed against something heavy, and he slid into the room through the partial opening. Inside he immediately saw what the obstruction had been; the office was filled with stacks of books in both English and Chinese.

"Your little school is going well?" the commandant asked. Salmon ignored the condescension in the man's tone and nodded as his eyes scanned the book titles. "You and your friend Mr. Tucker are very enterprising. I have always found Westerners to be lazy people, but sometimes you surprise me."

Salmon gave no response to the man's stare. The commandant waited several seconds before gesturing very suddenly at the books around him. "These have been confiscated from libraries around Shanghai. They are of no interest to me; you may have them."

Salmon rushed out to gather a half dozen volunteers to move the books to their quarters. He imagined the commandant was helping them because their school was helping him; a strange alliance had been formed. The commandant eventually collected about two thousand books for the internees. By this time, Tucker and Salmon were able to set up a real library in the old dynamo room. Guards could also be of help; they occasionally sneaked in a box of chalk for the students and teachers. Salmon finished off the walls of the mess hall with dark green paint to be used as chalkboards.

Next, the prisoners considered entertainment to conbat tedium. One afternoon Salmon came into the mess hall to find a tableful of singers belting out a popular American hit. The other internees grinned, tapped feet, and sang along until a few admitted they had brought musical instruments, which were now collecting dust under their beds. The Japanese had seized two professional musicians of separate jazz bands as well as the entire orchestra of the ship the *President Harrison*; these men had all brought their instruments with them, making a small prison orchestra.

An ex-bandmaster from the British Army also joined the group. Soon they were trumpeting, drumming, and strumming familiar tunes for the war-weary prisoners. The musicians put on their first performance after a week's rehearsal, and it was successful enough that they offered a concert every second Saturday evening.

The other internees joined in the spirit, putting together plays or travelogues to present at the functions, and most of the prison population showed up for these events. One man whose father had been a beefeater guard at the Tower of London give a presentation on the historic castle. He constructed an elaborate model of the tower out of old cardboard cartons. Another group put on a production of *Julius Caesar*, doing their best to play both the male and female roles.

All the programs were screened by the commandant before they were ever presented to the prisoners. Japanese guards stood by throughout each production to ensure nothing anti-Japanese or pro-Western was expressed on the improvised stage, banning national anthems or popular songs such as "Tipperary," which the band managed to play anyhow. Forming a complex medley of tunes, they would play part of one before breaking into another. In that way, the guards could not recognize hated songs such as the "Star Spangled Banner" and "God Save The Queen."

The band first put the songs together on a day when prisoners assembled before them were in especially low spirits; by the end of the evening the audience, more boisterous, was singing along to tunes such as "Carry me back to Old Virginny" and "Do ye ken John Peel?" When "America" or "Rule Britannia" was snuck into the midst of these medleys, the men cheered while the guards stood by, oblivious. That night the prisoners returned to their beds with renewed hope.

CHAPTER 9

As spring of 1943 brought a warm thaw to Shanghai, the crowds inside the tobacco factory walls grew. Prisoners arrived at a rate of several dozen a week, while none were taken away. Salmon and Tucker began walking regularly around the main building for exercise, determined not to lose strength.

Beale followed them one day and decided to join them. "You do this everyday? I can't imagine anything more boring than walking around and around the same building," he commented.

"Except perhaps sitting around in the same room," Salmon responded. Roper joined Beale, Tucker, and Salmon the next day; after that several bishops, a butcher, and a ship's captain joined in step.

Others, watching these daily calisthenics, began hiking along until hundreds were walking around and around in both directions. Salmon brushed past the other hikers each day, and he began worrying that soon there wouldn't be room for the growing crowd to circle the building regularly. Fortunately for him, the majority still chose some other activity to occupy them. To the north of the walled compound was a wasteland of several acres full of rubble piles. It had been a village for the Chinese workers before it was utterly demolished by bombs in 1937. The Japanese had done their job so well that there were not two bricks still together in the heap of rubble.

One May morning, on his first lap around the building, Salmon stopped; Tucker came up beside him, staring out at the trash heap. The Japanese guards were at work there extending barbed wire around the yard. Tucker let out a laugh as Salmon said, "Now what can they possibly be up to there?"

By the afternoon, the fence, with a door cut into it, surrounded the yard. One of the guards, with the help of a ladder, posted a sign above the new compound on a piece of discarded wood. The internees gathered to read the sign but had to wait until the man stepped down. When he did, Salmon read the scrawled letters several times in disbelief.

"Happy Garden," it was labeled in plain, black letters, still dripping with ink. They awaited the statement from the commandant, which came over the speaker system a short time later. "For your amusement and at the request of several of you, we have established a place for recreation. I hope you find much pleasure in the Happy Garden."

Salmon and Tucker, with most of their fellow internees, laughed at this weak gesture, but they were glad to have the wretched site. They were two of the first to roam through the barbed wire gate and poke around the yard. Salmon nodded as he murmured to himself, "Yes, I think there may be potential here."

Many of the prisoners clamored with ideas for the property, and they soon went to work clearing debris. For the first time in a while, Salmon woke each morning facing a mission, and he found himself sleeping more soundly through the cool Chinese nights.

The men first leveled an area to make a ball field. Men who had no interest in the adult school and had instead languished on their beds or bickered over card games could now run bases. The shouts of their games, as soon as they had made themselves a ball from loose fabric and whittled boards into bats, filled the compound daily. Salmon watched his American friends Tucker and Hughes play the game but was unimpressed. He preferred tennis—a good English sport. Once the ball games were under way, he began surveying the rest of the property for additional uses.

Immediately next to the compound the men agreed to set up one portion, fitted with concrete benches, water taps, and electrical lines for laundering and hanging wet clothes.

Salmon suggested that the rest of the wilderness be divided into gardening lots for those willing to clear away the debris and plant a garden. Here he orchestrated the planting of vegetables for anyone who could get his hands on seeds. He dug his own plot about twelve feet square, stopping short one sunny morning as his shovel hit a flat obstacle about two feet down. Clearing the dust away, he discovered the floor of a house demolished by the Japanese bombing years before. With the broken bricks of the house foundation, Salmon went to work constructing a wall and seat along the north and northwest corner where he could sit in the sun, sheltered from the cold winds. This became a popular place to escape the noise and crowds, and prisoners came to the garden-making prisoner asking for a turn in his quiet area. Because the concrete floor under the rubble brought a stop to his digging, he located rich Yangtze mud in a large hole at the corner of the yard and used it to the cover the concrete while he dumped the rubble in the hole he made.

Salmon later asked a guard, who had done favors for some of the men, if he could contact some Chinese friends of the Englishman in Shanghai. Soon Salmon received letters from friends he hadn't heard from in more than a year. He then asked for seeds, and the guard would hand them to him with a quick, furtive movement. The smuggling provided him with tomatoes, lettuce, and thick-growing amaranth, as well as melons. To the surprise of both the commandant and the internees, by summer the rubble lot actually was a happy garden, where the majority of the compound population spent all their free time.

CHAPTER 10

As the war continued, the men began their second year of captivity and noticed a slow but frightening change. Each day their food rations were growing smaller and smaller. The cooks warned that soon there wouldn't be enough to maintain the survival diet they now ate.

When the men first arrived, a camp supply of cracked wheat was available from the International Red Cross, which provided porridge during the noon meal. That food soon dwindled and was never replaced. The men ate two meals each day, one at noon and another at 5:00 P.M. The food supplies were brought to the camp once a week and delivered to the quartermaster, who divided them out daily as he chose. During the hot summer the meat often arrived rotten and blackened under a swarm of flies.

The quartermaster sought out Salmon for his knowledge of biochemistry, to examine one rank delivery, then began bringing in the newly appointed nutritionist to inspect each meat delivery before deciding whether to cook it or throw it away. On hot, humid days Salmon went to the mess hall bracing himself for the worst. Often the quartermaster's pinched expression foretold just how spoiled the meat would be. If Salmon found the meat was dangerous, the men buried it in the Happy Garden. The bones of some of the animals brought in indicated that they had died or had been dying of tuberculosis when they were butchered.

As the larder emptied, the level of protein in the men's diets dropped, and Salmon had to lower his standards. Leaning over a stinking chunk of unidentified animal meat, rife with tuberculosis, he shook his head and glanced at the chef and the quartermaster, who watched him with their hands over their noses and mouths. "This is fine," Salmon said.

"Are you crazy?" the chef exclaimed, but the biochemist ignored him.

"You'll have to cook it longer than usual, as a matter of fact I would cook this all day, but as long as you do there's nothing that would kill anyone."

The chef muttered to himself. "I never thought I'd be cooking anything like this."

Salmon smiled in response. "I would suggest using a little extra sauce on this one, maybe a marinade."

Each day the quartermaster reported to Salmon the weight of each item of food he had sent to the kitchen. With the help of a fruit company refrigeration engineer, Salmon calculated the amount of calories in carbohydrates, fats, and proteins and also the minerals and vitamins the men were consuming. Once a month he reported these to a health committee composed of two American doctors, one British doctor, and one Australian doctor. His findings became more depressing as the war continued. Eventually the health committee, based on the latest nutritional report, went to the commandant to report a dangerously low supply of vitamins B_1, B_2, and C. The commandant was unimpressed. "I think you forget, this is war time," the man responded. "As it is, you are eating better than many Japanese are."

The next day Salmon decided to meet with the commandant personally. "You might be surprised how simple it would be to improve the diet here," he told the man immediately as the commandant took his seat. The camp leader was no longer surprised by his visits from the small Englishman, who had become a ragged character in a tattered, tweed jacket and soiled shirt. Salmon realized, as he looked at the officer in the starched uniform, just how shabby his own appearance had become.

"Instead of bringing more food in, you could just make several changes," he continued. "Take the rice, for example. You are serving it to us in the cleaned, polished white form, but if we had it uncleaned there would be more of the B vitamins present." He added that the outer, greener leaves of the vegetables would be a better source of vitamin C.

The commandant, faced with the prospect of saving money in the interest of good health, agreed to these changes. Soon after the change, the men began to notice improved night vision and disease lessened. Nevertheless, some prisoners still fell sick. Salmon visited a young Dutch man who, pale and anemic, was suffering from beriberi.

"Aren't you eating the new rations," Salmon asked.

"Well, I'm not eating that filthy food if that's what you mean," he said of the more bitter, tough vegetables and unpolished rice. Salmon threw up his hands, leaving the man to his own misery.

It was the tedium of the diet that bothered most of the men. The chief steward of the *President Harrison* tried to bring variety to the rice and leafy vegetables with any available flavoring and spices. Salmon exasperated the chef with his approval of spoiling meat, but he also was the man's best source of new ingredients, between his garden and outside sources. When he could, Salmon would pass a new ingredient to the chef who would happily post a menu boasting in French of the improved cuisine. His signboard offered "a la salon premiere" one night, though most of the time the sign read "S.O.S."—same old stew.

CHAPTER 11

Despite the limited communication with the outside world, the prisoners could take a look at it whenever they chose. Through the window lay a tantalizing view of the Shanghai harbor and the movement of the Japanese and other international ships in the Chinese waterways. The shipping yard had once been the anchoring center of a half-dozen grand vessels, but now it was a place for the coming and going of small Japanese boats. There was one exception to that, however: the *Conte Verde*, an Italian luxury liner, was anchored permanently in the harbor where the Yangtze met the Whangpoo River. Salmon first noticed the ship when he arrived at the compound, and he would gaze at her majestic form and recall days when he was free—days he had traveled, times he had spent with his family, and before that, with Laliah, his journey to China as a young man.

The beautiful ship Salmon gazed upon had come from Rome the year before to pick up Italian troops in Shanghai but had been trapped there when the war with England broke out. To avoid certain capture by the British Navy, she remained anchored where she had been, there in Shanghai. Because the ship helped him through some of the darker moments of his imprisonment, the prisoner began to think of it as a friend. But it was a rough friendship from the start.

One morning he was startled when Tucker dashed through the door. "Come to the window; the *Conte Verde* is going down!" he shouted. They ran together to the window, ahead of a dozen others flocking to the portals, where they could see the harbor. As he looked out over the

Yangtze River port, he saw the *Conte Verde* and watched in amazement as the mast of the Italian vessel slowly tilted.

It fell slowly at first, then at increasing speed it came down to lie flush with the water. The huge funnels lay for a while on the surface of the river and then sank beneath it. Italy was no longer at war, and the crew had learned the news by radio. Rather than allow the ship to be taken by the Japanese, they opened the cocks on one side so that the ship listed to port and sank into the muddy river.

The men questioned the guards until a friendly individual told them what he knew of the ship. It could not have sunk in a more inconvenient place for the Japanese who used the Shanghai port, since it blocked all boats from entering or leaving the naval yard. The Japanese were furious and the guard told Salmon that they arrested the ship's officers and entire crew for sabotage. Not only did it prevent their use of the magnificent vessel, but it effectively blocked their use of the Kang Wan docks, where the Japanese were refitting and repairing destroyers and other warcraft. Since the Whangpoo was a tidal river with thick layers of mud, this large obstruction affected the currents until they threatened to undermine the Shanghai Bund. From the window, Salmon watched the Japanese disaster, feeling both amusement and disappointment at seeing the beautiful ship sink into the depths of the muddy river.

Several days later he watched as the Japanese tried to remove the ship. He stood at the window, engrossed by this unusual entertainment. They attached a winch and giant chain to the superstructure, then anchored a machine, braced against the shore by an immense cable around an entire block of buildings on the Bund, to lift the ship.

As the powerful machine tightened the chain, it writhed, groaned, and jerked spasmodically until suddenly the weakest link gave way. From where he watched Salmon could only guess at the outcome, but by the next day most prisoners had heard that several Japanese were killed by the snapped chain. After this fiasco, Japanese divers worked for more than three months to remove the ship. They placed airtight tanks in the holds and pumped in air in order to raise the rusted hull.

The ship was finally raised one evening, and Salmon watched with a sense of nostalgia, pleased as if an old friend had come back to see him. The next morning he was awakened by the buzz of an airplane over-head. It did not sound like the small Japanese fighters, but there was no anti-aircraft fire. As the sun began to rise, the plane circled over Shanghai once, and again passed over the camp low enough to bring the heads of Salmon's roommates up from their pillows. He ran to the window and was just in time to see a column of steam and water shoot up from the middle of the *Conte Verde*. A lone bomb had undone the patient work of the divers. Its mission completed, the mysterious plane disappeared.

It took another six months to raise the shattered hulk of what had been one of the world's most luxurious liners. It was then towed down-river, and Salmon watched it go, imagining that it would be broken up for scrap. Unknown to him at the time, the Japanese salvaged the ship and painted it the colors of a hospital vessel before using it to move Japanese troops.

CHAPTER 12

As the days passed, the most common unspoken question was when would this ordeal end. From time to time rumors circulated that there would be a prisoner exchange, but usually those rumors were wrong, and the disappointed prisoners returned to waiting.

In September 1943 the rumor reemerged and Salmon chose to ignore it. He was surprised then, when the commandant announced that 150 of the internees would be shipped out to Goa on their way to freedom.

Ellis Tucker, with a hernia, was among those to go. He came to his longtime friend and grinned with enthusiasm tinged with some regret for Salmon's sake. "I hate to leave you here, Salmon," he commented, "You only have your blasted good health to blame."

The Englishman smiled and nodded, disappointed but unwilling to show it. He knew, if Tucker was leaving, there was hope that the rest could go at any time themselves.

"Send a letter to my family in Minneapolis," Salmon said. He had no idea where his wife and two daughters were living there, but knew his wife's sister would send on any letters. "Don't say anything to worry them, and maybe you can pass a few of my own letters through," he urged. He wrote new letters full of good cheer and stoicism and sketched some pictures of the trees around the camp for his girls. The letters were confiscated, but the pictures later reached their destination.

Tucker, who had been the leader of the university in the compound, turned the controls over to Salmon, who accepted them reluctantly. "You're the obvious man to run this school," his friend said. "You've done most of the work putting it together; who else could keep it running?" Salmon agreed, and Tucker brought his course listings and books to him, where they sat piled by his bed.

It was a joyful day for those leaving when they woke at the compound for the last time and packed up their few belongings. They celebrated and cheered as they left. Salmon stood in the yard before the Happy Garden, shaking the hands of his departing friends and watching them walk away. Tucker let out a triumphant shout and salute to his friends and turned to walk away with the large group. The tall man stood a head above nearly everyone, and Salmon watched him go until he was out the gate and on his way to the waiting ship. The remaining prisoners returned to their rooms and activities with an uncharacteristic hush, and they later ate dinner in the mess hall in subdued silence. Salmon looked at the expanse of empty tables around them and hoped that maybe he would be next.

Two years had passed since his arrest, and he could imagine how much things were changing in the outside world as he went about his mundane routine. For a few days he engrossed himself in reorganizing the school, taking courses off the roster when there was no one left to teach, and finding substitutes for other courses. Salmon also went in search of new members for the essential services in kitchens, baths, lavatories, and commissariat. While he and the others prepared to spread out of their cramped quarters into the newly empty spaces, the Japanese stopped them. Instead, the guards ordered them to vacate some rooms and move closer together into the remaining quarters.

One week later, on a dull rainy day, a neighbor burst into the room where Salmon was teaching chemistry. "Women are coming!" the man exclaimed.

Salmon joined his roommates as they rushed to the windows on the south side of the buildings. There, a procession of tired, bedraggled females and some children trudged along the muddy, narrow lane and filed in at the iron gate. They were being moved from the Yangchow camp to fill places left vacant by the repatriates; as they made their slow procession, a few young boys and older men could be seen carrying some of their baggage.

Clean-shaven men were unique in the camp since razors were rare, the water was frigid, and soap was hard to find. Salmon imagined that it must have been a depressing sight for those tired travelers, entering the dingy, barbed-wire-encircled factory, to view hundreds of bearded, gaunt faces peering down at them from three rows of bare windows.

Two rooms housed all the married couples among the resettled prisoners. It was left to them how best to devise cubicles from boxes, curtains, and cords. The single women and some of the girls were kept in another room; the teenage boys were scattered among the men's rooms.

Salmon awoke the next morning to a huge change in morale. The quest for razors or the means of sharpening old blades had begun. "Hey, wait a minute," one of the Americans sitting beside Salmon in the mess hall said. "How have you kept that face so clean?" Salmon had been able to shave regularly because he had brought with him not only a razor but a sharpener. As a result, he suddenly became the most popular man in camp. Stubble beards began to fade away, and local haircutting bees could be found in every room. But while it served to motivate the men to new levels of cleanliness, the presence of women also caused practical problems. Salmon created a new shower bath schedule with "ladies only" periods. When he saw several men leaving the shower naked, he shouted after them. "Are you walking back to your rooms like that?"

Taken by surprise they stopped. "Hey, you think the ladies will mind?" one of them joked. Salmon issued a rule that no more "bare skins" be permitted outside the shower.

There were about fifteen children in the camp; they were easily incorporated into the school program with their own age-level courses that rivaled the classes they took in public schools. Salmon found the new group offered some variety to his adult education programs too. The latest prisoners were incredulous over the elaborate school system they were joining; the Englishman had to first convince them they had experience worthy of sharing with other restless, bored prisoners.

With that in mind, many more teachers and speakers found themselves signing up. A naval engineer who, with his wife, was an artist, lectured about his travels to remote spots in China and made them more entertaining by illustrating with rapid sketches on a blackboard.

Professor Drake of Chi Lu University needed no convincing to offer his own course; he was an artist who knew the Chinese classical history as few non-Chinese or even Chinese did. He kept his large audiences enthralled at night with accounts of the old tyrant Chin Shih Wang, who established the short-lived Chin empire by bringing the downfall of the old fuedal states. The parallel's between Hitler and Chin were clear enough for the students to notice, but the class seemed innocuous to the Japanese commandant.

With their help, Salmon breathed new life into the Pootung "University." He now offered seventy classes with about four hundred students and forty instructors; and new programs such as Chinese art and papier-mâché were added to the curriculum. Salmon was in awe of one student, known as Miss Graves, who showed an amazing talent for papier-mâché. She produced a believable reproduction of a Greek vase out of an old tin can, some newspaper, and a little soft-boiled rice as glue.

The English scientist found the opportunity to work on his own creativity. He used bits of toilet paper and a hand-whittled pen to make Chinese landscapes, which he planned to bring home one day to his daughters in America. He practiced calligraphy, whittled himself an entire set of pens, and smoothed out a slate for mixing the ink.

• • •

The women were unimpressed by the all-male Shakespeare productions, and a dozen of them offered to breath some life into the theatrical efforts of the camp. They produced colorful seventeenth-century costumes from fragments of bathrobes, scarves, and other clothing; the kings and queens in Shakespearean productions wore crowns and jewels made out of papier-mâché, wire, broken thermos bottles, and rice glue; soldiers carried shields and beaten plates made of cardboard covered with aluminum foil from cigarette packs.

The arrival of women also brought soprano and alto voices for a choir. At Christmas 1944 hundreds of prisoners put together a pageant of the Christmas story while Salmon helped piece together the stage. When it was finished, even the Japanese guards applauded. During Easter, the new choir sang a portion of Handel's "Messiah."

Shortly after the new internees arrived, however, Salmon noticed that the helpings of rice and cooked greens grew smaller. While there had been barely enough to subsist on before, now people began to fear starvation. The biochemist dug out all the plants he could from the vegetables he was growing; if he hadn't, he knew someone else would have. The only relief came every six weeks with Red Cross packages. Some of the food provided in them had to be cooked, and for weeks it went uneaten because the kitchen had no room to accommodate them.

Salmon suggested an outdoor grill; that afternoon about a dozen men built a large one with spare bricks and iron plates. From that day on, the grill was kept hot from early morning until 10 P.M. and was usually surrounded by internees. Soon after Red Cross parcels arrived, the grill was besieged with prisoners cooking hot soup, frying bacon or meat, or roasting a potato. Many of the better foods came through payoffs to the guards; those with the most money could usually be found spending the most time at the grill—they also seemed to be in the best health.

Salmon, without money for these extra delicacies, looked on with a groaning stomach. His luck changed though when the Red Cross sent colored beans in its packages. The beans provided nutritious food but looked dirty and smelled rotten when cooking. Many would cook the beans, examine them with distaste, then throw them out while Salmon looked on, shaking his head at their poor judgment. While others gave up on their Red Cross packages, Salmon prepared a feast with the scavenged red beans. He reheated them for the first hot supper he had eaten in months. By this time the temperature of the rooms was below 40 degrees; it was the winter of 1944, and Salmon, thin and chilled, found a solitary moment of comfort as he ate quietly in the dark.

Sitting there, he considered the picky eaters in the camp and remembered the tough training of his grandmother Gertrude—she would be proud of him, he guessed. That determined training led him to eat the maggots and other insects found infesting his evening rice. Many of the prisoners picked out the bugs while Salmon made a pointing of eating them, knowing he was getting the protein their regular diet lacked.

The health of camp residents worried everyone, whether they were sick yet or not. The four doctors in the complex had managed to smuggle in some medical equipment, drugs, and chemicals. By pooling these essentials, they were able to diagnose most problems with simple blood or urine tests. Among the women were several nurses, and with their arrival, the prisoners set up a small infirmary for the very sick.

One of the new women to join them captured Salmon's immediate attention; she arrived with the help of a teenage boy and an older man, each holding her by one arm as she tried to keep up with the others. By the next day, the middle-aged woman was unable to even stand without someone rushing to her side to assist. When Salmon first approached her, she gave him the apathetic look of a dying woman.

"I'm going to see that you get some help," he promised her and went in search of one of the camp's doctors. After only a perfunctory exam the doctor diagnosed extreme anemia and ordered liver extract through the Red Cross to treat her. But as the days passed after her treatment, Salmon saw her continue to decline. The disease was all too familiar to the biochemist who had seen similar symptoms among the undernourished Chinese before the war; he recalled that the purified liver extract of Western medicine didn't work as well as the cruder Chinese version.

He had formed a careful alliance with some of the guards and knew those who smuggled at the gate; so by hovering there with the Japanese, he procured some Chinese liver extract. After the woman swallowed the foul-tasting medicine with dull compliance, Salmon returned to her bed the next day to find her sitting up with a more alert expression. A week later he saw her in the mess room, pale and wan, but eating her bowl of rice with measured enthusiasm. When she noticed him, she offered a wave of gratitude. He smiled with a satisfaction he hadn't felt in years.

It wasn't the first time, however, that the scientist had seen local remedies work after Western medicine failed. During the worst of an Asian hot spell, the pharmacist in Salmon's room fell with a hard case of diarrhea. Although he took sulfa he had brought into the camp, it didn't slow his constant rushes to the latrines.

Salmon watched the man grow weaker and more miserable daily. At last in despair the man consented to eat a glob of unpolished, soft-boiled rice and some wild amaranth leaves Salmon had grown in the Happy Garden. Salmon cooked the vegetable on the grill and handed it over while the reluctant patient sniffed it skeptically, then ate it with distaste. From that time on, his malady vanished, and Salmon gained some pleasure in noticing that the man slept through the night without any nocturnal latrine visits.

After Salmon's cure of the anemic woman and the pharmacist, increasing numbers of his fellow inmates sought him out for medical advice. Scott, the engineer at the end of Salmon's room, came to him in distress one night. "My hand is becoming completely numb, Dr. Salmon," he said. "It started in the finger tips, and now I can't feel my fingers at all." He held out his right hand and wiggled his fingers before him. "I once severed the nerve in my elbow about ten years ago," he said. "I think it's atrophy of the nerves. What am I going to do?"

Salmon guessed the man was short on vitamin B_1. He knew one plant that offered this nutrient, the common plantain, the seeds of which the Chinese had used for two thousand years for common ailments. He had no trouble finding the plants growing wild on the perimeters of the garden.

The nutritionist dropped a teaspoonful of seeds into boiling water to make a cup of tea which he gave to the man daily for six days. By that time, feeling was restored in his fingers. Salmon's friend was so impressed with this cure that he brought another prisoner who was suffering from stabbing pains in his legs at night. Since this was often the first symptom of beriberi, another disease of acute B_1 deficiency, Salmon gave the same prescription: again the common seed ended the problem.

Salmon's next patient was an older man whose troubles predated the war. He had suffered chronic constipation so badly that his doctor had medicated him with physostigmine, an irritant bean extract. This drug was unavailable at the camp, and the problem had returned. Salmon guessed from the size, age, and overall bad health of the patient that even if he could have continued on the doctor's prescribed drug, his heart would not have tolerated the continual high doses of the toxic extract. On the "Robert Salmon Plan" of eating soft-boiled unpolished rice with amaranth leaves he was soon feeling better than he had for years.

The children always enjoyed the best of what the camp provided, both nutritionally and educationally. Some of the teenage students, who were university material, came to Salmon, now named education director, asking for a chance to take the Cambridge entrance exam in the event the war would end by the following school year. Challenged by this proposal, Salmon requested the camp commandant to allow the teens a Cambridge School Certificate Standard Exam. With the commandant's approval he then wrote to Cambridge in February 1945; this letter not only reached the college, it was answered. Eleven students took the exam through the neighboring Lungwha School, and all but two passed. Despite the war, the confinement, and the starvation, these children were eventually going to Cambridge.

CHAPTER 13

As the internees struggled with bad health and hunger, the war blazed on outside their walls. Though no one knew much about the war's progress, everyone pursued each rumor that passed through the camp.

Salmon was not completely in the dark about the outside world. He learned some of what was happening in the war by watching the wharf and the skies through his window, and there were other forms of communication as well. Three copies of the *Shanghai Times* were allowed in each room by the Japanese. This newspaper, published in English, had always been well respected by those living in the city but, after the war began, the Japanese took the paper over and made it an organ for their propaganda.

While reading the paper, Salmon often shook his head or laughed out loud, reading the more ridiculous statements to his neighbors Beale and Roper; he soon became an expert at guessing the truth behind the lies. One morning in 1944 he read that the Japanese had carried out a devastating air raid on a Pacific island. But Salmon recalled that several weeks before the Japanese had boasted of the area being in their possession. Obviously, he surmised, the Japanese had somehow lost control there.

"Listen to this," he said as he read another story while sitting on his bed, Beale sitting beside him looking over his shoulder. "According to this story, the Japanese had a successful advance to the rear.'"

He laughed as Beale commented, "I don't think the Japanese understand the word 'retreat.'"

Salmon, like his fellow prisoners, read the paper ravenously to interpret this hodgepodge of disinformation. The number of copies of the paper was eventually cut to fewer than one per room; in their place the Japanese distributed a small typed sheet dubbed the "headliner" which summarized the main reports and was circulated to each room. The "real" news was available too, but came from a variety of sources; Salmon noticed often the truest information arose as spontaneous rumors.

Radios were forbidden, but the radio operator of the *President Harrison*, a man known as Sparks, smuggled a small receiver in with his belongings and could pick up San Francisco stations. A small group of companions would then obtain the news from him and transmit it by word of mouth to the rest of the inmates. Sparks soon became popular throughout the camp, but his popularity backfired. After a stool pigeon in his room reported him, three Japanese officers dragged him and two friends out of the camp; he was thrown in prison for six months before returning to the compound.

Once Sparks left, the news tapered off, but one of Salmon's roommates would often lie on his bed with the covers over his head as faint voices seemed to come from under the covers. One night Salmon approached the bed and whispered "What is that, you have— a radio?" The man admitted he had stashed a radio in the springs of his mattress and could hear a New Delhi station. He was hesitant to reveal what he learned on the radio, however, and usually the information he gave in a whispered tone in the hallway outside the room was sketchy and hard to interpret.

As the Red Cross parcels came into camp, another source of news opened up. Some of the men had Russian wives who were not interned; the women would send in food wrapped in Russian newspapers, which provided detailed accounts of news concerning European and African theaters of war, so that after D-day the internees were so well informed they kept a map of France on which they stuck pins each day to mark the advance of the Allied forces. The Russians, however, had a treaty of friendship with Japan so there was no news whatsoever about the Pacific arena. With the exception of the sinking of the *Conte Verde*, no air activity occurred during the early part of Salmon's internment.

The first air raid by American planes occurred on Armistice Day, November 11, 1944. The prisoners woke to a beautiful and unusually warm day with low, fleecy clouds. Starting at nine o'clock, pairs of B29 planes sailed above the clouds, momentarily appearing and then disappearing again. There was no opposition, and they dropped their bombs on chosen targets and flew on their way.

The Pootung internees were energized by this new excitement, the best sign they had seen since their arrest two years before. They gathered transfixed at their windows as a fresh pair of bombers returned every half hour until 1:00 P.M. Salmon watched the first pair sail gracefully overhead to release five bombs on a strong point the Japanese had constructed in Chapee about a half mile across the river from the camp; the entire roof shot into the air. Salmon's roommate told him the next morning, after listening to New Delhi radio, that the bomb had killed several Jewish refugees from the Nazi purge in Europe, who were living in quarters close to the Japanese fort.

The second target they hit that day was an alcohol distillery about a mile from the camp on the Pootung side of the river; the building went up in a mass of flames. The third successful hit exploded the docks where the Japanese were repairing small war vessels. A dugout had been made for the protection of workers from air attack, but only the Japanese workers were allowed to take refuge in it. A heavy bomb made a direct hit on it, killing all the Japanese occupants and delighting the Chinese who saw in it righteous vengeance. The bombing increased the danger for those in the camp, but they silently cheered it anyway; Salmon welcomed each air raid as it came closer within striking distance.

That night, the now jittery Japanese imposed new restrictions on lights after dark: they directed the internees to put screens of Chinese matting in the windows of the mess hall and to paint a large red cross on the roof of the main building of the camp. In the coming days raids became more frequent, and the Japanese struck back with more violence. Salmon now spent his nights between his bed and the window, where the war thundered before him.

One night a Japanese fighter chased after the Allied planes and was struck fatally. As it plunged downward, Salmon and the internees began shouting in horror, watching the plane barreling directly down toward the camp. It passed, however, narrowly missing the river and striking the street behind a post office.

Another night the camp residents watched an air fight to see an American plane burst into flames over the camp. It was a doleful spectacle for Salmon, who watched mesmerized as it fell a mile or more to the east. After the war he was told that some internees walking in that direction found the graves of the airmen whom the Chinese had found and buried.

Spring brought the war even closer to the camp as American escort fighters began to appear with the bombers in daylight raids. Some of these were jets that amazed Salmon as they dive-bombed the anti-aircraft emplacements around the camp and zoomed away with smooth, lightning speed and grace. Their display left Salmon and his campmates stunned.

One bomb hit about twenty-five yards off one side of the camp and another about fifty yards on the other side. Salmon guessed the raiders knew just who was living between the two bomb sites and were sending a message. "Maybe they're trying to offer us assurance for the bombing ahead," he told a nervous ten-year-old boy standing beside him that day. "They're going to show us just how accurate they can be."

Salmon didn't know that an intensive attack was scheduled for August 8 but had to be postponed because of a typhoon in Okinawa. The dramatic raid everyone expected never came—the war ended first. As the summer went by, all sorts of rumors and speculations traveled through the camp.

Frequently on clear hot days, when it was a great relief to go into the Happy Garden to get fresh air, wispy, white clouds appeared high in the sky. At first, Salmon paid no attention; later his friend Hughes came by the garden and sat with his hands clutched at his knees, staring for several minutes at the sky. He finally said, "You know there's something strange about those clouds. They appear for awhile, and then they disappear." They both stared up at the sky, frowning against the sun's rays.

"You're right; there is something odd about them. Do you know, I think they are actually appearing in formation. Like the letter V." It was the first time Salmon had seen sky writing, but he now wondered if this were some miraculous message from the Allies, meant to give him and his companions hope.

CHAPTER 14

On Sunday afternoon, August 13, 1945, Salmon was again sitting in his little plot in the Happy Garden when Hughes sat down beside him. The two friends had spent hours here almost daily, talking about Salmon's chemistry class, Hughes's German class, and the progress of the war. That Sunday was different, however, and they spoke with hushed and serious tones, believing something was happening that would soon change their lives forever. That morning Salmon had been watching his window as usual and was taken aback by a strange sight at the Russian and French consulates—friendly buildings he had spent many hours watching during his captivity.

During the war the Vichy flag of German-occupied France had flown over the French consulate. That morning the Englishman watched as the flag lowered, and the old tri color was raised in its place; it had flown there for an hour or so when it was again lowered. He continued to watch the hammer and sickle over the Russian consulate, waiting to see it lowered, since he was sure that with the end of the war, the Russians would cease their alliance with Japan.

Salmon had heard that a strange new bomb had been dropped on Hiroshima, but he did not know that Russia had turned on Japan two days later. After the two friends shared their predictions, Hughes rose to go, patting Salmon on the shoulder. "There will be great news tomorrow," he forecast.

"Why do you say that?" Salmon asked, but Hughes only shook his head and smiled.

"I've got a good feeling this time," he said.

Monday morning dawned bright; something seemed different the moment Salmon raised his head from his worn, unwashed pillow. He dressed as his roommates began the day like any other, but he noticed when he stepped out of the room, the customary guards were no longer in the hallway. He exited the building with an unnerving sense of freedom and looked out the gate at the Chinese passing along the street. He was taken aback by what they were doing. The people he saw were smiling, and they shouted happily to each other as they passed. As he stood staring, the prisoner caught the look of the Chinese watchman across the street. To his amazement, the man waved and grinned, gesticulating as though he was either drunk or insane.

It turned out to be a very hot day. About eleven o'clock Salmon noticed all the closed shutters of the windows of the Japanese guards' quarters across the street from his building were closed except one. Through this one he could see the Japanese standing at attention: their heads hung downward and some seemed to be in tears. Had he ever seen anyone as unhappy as these men, who were listening to their emperor's orders to surrender? Soon they left the window, and he did not see them again.

At about two o'clock the persistent clanging of a piece of steel used as a gong for meals or hot water rations signaled that something was happening. Japanese-appointed prisoner leaders burst into the rooms and announced that the guards had left.

"Who's in charge?" Hughes asked and one of those leaders responded: "The Red Cross is. We are supposed to stay here in the camp."

Men began to mutter to themselves, but the leaders cut them off. "We don't know what might be happening in Shanghai right now. It's safer to stay here."

Later that day the gong sounded again, and the residents huddled together in the mess hall where American officers met them. They spoke with the internees, eager to find out about their health. Though many were still sick and everyone was hungry, the American suicide at the beginning of their stay was the only death at Pootung, as the commandant had predicted.

Salmon, the Americans said, was in excellent health, if seriously underweight. Many of the prisoners were weak and ailing from Asian diseases, but the officers attributed the general good health of the camp to Robert Salmon and the four doctors who had treated the sick prisoners.

The officers also questioned each resident in search of several men who were on the international "wanted list" for a variety of crimes. The names were familiar, but these wanted men hadn't been seen for several hours; they had slipped away in the afternoon when the others had been advised to stay where they were. One of these men was a surgeon who was wanted by the FBI for his operations as a Russian spy before he skipped the United States on the eve of his country's involvement in the war with Japan. Before he left the camp, he took the camp records the Japanese had dumped out of the office.

The residents were still advised to stay where they were, so Salmon went back to his room to stare at the walls. A few days later American bombers flew from Okinawa and parachuted large oil drums filled with canned fruits, chocolate, and cigarettes on the camp. It was a sunny day, but a strong northwesterly wind blew over the compound, so many of the drums fell outside the walls on rooftops. Some of those packed with canned foods overloaded the parachutes and fell like bombs, breaking windows and roofs and scattering the precious contents.

After the passage of each bomber, parties of inmates made sorties to rescue the contents of the drums. Salmon joined one of these groups, and as he chased down food he looked around him, catching his breath with the realization that he was outside the camp walls for the first time in three years.

In the meantime, the women went to work opening battered cans of peaches and apricots. It bothered him to see that much of the food was completely wasted since they couldn't reach it. As the Japanese remained in control of Shanghai, a regular steam launch ferry chugged into service. They watched it cross the river to the city. The Whangpoo River was almost deserted, but the streets of the city were thronged with pedestrians as usual. There were some flags waving as a sign of rejoicing.

The streetcars and trackless trams were running, but they were so crowded it was impossible for the average Chinese to get one. The minimum fare was $500 local currency, which was also the price of a newspaper— a single sheet of mimeographed paper. The paperboy had to carry large netted bags to hold the hundred dollar bills he gathered. All of this, Salmon watched from behind the walls, still waiting for the word that it was safe to finally leave his prison.

A Chinese friend came to the camp soon after VJ Day and gave Salmon a million Chinese dollars to cope with inflation. "My first million!" he commented wryly as he sifted through the bills.

On the streets now an occasional truck pulled through, piled high with sacks of rice or bales of silk. The trucks were driven by Japanese soldiers while others holding fixed bayonets or machine guns sat on top of the load. Although they had been conquered, they were able to continue "harvesting" the loot for several weeks after VJ Day.

• • •

Toward the end of August Salmon decided he had had enough. Hughes said he was waiting for the American liberation, but Salmon decided the time had come to leave. He packed only one bag now, of the few items still worth carrying, and with no ceremony he walked through gates that had stood open for several weeks. A handful of friends watched him go, but planning to see him again soon, they said only perfunctory good-byes. With the sun in his eyes, he left without a second look at his home or at his quiet plot in the Happy Garden. He was three years older but felt he had aged a decade.

Robert Salmon secured a room at St. John's University, preparing to continue teaching and anticipating the return of his family, now anxiously waiting in America. His former home was now occupied by a Chinese family, and the best part of his furniture had been taken by the Japanese. He lived in a room, therefore, on the top floor of one of the student dormitories.

For about a week the two lower floors were unoccupied, but that changed on September 7 when the first Chinese Nationalist troops moved in. Their arrival had been delayed by Communist troops who had infiltrated Shanghai, and the nationalist forces had to be airlifted into the city. They were then billeted at St. John's; the two lower floors of the hall where Salmon was living were filled with them.

The arrival of troops did nothing to aid Salmon's sense of security. This was not the Shanghai he had known, and the Englishman became increasingly uneasy. On St. John's campus lurked some Japanese troops and a few American Marines. Since all were fully armed, a feeling of danger and tension hung over the campus.

Salmon was surprised when his closest Chinese friend, who had supplied him with vegetable seeds and more recently a million Chinese dollars, would not speak to him. The man had joined the Communists and would have nothing more to do with the capitalists of the West.

St John's campus and Jessfield Park were for Salmon a sad sight when he compared them with what he had left three years before. Paint was peeling and waterspouts hung loose from many of the buildings. The formerly trimmed lawns were poorly kept, and the flower borders and shrubberies were full of rank weeds.

When he tried to go out, the only form of transportation was his own feet. He did not go into Shanghai often, but by chance happened to be on the Bund when a Western fleet came up the Whangpoo. He smiled now to see the river once again become a busy thoroughfare.

A few days later Salmon learned that the hospital ship *USS Refuge* was to leave shortly with the fleet and had a vacant space. He rushed to the ship to secure that space and was then on board the first vessel to sail from Shanghai after VJ day. He was finished with China, for good.

The ship took the war-weary Englishman to Okinawa on the heels of a deadly typhoon. Several ships lay on the shore, and the rest were standing offshore preparing to ride out the approach of another predicted typhoon. Salmon quickly transshipped to the *USS Constitution*, which sailed immediately. By now it was obvious another storm was on its way; the sky had turned a somber, copper hue that boded trouble.

After passing through the storm to Guam, Salmon learned that within a few hours after he left Okinawa a disastrous typhoon had destroyed aircraft and ships. Any plans to stay in Asia were now dashed, and Robert Salmon happily trained his eyes and his thoughts on the West, where his wife and two daughters awaited him.

PART THREE

Making News: A Reporter Defies His German Captors

CHAPTER 1

With his breath bursting out of him in cold clouds, PFC Edward Uzemack scrambled up a frozen and heavily wooded hill surrounded by his fellow riflemen of Company B, 110th Infantry, 28th Keystone Division. Their mission was simple—to wipe out a German pillbox at the top of the rise, allowing movement of the Allies toward the Rhine. There was a high risk of sniper fire, and the men stayed low to the ground ready to be fired upon, most likely from the pillbox they were making their prey. Uzemack's eyes darted behind his thick glasses watching for enemy movement while his lungs hissed with tension. He shouldn't have been there in the Belgian woods risking his life; he was far from a career soldier and had never expected to be on the front lines seeing this kind of combat.

Uzemack's tour as a soldier began when he was called up for duty from his home in Chicago. It was 1943, and the *Chicago Times* news and feature writer was twenty-eight years old, launching a successful career. He had bad vision and was confident he wouldn't be sent into action. Back in Chicago the military physician had examined the writer's eyes, tested his vision, and agreed that without glasses Uzemack couldn't see more than his hands before his face. His vision was 20/400, enough to label him a 4-F, not physically fit for service; but Uzemack was in excellent health, and the doctor seemed reluctant to let him go that easily. So as Uzemack sat on the examination table waiting, the doctor took the nearsighted man's glasses, peered at them, held them up to the light, then nodded, handing them back. "I'd say you're 20/200," he said. Uzemack knew what that verdict meant; 20/200 vision allowed a man to be marked for limited service—a backup soldier, but a soldier never the less. Uzemack was a married man with a job he liked and a baby on the way; he left for the war in Europe as company clerk for two hundred riflemen replacements with no great enthusiasm.

When the new soldier arrived in France, he followed in the wake of D-day and its heavy casualties; there would be no question of secondary status. Every able-bodied man would be put to service as a rifleman. Five months later Uzemack was here—stuck on a hill firing at the German pillbox. Rapid fire from behind exploded over his head, and he realized the shooting was coming not only from the target, but from all around him. His unit had been booby-trapped by the Germans who had lured the American soldiers there and surrounded them.

The order came from the company lieutenant and gave them little time to hesitate. "Take cover! Get out, and don't stop for the wounded," the officer shouted as bullets pierced the air around them. The newsman, a tall, 198-pound man, dropped low enough to the ground to run, yet make an elusive target in his retreat. The ground was slick with ice and snow; the trees loomed dark around him as he stumbled for his footing, then slid into the trunk of a tree. At the same time bullets bore holes in the bark and woody flesh just over his head. His helmet, which he secured on his head without its chin strap, fell loose and landed on the bridge of his nose, sending pain jarring through his face and his glasses flying to the ground.

Suddenly blinded, he fumbled for the remains of his glasses, feeling little more than the frame with his anxious hands. When he put the glasses back on, he found that one lens was crushed, the other badly cracked. With this marginal vision he barreled on down the hill and reached safety, losing many of his fellow soldiers behind him.

Another Army physician looked Uzemack's eyes over when he took his R and R days later. "All right, we'll order you another pair of glasses," the doctor announced.

"Great, when can I get them?" Uzemack asked. "I can't see a damn thing."

"Well, they have to be ordered from Paris," the officer responded.

Uzemack grinned at the blurred image before him. "No problem, I'll go to Paris to pick them up." Uzemack couldn't be sure if the doctor grinned at his joke, but he sent him away with the same pair of glasses to await the new set.

When Uzemack returned to his own men, they advanced to hole up in Luxembourg homes near the German front lines. Uzemack hoped to avoid any service until he could have his vision restored, but in the meantime he found some medical tape to strap over the useless lens. His vision was blocked over one eye and through the other he saw a fractured world—spidery, veinlike patterns running before his eye. Not only was it hard to see, it gave him a headache.

By Friday night, December 15 he hoped to have the new pair of glasses soon. He and his men awaited their next orders in a deserted inn. With idle time on his hands, Uzemack wandered into the kitchen. There, a working stove inspired him to prepare pancake batter from his K rations, and the men in the platoon planned a breakfast feast for Saturday morning complete with hotcakes, fried eggs, and cereal.

• • •

On Saturday morning he stirred from a peaceful sleep anticipating the carefully planned breakfast; moments later he leaped out of his bunk to the roar of a predawn artillery barrage. The men waited in the inn for more than thirty minutes as the war raged around them demolishing several buildings. Some of those buildings, housing troops, were set aflame.

Uzemack and his platoon took cover on the floor as artillery came through the walls of the cellar at their inn; it seemed the war had come back to them. The division was strung out in a thin line over some twenty-five miles of hilly terrain along the Our River, which separates Belgium and Luxembourg from Germany. Uzemack's company was located near Clervaux in the approximate center of the line. The men were facing into the teeth of the Siegfried line across the river, but they had been confident of enjoying a pleasant Christmas in the evacuated Luxembourg villages that they occupied.

Something was wrong, Uzemack realized. It had been weeks since any of the men had undergone an artillery attack, and until that morning the Yankee units had exchanged only a few token mortar shells with the enemy each day since Uzemack lost his glasses. When the battery ended, the silence fell ominously in their ears, then machine-gun fire rattled from the direction of the left flank where the third platoon was anchored. Soon a runner came to the men of Company B shouting for help, and the squad headed down to join history as part of the Battle of the Bulge.

Uzemack helped his platoon fight off the German infantry throughout the day. Despite heavy German casualties, the enemy persisted, sending their infantry forward until nightfall. With the coming of darkness, the men hunkered down and agreed to take the breather they had been waiting for since dawn. But dashing in through the night air, a runner tore into the command post, another private home that was abandoned to the Americans, with the breathless announcement, "A mess of Jerry tiger tanks are coming up the road."

The men doused the lights and piled down the back stairs into the cellar. Within a few minutes the ominous din of heavy tanks surrounded them, and Uzemack sat listening to the clatter of the tanks coming up the road past their house. The riflemen believed the Germans were headed for Clervaux, and they hoped to be overlooked entirely. But the men soon discovered that this was more than a few passing tanks. As they waited for the sound to die down, they looked at each other, first hopeful, then confounded as the clatter turned to a never-ending roar. Tank after tank after tank was making its way past their house. With increasing apprehension they heard the huge vehicles parking around the various buildings in the village, followed by guttural German commands directing searching parties throughout the town.

"Well, it looks like we'll be making a night of it in the cellar," Uzemack said. The Germans once again were interfering with his comfort, and he considered the irony as his platoon guide suddenly stood.

"There's hot chocolate steaming in the kitchen," he reminded them. They all nodded, wondering if the presence of warm chocolate on the stove would give them away. But that was not the reason Sgt. Edward Reichert had brought it up. "If we're going to hole up here all night, we're going to want that hot chocolate," he said.

"You're crazy," one of the men shouted after him as he sauntered up the stairs. They could hear him walking on the floor above them, and they waited for what seemed hours until the sergeant returned with the hot kettle in one hand and blankets in the other.

"You risked your own hide for a kettle of hot chocolate; this better be good," one of the men commented as Reichert took a cup and began pouring. What came from the kettle, however, was clear and runny, not thick, dark, and sweet. The cellar filled with the curses of Uzemack and his companions; Reichert had risked his life to rescue hot chocolate, then in error had grabbed a kettle of water.

The Americans fell silent as they recognized the sound of tanks surrounding the house. One vehicle rumbled to a stop in a nearby barn; several more tanks pulled in immediately beside the building. The noise from the barn resonated in the cellar, which was separated from it by only a thin, wooden partition, and the men held their breath. The Germans then moved into the house, beginning a systematic search from attic to cellar. Their heavy boots clumped up and down the stairs as they barked commands at each other.

Throughout this the eighteen Americans sat silently, waiting for the cellar door to swing open and a German rifle to be pointed their way. Instead, the Germans were fooled: the house had two cellars, and somehow the Wehrmacht soldiers searched only the empty one. Believing they had combed the entire building, the Germans became jovial, kidding each other and laughing about the battle they had won. The Yanks knew enough German to recognize comments about the "stupid Americans" and to hear the joviality of the talk over their heads.

With the Germans so near, the men couldn't afford to make a sound. They sat silently for an hour or more, and they knew they may have to wait out the night before the Germans continued on. Surrounded by dumped crates filled with crockery that clattered with the slightest movement, they stopped talking and stifled any coughs or sneezes. When the night dragged on, some fell asleep only to be awakened to stop their snoring. The Americans could easily hear the Germans talking and rustling through the wooden partition and could also make out the sound of the men rummaging through their personal belongings upstairs. No doubt they were enjoying the hot chocolate in the kitchen, Uzemack thought, while the night stretched longer and longer.

But the men were not entirely helpless. They had a radio in the cellar with them, and Reinhart whispered communications to their commander. They received their last Army order at about 2400 hours. "Stay put. Help is on the way."

The radio then went dead. The men agreed to stay where they were, waiting until morning for help. Their plan was to attack the Germans from the rear as soon as the relieving forces came to engage them. The help never came.

Chapter 2

On Sunday morning a lone German poked his nose into the cellar, having suddenly noticed its door. He carried a burp gun and almost immediately spotted one of the Americans hiding among the crates by the door. He shouted in German at his new prisoner to stand and the American did, nervously walking toward the doorway under gunpoint. At the same time the arresting soldier hollered for help, then turned to face the other Americans hiding in the cellar.

"You have a choice," he shouted in English. "Come with me now, or wait for the tanks to blast you out." The men stood, their hands in the air, and filed out of the cellar, ending their careers as soldiers and beginning their lives as prisoners of war.

Once outside, the men blinked at the bright light and looked upon the heavy machinery that was the basis of the German offensive in the Battle of the Bulge. They had been captured by a crack German Panzer outfit: Uzemack noticed these tanks were in excellent condition and that the enemy soldiers appeared to be sharp and well-trained.

Their first captors treated the Americans with a startling politeness that made Uzemack think of the term "gentlemen." The black-uniformed men were young, clean-shaven, and smartly dressed; they were efficient and cocky as they went about their searches and prepared the prisoners to march out of the tiny village. They were proud soldiers and not above gloating over their capture—Uzemack heard them attribute the capture of these Americans to their "Aryan superiority."

The young journalist, wearing his broken glasses, was permitted, together with his eighteen companions, to secure blankets and overcoats for the December march. Uzemack learned later what a rare privilege that was for a POW. It was a bright, sunny day, and the sun helped mellow the chill in the air as they stood waiting. Parked around their hiding place were three Tiger tanks and one German half-track.

Uzemack peered down the road through his cracked lens; he could see well enough to notice similar vehicles parked before nearly every building. He could also hear the roar of tank motors moving up another road not far away. As they began marching, Uzemack saw American soldiers being rooted out of the other buildings to join the ever-swelling column of POWs. They were marching to the German rear and headed toward a highway.

When the men reached the highway, Uzemack could see just how mighty this German offensive was; the highway was jammed with Nazi war equipment rolling toward the Allied line. Also weaving through the cavalcade of tanks and marching POWs were Red Cross ambulances, which stood out in the midst of this display of military strength. Uzemack peered into a few of these ambulances as he marched and saw armed German troops packed tightly inside.

Tanks, artillery pieces, and ambulances rolled endlessly past the men as they marched. But the vehicles further behind in the column began to drop in quality; these vehicles lacked the impressiveness of the first shining heavily armed tanks and trucks. The prisoners saw that the ambulances and infantry trucks looked especially weathered and heavily used.

The German officer in charge of the POW column was a character out of a storybook, Uzemack thought. The man wore natty riding breeches, boots, and a monocle; he swaggered as he swung a riding crop at his side. In his early twenties, he seemed slight to the point of being effeminate, but his attitude toward the prisoners was stern. His cool indifference to their hunger and suffering amazed Uzemack.

Around noon the group stopped in a small field behind a hillside air-raid shelter. The guard searched the men and relieved them of all their tobacco, rations, personal jewelry, and other items that could serve as German souvenirs. Many prisoners hid their watches or personal effects and managed to sneak them past their captors.

When the guards had confiscated a pile of cigarettes, food, and memorabilia, they herded their prisoners into the air-raid shelter. As he neared the door Uzemack paused, facing what looked like the entrance to a dungeon. This hesitation was not lost on one of the German guards who said in English, "Take a good, deep breath, Yankee. It will be the last fresh air you'll get for some time."

Uzemack's prison proved indeed a dank dungeon, crowding four hundred men into space that could more easily have held two hundred. He soon learned that the prediction of the German guard had been correct.

The shelter was a pitch-black cave with fetid air smelling heavily of urine and sweat. This dark place became Uzemack's home until Tuesday morning, December 19. The men slept on wood slats, with two or three to a bunk built for one. They lay in the dark day and night with no food and little water.

As time passed the air grew more foul, and the stench of excrement choked the dripping cave. Hunger led to exhaustion, irritability, and illness. But Uzemack spent his time on his back, his eyes closed as he allowed visions of food to float before him—visions that would become his closest acquaintances during the following months, appearing to him every time he had a moment to think.

While the Americans were held at the air-raid shelter, a German officer came to interrogate them. The prisoners in the cave could hear the Nazi war machinery rumbling past the shelter every hour of the day. When they finally emerged Tuesday morning, the Nazi equipment was still moving toward what was once the direction of the Allied lines. Uzemack was staggered that the war had changed its course so dramatically in the past few days.

But the vehicles looked to Uzemack like something driven straight out of a trash yard. The Nazis had used their best fighting power in front, and their rear looked like every remaining vehicle still running in Germany. "What a pile of junk," he muttered to the man beside him.

Hoping for food, Uzemack kept his eyes on his captors but found the Germans felt no compunction about not feeding these men—despite the fact that they had been prisoners for three days. Instead the Americans marched until evening past the Nazi column, dodging half-tracks, tanks, and trucks piloted by sadistic Germans who made a game out of aiming for them and making them jump. Around them horse-drawn carts, trucks, and autos that had to be towed by other vehicles all made their sluggish way toward the front lines. Apparently the Germans were gambling with everything they had, the prisoner thought.

Hunger was Uzemack's only concern now. In the afternoon he watched a German toss a small, partly-eaten apple into the muddy road as the prisoners passed, and Uzemack leaped on it, devouring the unappetizing fruit before he considered what he was doing. He vowed never again to act so desperately.

The men reached a German village thirty kilometers from their starting point that evening. Soldiers pointed at the muddy field where they now stood and spoke German, which one of the POWs interpreted. "We have to spend the night here," the bilingual POW told his comrades.

As the prisoners prepared to settle down, seeking dry spots in the field, the Germans changed their minds and forced them into a small church. Here the guards handed out the first meal since their capture on Sunday. Uzemack snatched up his ration, which consisted of a half-loaf of bread, a small piece of cheese, and some jam. Along with most of the men, he gulped down his food only to learn the next morning that they had been expected to make it last for several meals. There were no latrines or facilities in the church, and some men eventually used their helmets, leaving them behind in the church when they marched out again the next morning.

Uzemack still managed to hide his precious belonging from the Germans—a small address book with blank pages that could serve as a journal. If he could only locate something to write with, he would record everything that was happening to him. The three days of marching dragged on interminably; he later wrote of it as a never-to-be-forgotten nightmare. By the end of the fourth day, the men had marched 100 kilometers, the guards as weary as the starving prisoners.

The night of December 20 the men again slept in a village church, where they were given about a mouthful of ersatz coffee for supper. They survived the day on a slice of bread about an eighth of an inch thick and a half inch wide. Their captors gave them the bread as their noon meal, and this time the men realized it was expected to last all day. When the group stopped in another frozen field, after walking twenty kilometers, they learned that 980 men were to share twenty loaves of bread and four cans of marmalade.

On the morning of December 21 they left the church and set out on the road again. They had marched no more than one kilometer when the column was halted by the natty officer whom Uzemack thought of now as someone out of a comic opera. The little man charged up the road, shrieking at the top of his lungs and flailing his arms wildly. Uzemack learned through translations that the officer wanted them to clean up the mess they had left behind in the church; he sent about thirty men back to use their own shirts and hands to mop up human waste.

In the meantime, nearly a thousand men stood in the frigid field on the outskirts of the village, waiting for the cleanup detail to finish. It took about two hours for the men to finish their chore and, while they waited, the officer ordered all the GIs to turn in their money. The loot he collected from the men amounted to several thousand dollars. No receipts were given to the prisoners, and Uzemack imagined that the money was destined for the officer's personal pleasure.

That night they reached a town about fifteen kilometers west of Gerolstein. They were told they would eat there before boarding trains to head for a POW camp. Instead, they were crammed into sheds along a railroad siding with fifty men to a room about fifteen by twenty feet. The starving men were given neither food nor water and were left to sleep as best they could in the unheated shed. There wasn't enough room for anyone to lie down, so they slumped against each other for warmth and support as they dozed standing up. The air quickly grew foul from body odor and lack of oxygen.

CHAPTER 3

The next morning the same tired guards flung open the doors and ordered them to hike another fifteen kilometers to Gerolstein. Here the men finally received another crust of bread, and they were ordered onto a freight train, recently vacated by a shipment of horses, with fifty or sixty men to a car. Though there was little room to lie down, those who could lay in manure and clumps of straw.

The train took an aimless course as it shuffled through the night. The next morning Uzemack, stiff, tired, and starving, found himself with his companions at a standstill just outside a small city. Again he hoped for food, but again the Germans showed no indication that they would be feeding the captured Americans.

Instead, the guards told the prisoners their journey was being delayed, because an air raid had torn up tracks just ahead; they heard this story several times throughout the subsequent days. Suddenly the city's air-raid sirens would sound. Uzemack would hear the roar of airplane motors a short time later and earthshaking explosions of blockbusters not far away. The train would shake with each tremor.

One plane, Uzemack identified as an attack bomber, roared low over the train. He zoomed up and away only to return a few minutes later, and with dread the men realized this pilot meant business. He proved it too, with a staccato of machine-gun fire, and as the motor roared closer and closer, several explosions confirmed Uzemack's worst fears—the train was under attack. Panic assailed the men as suddenly as did the fighter plane; some pounded on the walls, screaming to be released from the sealed cars, while others hugged the floor trying to dig through with their fingernails.

The guards vanished, and suddenly the door was flung open by several medicos who had broken free from the car behind them. Men streamed out of the cars shouting in terror, which changed to awe when they saw what was awaiting them there in the fields.

While the planes flew over head, firing on them, the men began digging up vegetables growing in the rich German soil and shoving them into their mouths. Uzemack, joining in the vegetable and dirt feast, paused only momentarily to wonder at the bizarre sight of men on their hands and knees in the fields, oblivious to the shooting that bounced around them.

As soon as the planes had passed and disappeared from sight, the Nazi guards emerged from hiding and ordered the prisoners back. Some were reluctant to go, ignoring the orders as they grabbed for one last beet or turnip, and the guards frantically opened fire. Uzemack cringed in horror as one GI was shot in the back. The guards swiftly ordered the man hauled back into the car, where he died of exposure and lack of medical care.

It was Christmas Eve, and the men again received neither food nor water. Uzemack spent the day in the railcar lost in prayer and reminiscence. He conjured the faces of his wife and loved ones celebrating Christmas at home, imagining he would not see them again. The images of food continued to dance past his eyes while his stomach growled over the tiny fragments of dirt-coated vegetables he had offered it.

A handful of men tried several times to engage the others in singing Christmas carols, but the effort failed miserably as grumbling tapered into collective silence. Instead, Uzemack found consolation in the Bible, especially Psalm 22, which a prisoner offered in prayer.

On Christmas Day the men entered Frankfurt, and again their hopes rose as they anticipated food. Rumors of a holiday meal coursed through the cars; no food materialized. That evening they neared Bad Orb and spent the night on a siding where a guard told them that they would disembark in the morning.

The men again ventured a few Christmas carols, beginning with the sad but heartfelt strains of "Silent Night" and "Adeste Fideles." This time many of them joined in, forcing a festive spirit in recognition of the holiday. The effort ended as abruptly as it began though, as quarrels and bickering set in over where and how the men would sleep.

Shortly after midnight, the Nazis tossed eight loaves of bread and seven cans of meat into the car. The food scattered, and the prisoners scrambled for it, jostling each other and shouting as they grabbed in the dark. They eventually agreed to turn the food over to one man who would divide it equally among them.

Taking advantage of the invisibility of night, one POW stole a can of meat, so the fifty-six men inside the car shared the eight loaves and six remaining cans. Shrouded in darkness, the men managed to distribute evenly the food that was left. Uzemack, like the others around him, concluded that this was the best Christmas meal he had ever eaten.

The following morning they left the train and began the next phase of prison life—an existence far from what Uzemack had expected after observing enemy prisoners in the United States.

CHAPTER 4

On December 26 Uzemack had been a POW for nine days, and he was overjoyed to finally climb off the train and draw in a lungful of cold, fresh air, knowing the torturous journey had ended. The human freight arrived at Bad Orb, a small western German city, with four thousand GIs captured during the Battle of the Bulge, and they poured off the train to march up a steep slope to their new home. But Uzemack's pleasure was short-lived.

The men were destined for the crowded and growing Stalag IX B, primarily a detention camp for escaped prisoners. The compound sat on a windswept hill overlooking the city of Bad Orb in a strangely picturesque winter setting. For Uzemack though, taking his glasses off, then returning them for a glimpse through a cracked lens, it was an uninteresting blur. As they passed through the gates, they entered what was intended to be a temporary holding camp until permanent places of confinement were found. For most of them, however, Bad Orb would be their final destination.

Stalag IX B began its service in World War I, when it housed German criminal prisoners. Before World War II it served as a children's rest camp and a concentration camp. Later it was used for Allies captured in combat and finally returned to its original use as a POW camp.

As he marched into the center of the compound, Uzemack got an ugly glimpse into the suffering of the Jews and the reign of terror Hitler had forced on Europe. He knew enough German to understand the signs looking down upon the prisoners, carry-overs scattered throughout the camp that declared "Juden Baracken" (Jewish Barracks).

Before he had much time to further consider his surroundings, Uzemack and his fellow GIs were ordered to strip for yet another search, though there was little left for the captors to seize. When the men had redressed, the Germans allowed them their first hot meal in nine days—carrot soup—then divided them into groups of one hundred and assigned groups to their barracks. Uzemack joined his new bunkmates in a dilapidated wooden building with the number "31" on the front. To his astonishment, three groups of one hundred men were crowded into it with him. Inside the barrack, the men found a gaping expanse devoid of furniture—its only luxury being a thin layer of excelsior strewn on the floor as bedding.

The guards organizing the men all appeared to be World War I veterans, in their forties—too old to fight in this war—and they watched the disoriented prisoners with measured patience. "No bunks, no mattresses, no blankets?" a prisoner asked of the guard standing closest to Uzemack. The guard shot back in English, "You will have clean straw to use for beds . . . later."

The men immediately began scrambling for sleeping space in the cramped quarters; Uzemack joined the crush, finding himself some tight space near the wall on the soiled straw. He was tightly wedged in with the other men, while those unfortunate enough not to mark their own territory in time were forced to sleep in the center of the room, where the floor was completely bare.

Every foot of floor space was occupied when the men lay down to sleep. The cold December wind easily penetrated the ramshackle walls, and Uzemack was glad to have men squeezed against him on either side. Without the close quarters, many would have suffered from exposure.

The barrack was divided into two sections, separated by washrooms. Barrack 31, like most of the other barracks, had about one hundred fifty men in each section; and the washroom included one sink to be shared among the three hundred of them. The water was frozen in the pipe most of the time, so Uzemack ignored it. Of greater importance was the toilet, which consisted of a small hole in the floor about six inches in diameter. The dimensions of the hole would gain importance to him over the first week, because soon after arrival, about 75 percent of the men suffered from chronic diarrhea.

For the first two weeks, Uzemack and his new roommates stayed locked inside the barrack and were never permitted out for fresh air. The filth and stench of three hundred unwashed men using a tiny hole for a toilet grew nearly unbearable. With the door closed and no windows, there was no hope of air circulation. The men, bored and anxious, continuously fought over space on the floor. Uzemack watched two men seated near him break into a scuffle as one caught the other with a handful of excelsior that didn't belong to him.

The guards deloused the men the day after their arrival—the only bathing they would have. Since they had no towels, most of the men dried themselves on their dirty clothing. Whatever lice were eliminated the first day soon rehatched and thrived among the crowded, unwashed bodies in the camp. The lice had plenty of parasitic company. Fleas and other insects feasted on the itching skin of Uzemack and his companions, jumping and wriggling through clothing, hair, and even eyebrows . The men would pick them off to flick them away; but no matter where the bugs landed, they had their choice of new hosts in the crowded barrack. The men's clothing had not been washed since the day of capture and laundering was an impossible luxury, so Uzemack scratched at his irritated skin and became accustomed to the stink coming from his own clothing.

The Germans also made no effort to provide eating implements. Because most men had relinquished their mess equipment during their capture, it was up to their ingenuity to find a way to eat the daily soup. Uzemack thankfully had not used his helmet as a chamber pot during his travels, and he was relieved to have it. The helmet became a useful bowl for his soup and served him for several months. Those who had left their helmets behind scrounged in the scrap pile in the camp for tin cans, flower pots, and any other containers they could find. Grimy fingers often served as utensils until a prisoner fashioned a crude fork and spoon from wood slats torn from the barrack walls.

In the barrack four small stoves pumped out meager heat. Each day the Germans allowed the men an armful of wood—sufficient fuel to keep the stoves going for only a couple hours. For the remaining time the men huddled together as the embers cooled, their oily, soiled blankets, if they had them, pulled over their heads and bodies.

Uzemack still held out hope of being moved. The guards, when asked, always said they would be sent elsewhere soon, but there was no sign of it. If anyone complained the Germans advised them not to worry. "You'll be shipped out of here soon," they said. But no one seemed to be going anywhere.

The days dragged along, and Uzemack began to notice alarming changes in himself and his fellow prisoners. The weight loss was enormous. Not only did the flesh seem to dissolve from their bones, many suffered severe diarrhea and in some cases, pneumonia.

Lt. Joshua P. Sutherland of Haysi, Virginia, was the camp's only medical officer, and he set up his makeshift office in the wretched and overcrowded quarters that served as hospital facilities. Sutherland, because he was an officer, was offered internment at an officer's camp, but he chose to remain where he was. "I'm the only person with medical training," he said. "It may not be much, but you have to have some kind of doctor."

In the same spirit, two of three ministers also agreed to remain with the enlisted men. Lt. Edward J. Hurley of Detroit, a Catholic priest, and Lt. Samuel R. Neel of Jackson, Tennessee, a Protestant cleric, stayed with the men, while a third minister happily moved to the better accommodations.

The ministers needed only their Bibles to carry out their work; Sutherland, being a physician, was not as lucky. He was equipped with one needle holder, one forceps, one pair of scissors, small doses of novocaine, and a spool of cotton thread for sutures. He went from barrack to barrack collecting sulfa tablets and managed to acquire three thousand of the horse-tablet-sized pills.

Sutherland immediately made effective use of the sulfa tablets, doling them out to the men suffering from severe pneumonia. Hunger was the greatest scourge, though. Weight loss averaged twenty-five to thirty pounds, though some prisoners lost seventy pounds or more. In the period from December 26 to February 20, Sutherland treated more than eighty pneumonia cases, and only one of his patients died.

But the men were doing more than just losing weight. With little to do but think of home and food, minds began to crack. Uzemack's most common source of entertainment was pondering the pancake breakfast he had been planning the night before the Germans began moving in. For others, the hunger and depression took control. One evening Uzemack watched a group of men huddle around a stove; their breaths, gathered in clouds before their faces, and the air was so cold that shivering had become an ever-present condition. These men, however, were enjoying the heat coming from the stove, despite the fact that the stove had burned out hours ago. Uzemack watched in amazement as the men went through a routine of warming different parts of their bodies near the stone-cold stove. One man leaned forward, rubbing his hands together as if soaking up the non-existent fire's heat.

Those whose behavior seemed the most bizarre were the same ones who spent the majority of their time lying on the floor trying to find refuge in sleep; a few never woke up. Throughout the first few weeks tempers sharpened and bitter arguments erupted over things such as bread crumbs. Sometimes the fight would come to blows, and others gathered around to watch and drag the adversaries away. There was never much harm done to either participant in the fight; by now they were too weak to cause any damage.

CHAPTER 5

The Germans did not beat American prisoners at Bad Orb, nor did they subject them to conventional torture—they simply starved them. But the men hungered for more than food. With nothing to occupy them, they thought of family and loved ones at home; they also thought of the basic comforts they used to take for granted. Now they existed without the cigarettes that most of them used to smoke regularly and without clean clothes, baths, and beds. Uzemack most of all wanted something to do.

The doors to the barrack were eventually opened during the day, but all prisoners had to return to their enclosure by nightfall. Wandering through the camp seemed to have little purpose, since no matter where he went, Uzemack found only men hungry and idle like himself.

The camp itself was surrounded by beauty. Perched on a steep hill, it allowed a view of snow-covered pine trees and a canyon where the men could look out toward Frankfurt—about thirty miles to the west. The contrast between the picturesque view and the misery inside the camp struck the prisoners with bitter irony. If Uzemack complained of the conditions to the Germans, he was usually told it was the fault of the Americans.

"Your American bombers," one English-speaking guard commented to Uzemack one cold day, "blame it on them. They blow up our homes, our railroads, our highways. You are hungry because you brought it on yourselves."

The Germans blamed the same bombers for the fact that the prisoners never moved from the overcrowded camp. The guards offered descriptions

of the supposed American POW camp where they were eventually
headed—a camp with many of the conveniences they missed most, as
well as Red Cross packages and work to do.

Uzemack was sobered by men around him slowly losing their grip
on reality; fearing that boredom could make him head in their direction,
he took to writing. He found a short dull pencil among his fellow prisoners
and pulled the tiny address book from his pocket to do what he did best—
write. The first entry he made in the diary was on December 28, when he
scribbled just a few words. "Have been eating regularly at Stalag. The first
meal we had here was a soup of carrots, turnips, and other dried vegetables.
Our menu is the same each day—ersatz coffee in the morning, soup at
noon, bread and ersatz tea for supper." Supper came at 2:00 P.M., after
which the men must wait until morning to eat again.

On January 1 he noted the changing of the year as well as a snowfall.
The snow blanketed the camp, and the cold penetrated the men's sleep
as they endured the nights in the unheated barrack. Uzemack was lucky:
he was one of those who had saved an army blanket, which he wrapped
around himself on the cold floor at night.

On January 3 Uzemack watched the Germans drag a dead horse into
the camp; he wandered close enough to pick up a strong smell from the
carcass as they tugged it into the kitchen. The next morning he walked
behind the kitchen to see a horsehide and hooves thrown in the rubbish
pile. At lunch, the soup, usually of vegetables alone, included the distinct
taste of meat. Uzemack had never eaten horse meat before, but he was
glad to have it at this point. "Even a dish of cat meat would look good to
me now," he scratched into his diary that day.

On January 13 the Germans removed the Russian kitchen crew and
allowed GI cooks in the kitchen. Uzemack was impressed with the
improvement in flavor and actually enjoyed his bowl of soup. Later he
wondered at that attitude, since he could never describe the food as
much more than "one jump ahead of garbage."

Trading ran rampant throughout the camp, and treasures seemingly
emerged from nowhere. Men suddenly revealed watches they had been
hiding, which they traded for a loaf of bread or a pack of cigarettes. Stealing
food was so common that no one could consider himself safe until he
had eaten whatever he had, but some traded to the point of starving
themselves. Often Uzemack saw men walk zombielike through the
muddy camp with grimy blankets over their heads, shouting in hoarse
voices "Bread for cigarettes—bread for cigarettes."

On January 16 Uzemack believed his luck was changing; a new batch of American POWs arrived, fresh from the war, who reported the Americans were closing in on Germany. Norway has attacked, they said, and the war should be over in two weeks—but there seemed little change.

Two days later German officers announced that Jewish prisoners would be separated from the others to live in a barrack surrounded by a barbed wire fence. Later they were shipped out, and Uzemack learned they were sent to Berga an der Elster, a camp near the Czech border where prisoners dug a cave complex for a German atomic weapons project. They worked eight-and-a-half-hour days, seven days a week, with no medical care, moving blasted rock and pushing rail cars. Many died from disease and beatings.

Meanwhile, the IX B men continued bartering for cigarettes with sales reaching outrageous prices—up to 2,000 francs ($40) for two French cigarettes. Uzemack resisted the urge to make such deals, considering other uses for his food. He began using his ersatz coffee to bathe himself, commenting to a man he met in the barrack that it was a better use than drinking the foul-tasting liquid that in no way resembled real coffee.

• • •

Just as refuse tossed into a pool floated, friendships surfaced in the camp for Uzemack. In this way, he befriended a librarian in his forties from New Mexico named Val Cosado. Cosado, who had been drafted only a few months before, found the young soldier and newspaperman interesting, and they soon struck up a conversation. Sharing an interest in writing, history, and politics, they held long discussions about anything that would distract them from their nagging hunger. Like Uzemack, Cosado had a wife and children at home and had only been drafted as the military began calling up just about every able-bodied American male after the heavy losses at D-day in Normandy.

But food was still foremost on the young journalist's mind. January 20 was a special day for the prisoner, since it was the day he discovered an entire neck bone floating in his soup. Meat and vegetables found in the soup were rare and treasured and prompted men in the chow line to call out, "Dig deep in the barrel." It was an icy walk back to their barrack, from the kitchen; if the men slipped and spilled their soup, there would be no replacements.

As the Americans waited in line twice each day, they still conversed about their hopes for release. Good news about the war was trickling in;

Uzemack heard that the Russians were within forty miles of Germany. The story was that Russia started a winter drive on January 16 and gained 120 miles in five days. Uzemack's information was sketchy, however, and his sources unreliable. As a journalist he knew the difference between rumors and news.

CHAPTER 6

Four days later the Germans moved Uzemack and Cosado out of Barrack 31 and into Barrack 26. Their lifestyles improved radically. Here, with more space, the men could stretch out on their own bunks, and Uzemack lay down with comparative luxury on the bed he claimed. It consisted of iron supports, with wooden slats for bedsprings and a mattress comprised of some loose excelsior ticks. Because the bunks were stacked three-high, Uzemack had two men sleeping above him. Sharing his barrack with a new group of prisoners, the friendly Chicagoan began collecting men's stories about their lives in America. He was happiest to meet others from his hometown. "What do you say we start a club here?" Uzemack mentioned to a few fellow Chicagoans, and immediately he started recruiting twelve Windy City natives for the Stalag's only "Chicago Club." Together they exchanged stories from their neighborhoods, their schools, places of work, friends they shared in common, and some of the best restaurants and bars.

The journalist still wore his one-lens glasses with one eye taped over, relying on the vision of his left eye only. He would have been a comical sight in the United States, but here, where every man made do with what he had, no one questioned the taped glasses. He was becoming accustomed to peering at people through a cracked lens while the other eye stared uselessly at black tape.

This arrangement was far from perfect; he wondered if he was doing any permanent damage to his right eye, which he occasionally exercised by taking the glasses off and straining to make sense of the blurred figures and objects moving in front of him.

"Oh, the hell with it," he said one day, taking the glasses off for good. He had no trouble seeing someone close to him, and otherwise, sharp vision seemed to be of no use. He had nowhere to go and no reason to have long distance vision, so he resigned himself to an out-of-focus world.

The newsman wasn't ready to allow his vision to compromise his social life. He acted as chairman of the ever-growing Chicago club and was always seeking to recruit new members. The group was holding one of its meetings when the news came by way of a guard: Red Cross packages had arrived.

"Wotta treat!" Uzemack wrote in his address-book diary. For the first time in forty-three days he smoked an entire cigarette—with a spinning head he put out the butt and stowed it away for later. Uzemack wasn't the only one feeling giddy: the jubilation in the barracks was nothing less than a dull roar as the men rifled through their new treasures as if it was Christmas Day. The boxes, the guards explained, were on loan from Serbian POWs. They would have to divide one box among four men. Each box contained two chocolate bars, five packs of cigarettes, meat, cheese, fish, crackers, butter, raisins, sugar, coffee, powdered milk, vitamin pills, and soap.

After the feast, a prisoner in Barrack 26 shouted to the men to be quiet. "How about a thanksgiving prayer?" he called out. The men bent their heads in silence, then spontaneously sang hymns and Christmas carols. They finished by singing "God Bless America" and the "Star-Spangled Banner." The guards stood by and didn't make a move to stop them; Uzemack wondered how the off-key patriotic tunes sounded to their German ears.

That night the makeshift latrine saw heavy use. "Move over would you!" men hissed at each other as they awaited their chance over the tiny toilet. Uzemack cursed the narrow circumference of the hole in this latrine as the rich food began getting the better of them. The next morning many lay in their bunks groaning.

"Oh, why did I eat all that?" the man above Uzemack groaned over and over from his bunk. Sick or not, they were all happy.

With a new, valuable commodity circulating through the camp, the men began to play poker with high stakes. To help ease the boredom Uzemack agreeably joined in, taking a seat before a circle of other players. He was a good player in Chicago, and he discovered the same skill served him well here in Germany. In no time he had won himself nearly a dozen cartons of cigarettes. Though he enjoyed cigarettes, Uzemack refrained from smoking all of his winnings. Cigarettes were almost as good as cash in this Stalag, and he hid them carefully from the roving thieves who plagued the camp.

The card games soon became his downfall, however. Playing again soon after his big win, he sat squinting at a full house. With a marked self-assurance, he bet nearly everything he had, only to lose. He couldn't see the man across from him clearly but saw the hand well enough as the man held it up close to Uzemack's eyes for a good look.

This happened to the next hand as well before a friend came to stand behind Uzemack. "You better watch yourself," the man said in his ear, "you're being cold-decked." Looking closely, Uzemack saw that some of the cards were marked; slapping them down on the floor in a rage, he jumped to his feet. The same friend who had tipped him off now held him back from the other card players. Uzemack salvaged the cigarettes he had left and vowed to give up the card games.

CHAPTER 7

February brought the same routine for the prisoners, and Uzemack gave up hope of being moved to another camp. Discouraged and weak, the men accepted their routine as they finished off or bartered for any remaining goods from their Red Cross packages. No new packages arrived; and the hot, runny soup was their only solace throughout the tedium of each cold, raw day.

Uzemack sat on his bunk with his pencil poised over paper, considering how to describe his life in this prison. His hand came suddenly off the page as an explosion ripped through their quiet afternoon. The concussion came from somewhere in Bad Orb and was clearly a blockbuster being dropped in or near the city. It was the closest air raid yet, and the men didn't know whether to shout for joy or run for cover.

But the fireworks were not over yet. As Uzemack scribbled a description of the explosion in his journal, Cosado stood over the bunk. "You all right?" he asked and Uzemack nodded.

"That was a helluva blast, wasn't it?" They exchanged a joke about the pilots before they both froze, listening to the unmistakable buzz of a plane shearing down upon them. It opened fire on a rival plane, and in horror they realized the strafing was piercing the barrack. In shouts of confusion, men lunged for the ground, then started scuffling toward the door. Uzemack was with them, dashing wildly among hundreds of his fellow POWs. The Germans had instructed the men to dig trenches in front of all the barracks, and now these trenches were put to good use. Uzemack leaped into one and felt the slamming of bodies falling on top of him as others jumped for shelter.

When the strafing stopped, the Americans slowly picked themselves up and made their way back to their barracks. Uzemack was dazed when he saw that some of the men had been hit. Prisoners were carrying the injured to Sutherland's makeshift hospital; blood spattered sections of the barracks. The men who had returned to the barracks earliest had already cleared away Val Cosado's body from where it lay beside Uzemack's bunk.

His best buddy had been killed with one of the .50 caliber slugs ricocheting through the barrack. As men walked through the building checking for more injured, Uzemack sat on his bunk, stunned at the suddenness of his loss and the fact that he had somehow survived. Several inches above his head on the bunk was a bullet hole.

With a shaky hand Uzemack located his pencil and opened his journal. "This entry was broken by a tragedy I'll never forget," he wrote. A few days later the POWs buried Cosado on a quiet hill near the hated Stalag. He was joined by five other GIs, two of whom had died of malnutrition that day.

Uzemack had never volunteered for burial detail before, but he knew it was the last chance he had to do something for his friend. With three other volunteers, he tugged a flat wagon carrying Cosado and his companions in death through the gates of the camp. He wore his glasses, because he knew he would need his vision for this somber task. It was the first time since December that he had left the compound, but he felt no joy in this flirtation with freedom. Instead he stared directly ahead of him as they climbed up a slick, grassy hill several hundred yards from their camp. The troop, including four pallbearers, a priest, and two guards, stopped before freshly dug graves.

For the first time Uzemack evaluated this place, where his friend would be laid to rest. He was struck with the beauty of the scene around him. They stood at the top of a rolling hill that overlooked their camp, in one direction, and the snow-covered fields and the city of Bad Orb in the other.

As the bodies were lowered into their graves, Uzemack recalled the words of the doctor. "These guys," the doc said of those who died of starvation, "they didn't have to die. They could be alive if they hadn't traded their food for cigarettes."

The men shared the laborious chore of filling in the graves; Uzemack went to work with his shovel, pausing when he was finished to memorize the scenery around the grave. There was consolation in the beauty of the spot where these men were laid to rest (here, where the Germans would eventually grant a small, white cross in remembrance). Uzemack saw the lovely hills and peaks around the wintry countryside, and a peacefulness challenged the ugliness of the camp and the reason his friend died. When he had a chance to write to her, Uzemack told Cosado's wife that he had a scenic and tranquil resting place. "He never suffered," he said. "I was the last to see him, and we were laughing and enjoying a good joke before he went."

In the meantime Uzemack was sending home carefully scribed notes to his wife Eleanor; he wondered if even one had actually reached her. The prisoners had not received any mail in the camp since their arrival, and he wondered if she knew that he was a prisoner and not killed in action.

Talking to other prisoners around his barrack, Uzemack happened upon Dennis Murray, a cub reporter for the *Chicago Tribune*. Since Uzemack was a reporter for the *Chicago Times*, they soon got to the business of remembering their days covering stories in their native town. Another friend, John Dunn, was also a newspaperman who lived in Brooklyn until being drafted into the forces. Dunn was the first to consider the idea of finding recreation for the men.

"I'm something of a history buff," he commented to his friends. "I wouldn't mind giving a few talks on American history and, who knows, maybe a few fellas would be interested."

The idea intrigued Uzemack. Short of food, there was nothing the POWs needed more than something to occupy their time. The boredom bred rumors that ran rampant through the camp, giving men inaccurate information, false hopes, and unnecessary disappointment. The newsman realized that, with his pencil, he could change that. The Germans would never allow a newspaper at Stalag IX B—which made Uzemack convinced he should produce one. He discussed the idea with Murray and Dunn, who assured him that they should do it.

Waiting the next day in the chow line, Uzemack noticed a guard standing near his barrack with a diffident look. Most guards were unwilling to speak with him, and his limited German made communication almost impossible. But this one, who appeared to be at least in his forties, seemed to have an approachable expression and a gleam of intelligence in his eye. Coming out of the mess hall with his food, Uzemack wandered over to the man.

"How is the war going, any news?" Uzemack asked the man. The German snorted his irritation as he looked at the American.

"The only news I would like is that it is over and done with," he said. The man said no more, and Uzemack walked away, pondering this comment.

Uzemack made a point to speak to him again the next day. The German guard, a corporal, soon struck up a tenuous friendship with the prisoner.

He spoke English fluently and said he was a lawyer. "I hate that son of a bitch," he said of Hitler one day, "and I'll be glad when they finally put him away where he belongs. All of this," he said, sweeping his hand over the camp, "all of it is because of Hitler. Why would German people want this?"

The corporal, glancing at the other Germans before speaking, said he was watching the progress of the Allies as well as the Germans through the *Wehrmacht Sprecht* (The Military Speaks), a German version of the American military's *Stars and Stripes*. This news came to him via radio, and he diligently copied it down each day. When Uzemack said he planned to start a newspaper, the man agreed to feed him information for the sake of informing the prisoners. "We have to meet behind the kitchen there," the corporal said, gesturing at the wooden shack where the watery soup was produced daily. "Right after they begin handing out the rations each day, so that no one will be able to watch us."

CHAPTER 8

Uzemack did not need the corporal to tell him that the war raged ever closer to their camp. By February 17 the weather was improving, and an occasional early spring mildness brought relief to the wretchedness. The men wandered outside, where some sat, straining for the comfort of the warm rays of the sun on their pallid, sunken skin. Uzemack was startled by yet more American firepower, this time a procession of Air Force planes pounding targets several miles away. From his vantage point Uzemack could see the battle rage on and watched as a B17 was shot down by anti-aircraft fire.

Rumors whirled throughout the camp that the Allies nearly had the war won. One man told Uzemack that Berlin was surrounded. A great wave of optimism swept the camp as the men began making plans for their life when the war ended. "It'll be over in the next few days, mark my words," one man told Uzemack. These predictions made the young journalist even more intent on providing accurate news for everyone.

On one of the warm afternoons of mid-February, the Germans brought in another round of men, English and Canadian prisoners, who were housed behind a fence in another section of the expanding camp. It wasn't long before Uzemack walked over to the fence, trying to start conversation. There he met both Canadian and British troops who had more recent news of the war. But the best came from a very reliable source.

"One of the men here has a radio," a Canadian told the American prisoner. "He disassembles it during the day and keeps it in a banjo. At night he puts it together." This was crucial information, and Uzemack knew what value it could be to his paper.

"You get news reports?"

"Sure, we can get the BBC with it," the prisoner told him. With that, Uzemack now had two reliable sources of information.

Dunn, in the meantime, talked to the camp supervisors and secured approval for a barrack to be reserved for religious services and recreation. He had begun holding small meetings in his barrack to talk of American history. A handful of inmates dutifully gathered to hear stories of their homeland; each day there were several more men.

The men began cleaning the empty barrack to ready it for church services and other events. Prisoners passed through, wandering in to see what was happening, as Dunn supervised the cleanup. Hurley, the camp priest, used a table altar and equipment he borrowed from a French chaplain to offer daily mass in the hall and Protestant services were led by Neel. The prisoners gathered there with fervor—Uzemack noticed a strong return to religion for most men, no matter what their faith. Each barrack also held night and morning services while Catholics said their rosary every night.

• • •

Uzemack's days were consumed with the Chicago club, religious services, and preparation for the first edition of his one-page newspaper. Now he had a mission, and the work seemed to improve not only his outlook but his energy. Finding materials for his work was the first challenge; Dunn scavenged short blue pencils from other prisoners for writing the news but paper was an impossible luxury. The Germans provided each prisoner with legal-sized paper for toilet paper, and the three friends saved some for writing. Murray agreed to write a general column, while Uzemack would cover news of the war, gaining most of his information from the German corporal and from BBC reports.

He completed his first edition with several news stories on February 21 and posted it on the camp bulletin board in the recreation barrack. It was a single page written in longhand with his worn pencil. The stories detailed the progress of Patton's Third Army and included a column written by Dunn about the recreation activities in the camp.

With satisfaction the young publisher watched the stream of GIs gathering by the paper to read the day's news. The men agreed to watch for German guards, ensuring that the newspaper never fell in the wrong hands. At the same time, while trying not to attract attention, Uzemack wanted to draw as many readers as possible. When the day was over, hundreds of men had filed past the bulletin board, and Uzemack snatched it down again before the Germans could get a look.

"Hey, how about reading it to us?" a GI shouted to Uzemack one day as the usual crowd gathered for a look at the latest edition. This comment gave him the idea of encapsulating the news. The posted newspaper, drawing a constant flow of prisoners, could attract the attention of the guards while Uzemack offering a news summary in the barrack would go unnoticed by the Germans. While he would still post the paper daily, he would also offer a weekly "news analysis," quickly summarizing the news to the men standing around him and answering questions without raising suspicion from the guards.

The kitchen staff soon learned of Uzemack's latest actions. The kitchen had found itself a part of the news several times, especially when the Russian prisoners who had been employed there were sent away to be replaced by Americans POWs. There had been many Russians in the camp when the Americans first arrived; now they seemed to have disappeared. The fate of these Russians was unclear, but at least one GI, noticing the shower room's heavy doors that locked from the outside and strange showerheads, possibly holdovers from the concentration camp days, suspected they were killed.

When Arthur Schmidt, a German-American from New York was placed in charge of the kitchen, Uzemack quickly befriended the man the POWs came to know as Smitty. Smitty not only spoke German fluently, his parents ran a hotel in Germany before emigrating to the United States. He had worked as the chef in his parents' New York restaurant for eighteen years, until being drafted into the army. This new, ignoble chapter of his career meant a boost in prisoner morale, since many hoped that the food would somehow become more palatable. Although it didn't, there was more communication about just what was happening in the kitchen.

Every few days Uzemack began meeting Smitty behind the kitchen to brief him on the news. The chef would then relate the story to the rest of the kitchen staff. Smitty agreed to write his own column, "Meet the man behind the ladle," in which he argued that he could not be blamed for the quality of the food.

"In this job you find out you can have friends one day and enemies the next," he wrote. The chef noted that if a chunk of meat was floating in a man's soup, the man was sure to say "Wow, you're a pal." The next day the same man would be fighting mad over the same watery mixture that lacked any such "treats."

One day Smitty and Uzemack met behind the kitchen, and Smitty furtively pulled his news-writing friend from the view of the guards as he said under his breath, "We had some trouble in the kitchen last night, and you can put that in your paper. Don't expect the rations to get any bigger after this one."

The chef said he often overheard the comments of the German guards, gathering a lot about what was happening in the camp administration. This morning the guards had been talking about one of their comrades, the mess sergeant on night shift. Apparently, two POWs had hidden themselves in the kitchen during the night, intent on stealing food. The idea backfired when they were caught beneath a table by the night guard.

Afraid of capture and irrational from starvation, one of the men started swinging at the guard with the first weapon he could find, a meat cleaver. One prisoner tackled the startled guard while the other struck the man in the head nine times, but by this time the prisoners were so undernourished their strength was like that of children. The guard threw them off and managed to escape with nine deep gashes in his head. The POWs summarily were captured and no one knew what had become of them.

Smitty said the incident was the source of conversation for all the kitchen guards. "They were laughing about it," the chef said. "They were kidding about what a big fat head that guy must have to survive nine blows with a meat cleaver."

CHAPTER 9

"Third Army Advances" was Uzemack's latest headline as he distributed his paper in early March; he expected the Americans to be crossing the Rhine in a matter of days. His analysis was made more precise by the maps he shared with members of the Escape Committee, a group of non-commissioned officers who used the maps to help those intending to escape. There would be no escapes from the Stalag without the permission and supervision of this American committee. Anyone wanting to escape could go to them, and they would help establish the safest route and tell them when to make their break. So far no one had made the break yet.

By March even more prisoners were arriving, and the latest were the most emaciated Uzemack had yet seen. Many had marched one hundred kilometers or more since their capture, and they arrived too exhausted to do more than lie starving in the barracks. The days were gray and blustery, and the men, venturing outside more often, would sit idly, feeling their hunger more acutely than ever before. Hope of being released in a few days was effectively extinguished, and the war seemed no closer to an end. Meanwhile, provisions grew more and more scarce, not just for the prisoners, but for Germany as a whole. As the guards grew hungry, the prisoners grew even hungrier.

Every day a few men huddled behind the kitchen like starving vultures, waiting for the cooks to toss the day's garbage on an ash heap in the back-yard. The men pounced on it, digging for anything edible, which usually wasn't much. The cooks' refuse consisted of a few rotten potatoes, some old peelings, bones, or other scraps. Smitty said the prisoners were often caught scavenging, and then the German guard on duty would crack the men on the head with his rifle butt or kick them in the rear end. The men would stagger away, sometimes yelping like stray dogs.

The newpaper, in the meantime, was still gaining in popularity. The Soup Kitchen column often included stories of life in the camp, and Uzemack implored readers to submit their own stories. The typical column kidded about the conditions of food, listed the recipe of the day (consisting of weird concoctions of the men's favorite foods), and recounted stories of their fighting days before the men were captured.

One man wrote his own column suggesting the men petition the U.S. government upon their release to erect a monument to the potato in Washington, D.C. "Any former POW, I'm sure, would be happy to donate money for this memorial," he said, to commemorate the vegetable that had become the men's staple and yet was never enough to fill their hollow stomachs.

One of the more popular columns was the daily recipe, intended to tantalize the appetites of the already half-starved. One of the most popular recipes read as follows: "Slice a Milky Way bar in two, place a wiener between the halves, roll it in biscuit dough, crumble C-ration crackers over the results and bake it in the oven." The author was serious.

• • •

With the Escape Committee's sanction, two prisoners managed to escape the camp late one night by scaling the barbed wire fence. Not only were they unable to elude the guards, in their weakened state they couldn't muster enough speed to outrun the Germans when they reached the freedom side of the barrier. The men, Uzemack learned, went to hard labor in another part of Germany, possibly to join the Jewish prisoners in Berga.

Many American Jews had still managed to escape notice from the guards in the camp by hiding or swapping dog tags, and the other prisoners worked hard to keep their cover. Father Hurley was familiar enough with Jewish ceremony to provide the Jews with religious services—keeping these practices tightly behind closed doors when there was no chance of a guard stumbling upon them.

No matter what their faith, the prisoners all prayed for two modes of salvation: release from the camp or more to eat, but there seemed little hope of either. The unvarying staples were bread and potatoes; but as the winter turned to spring, the meager supply was cut and then cut again. One warm day, the men lined up for chow and were served a warm, cloudy mix minus any potatoes.

"What's the big idea of this?" men shouted as they spooned through their soup; Smitty and his companions only shook their heads. Uzemack downed the warm fluid but finished as hungry ever. Talking to the camp doctor, Sutherland, he wondered whether this cut in provision would mean the end of the men there.

"You know the men won't survive on this." Sutherland said.

Uzemack held his usual meetings with the chef and with the German corporal, both of whom told him the same story: "There aren't any more potatoes." The Germans had almost nothing to eat themselves. What they were serving was a mixture of flour and water, devoid of even salt. Sutherland offered a grim insight into the camp's future on this latest diet.

"If we continue this way," he said, "not many of us will make it more than six months." As it was, he worked ceaselessly, trying to breathe life into tired, undernourished bodies. Sutherland's predictions were quickly coming true as they continued on their flour diet. From December 26 to February 20 there were only three malnutrition-related deaths; afterward the number of dying soon reached two or three a day. The burial wagon rolled through the gates as a regular part of each day.

"What happened to the Red Cross packages; isn't that part of the Geneva Convention?" Uzemack asked the guards. But Germans blamed the Allies for the starvation of their own prisoners.

"We never receive the packages," a German officer told them, "because your planes have bombed our railways and made it impossible to bring them in."

Uzemack was skeptical, since the Germans had managed to bring the human cargo of prisoners to the camp. Moreover, the people of Bad Orb were clearly not starving or suffering from a lack of transportation. Instead he and the stronger prisoners kept themselves alert, finding activities to take their minds off the hunger. Dunn, who was the inspiration for the recreation barrack and the brains behind new activities, proved himself a boon to the men. At thirty-eight he was one of the oldest prisoners, yet he maintained levels of energy and enthusiasm that kept him healthier than many twenty-year-olds.

Dunn's lectures on American history had become so popular by March that he moved them to the recreation hall where hundreds of men crowded the former barrack to listen. A museum curator took his inspiration from Dunn and began delivering lectures on paleontology. Men from throughout the camp gathered for his lectures, filling the floor and standing crowded at the door for some organized entertainment.

As promised, the German corporal continued to feed news to Uzemack. They met furtively, unnoticed by other guards or the Americans, who were more intent on polishing off their soup and bread. His English was impeccable, and Uzemack found his information extremely accurate.

With the use of a map kept on the recreation hall bulletin board, the newsman was able to pinpoint exactly where the American and Russian troops were and could monitor their approach toward the Rhine. The men were starving for news, a fact which lent itself to Uzemack's popularity. The Germans often took advantage of the men's curiosity, though, feeding them discouraging rumors that flashed through the camp with lightning speed and convincing the POWs that some crucial event in the war had taken place that was bad news for the Americans. Uzemack urged his fellow prisoners to ignore rumors and trust only the news in his paper.

At first, when Uzemack pinned the newspaper to the bulletin board, he worried it wouldn't last there long. Since each man was rationed one small, small square ration of toilet paper, which was exactly what Uzemack used for his newspaper, anyone with a case of diarrhea was sure to come up short. Uzemack could imagine such a character coming by the bulletin board and snatching the paper down to use the fruits of his hard work for its original purpose. In fact that rarely happened. Instead, at the end of the day he stashed the paper away with the pile of other outdated issues under his bunk; he hoped to take the papers home eventually. Dunn and Murray took their own pride in the paper, with Murray working at the Daily Soup column and Dunn acting as the adviser—"the kibitzer," Uzemack called him.

On March 12 the trio printed a newspaper with a banner headline: "Yanks Cross Rhine!" Uzemack spent the day drawing cheers and pats on the back as he traveled on the "news analysis" circuit as if he himself was responsible for this conquest. The men were jubilant throughout the warm spring day while the guards seemed morose or indifferent. Most guards, Uzemack had discovered, were not only incurious about the prisoners, they were aging and dull. These were the men the Nazis could not use on the front lines, and by the spring of 1945 that meant only the most physically and mentally feeble.

In this atmosphere Dunn managed other diversion for the men in addition to the lectures and newspaper. He procured several instruments from the Germans and assembled an orchestra from the more musically inclined prisoners. The musicians obligingly blew horns and strummed guitars through concerts, jam sessions, and quiz programs. The audience would occasionally roar with laughter in the recreation hall as they tried to "name the tune," but the laughter offered only temporary distraction from their starving stomachs. None could obliterate the visions of food that tormented them even in sleep.

CHAPTER 10

On March 9, Lieutenant Sutherland discovered the first case of spinal meningitis. This deadly disease was so communicable that an entire barrack was quarantined as possible carriers. The first known case died from lack of treatment. Another case emerged in the next few days, and Sutherland put to use the remainder of the sulfa tablets gathered from the POWs.

Despite this latest health disaster, the men still found reason to hope. Walking to the kitchen one afternoon, Dunn and Uzemack halted to listen to a rumbling sound in the distance. Uzemack knew immediately what it was; he had advance information from the *Wehrmacht Sprecht* as well as the BBC, and now he had his own ears as confirmation: Patton's men were approaching. It was March 13, 1945.

"That's it, we're almost finished," he said.

"Don't be so sure, you want to make a wager about that?" Dunn answered.

Uzemack laughed at Dunn's foolhardy wager. Uzemack was the best source of information in the camp, and he was positive he could guess the time of liberation. But he waited on the bet.

By March 14 there was little doubt that the men had reason to hope, as long as they could survive a few more days. On March 28 the newspaper reported that there was still fighting in Frankfurt, where Patton's men were taking care of the remaining German troops. There was also action thirty kilometers west of Bad Orb, and other American units were forty to fifty kilometers to the north and south. This wasn't close enough for some men in the camp, who were hoping for a faster salvation. Some of the guards were disappearing; yet the gates to the compound remained locked, and guns were still trained on the men.

Prisoners started roaming out of their barracks in the dark despite the fact that regulations required them to be inside at night. Uzemack, however, still had a newspaper to put out. As the sound of the war drew ever closer, he and his friends prepared the camp's April Fools' Day issue. The real news was heartening: Bad Orb had been cut off and surrounded for the past three days. Battles were raging around them; it sounded as if, accompanying the sound of mortar fire, they were hearing the rumble of vehicles pulling out. The German Wehrmacht was giving up the city.

But the paper's headline read "Hitler Here! The Fuhrer arrives at Bad Orb and takes Command." Under the screaming headline Uzemack prepared his story. "Adolf Hitler arrived here at Stalag IX B to take personal command. It was also reported in the *Wehrmacht Sprecht* that the propaganda Minister Joseph Goebbels had joined him here. Herr Hitler addressed the gallant old farts defending Stalag IX B and commended them for joining the battle of the lice. He then hit the chow line for Herr Schmidt's famous pea soup.

" 'Prima!' Hitler started to say, then passed out. Doctors still don't know if the Fuhrer will live."

The April Fools' edition also commented on the massive trading going on with the new cigarettes and Red Cross packages that were circulating. The paper reported that General George Patton had announced that no box of K rations would be sold for more than one pint of blood. The former price of a right arm and leg, the paper declared, was no longer permitted. "'Blood is all we want and blood is all we'll get,' Patton said."

Uzemack was in a good mood as he pinned the paper to the bulletin board. He was ready to pack his bags for his release. Walking to the kitchen for dinner, he fell in beside his friend Dunn.

"You still care to wager?" he asked.

"Go ahead, make your prediction," Dunn told him.

"Sure, by Easter Sunday, if we aren't shipped out of here, we'll be liberated," Uzemack declared.

"You're on. How about putting 1,000 francs on it,"

"Done."

Making their bet, the friends continued on to the kitchen for the mid-afternoon meal of bread, sugar, and tea.

Dunn won the bet. The artillery seemed to roar closer, but for many of the men it was not fast enough. They were dying—several each day from hunger and disease, and Uzemack watched their decline bitterly. "Those goddamned Nazis," he commented furiously to his friend Murray. "They're murdering these boys as sure as if they shot them," he said. POWs continued to die from apathy as well as hunger. Many remained on their bunks all day, and even the recreational activities could not break them from their catatonic states. Some had been that way since they arrived in the camp, suffering from the horrors of the trip to Bad Orb.

• • •

Easter morning, April 1, began as a pleasantly sunny day, and the men teemed into the outdoors waiting for answers. Excitement hummed in the warm spring air. Men, recognizing the sound of retreating vehicles, began yelling and kidding among themselves, while a few started tearing wire off the windows. But rescue did not come. The day turned to night; the excitement quieted to frustration and then the restless silence of anxious sleep.

On April 2 Uzemack arose at 2:00 A.M. to help in the kitchen; he didn't want to miss the liberation. Once again he had money on a time of freedom, and it was in the next twelve hours. He walked to the kitchen in a cool, damp night and arrived to find the chef boyishly excited. The POWs, he said, had hung a white flag on the camp's clock tower. Bad Orb had been taken at 11 P.M., and the men need only wait for the Americans to get around to liberating them.

Uzemack helped prepare the food as usual, a few rotten vegetables boiled in water and bread for everyone. He finished his work at 7 A.M., as breakfast was called, and the few guards still remaining led the men through the lines to the kitchen. The newspaperman then walked back to his barrack wondering if he would print a paper today. At 7:30 A.M. he scratched an entry in his journal. "Everything is quiet," he wrote. By 8:12 A.M. men gathered at the fence as the first American troops came into view. Uzemack stood back and waited, watching as a handful of their liberators came through the doors and were greeted by thousands of starving, sick, yet happy men.

The first man through the gate strolled into camp, staring around him and shaking his head in disbelief. He stopped when he encountered the editor of the camp newspaper. "Ed?" he queried.

Uzemack looked closely at the GI who had lived next door to him in Chicago. For the first time the young journalist was at a loss for words when his more robust friend clasped his hand and pounded his back heartily. When they had last met, Uzemack had been 198 pounds and healthy; now he stood as a filthy, 145-pound beanpole with one cracked lens through which to watch the world. The two excitedly blurted out stories about the past few months, each with information the other wanted.

"Wait!" the friend and neighbor suddenly exclaimed. "We've got something for you, stay right here!" The GI rushed off and returned a half hour later with a crate filled with cigarettes and brandy. Around him was this carnival atmosphere, both festive and macabre. The prisoners who had not been standing at the gate to cheer their liberators were the ones who might not survive. These men were shrunken, dejected, and in some cases, ruined shells of themselves; the worst wandered around the camp with their blankets still wrapped around their heads, staring ahead of them with dazed expressions. For them the liberation had not yet happened and never would.

For the rest it was a time of celebration. GIs had found German warehouses filled with the Red Cross packages long ago intended for the prisoners, and they emptied them in the camp. Men who hadn't eaten more than a bowl of soup a day since December were shoving whole chocolate bars in their mouths. The drinking lent further chaos to the atmosphere. Most would soon regret their early revelry, and for some, whose digestive tracts could not suddenly process alcohol and rich food, it would prove to be fatal. Uzemack eventually made his way back to the Commanders Barracks, where he had been living for the past two weeks. Here he put together his last newspaper, which he would post on the bulletin board where so many had preceded it. "No News Today"—the headline declared.

Both GIs and prisoners came and went from the barracks throughout the day as the excitement continued. Uzemack sat back with a cigar in one hand and a bottle of brandy in the other, talking to members of the passing throng. In the afternoon a soldier poked his head in the door saying he was a war correspondent. "Is there someone around who can tell me what has happened here?" All turned to Uzemack, still sitting back, comfortable in his one-eyed glasses.

"If you want to know what's going on around here, there's the man to talk to," someone said. The correspondent walked toward the compound's newsman.

"My God, Ed Uzemack," the man said, and for the second time that day Uzemack sat forward, straining to see who had recognized him. "You're the *Times'* war correspondent." Uzemack had covered war news for the *Times* until he was drafted, and he recognized the fellow newsman's Chicago accent. The journalist was from the Windy City and had known Uzemack there as they covered the local news together. The GI sat down with the prisoner of war, and they talked about what had happened to the men. As other reporters arrived, the correspondent called out, "Hey, fellas, come here, I want you to meet another newsman."

Soon a half dozen journalists sat together talking spiritedly about the end of the war. "Hey, we've got to do Ed a favor here," the war writer said suddenly. "We can't send you off to the hospital with all the others; we'll ship you back to Düsseldorf with us. That's where we're headquartered."

"Düsseldorf?" Uzemack said, trying to comprehend this scheme.

"Hell, yes, you come on back with us, and we'll all have a party and talk old times." The men prepared a plan, which included dressing the liberated prisoner in a fresh uniform to disguise him as one of them.

That night Uzemack caught the sleep he missed the night before, and despite the usual hard bunk, he slept the deep, easy sleep of a man in a down-filled bed. The next morning he awaited the return of his friends to take him to Düsseldorf, but they never arrived. Later he learned they were unable to make the plan work. Instead he, with thousands of other prisoners, walked out through the gates and toured parts of Bad Orb, the town for which their camp was named, and wandered freely among the homes there. Here Uzemack noticed empty Red Cross packaging and realized that though some of the packages had landed in warehouses, others were going directly to German homes. This was the food the Americans, Canadians, and British had been forced to do without.

When he left, Edward Uzemack took with him everything of importance—that included his diary and most of the copies of his daily newspaper. Before leaving the camp, he took down the final paper declaring "No News Today" and tucked it with the others in his pocket. Taking the history of the camp with him, he walked away.

PART FOUR

Hitler's Youngest Soldiers

CHAPTER 1

The war was ending when eight German teenage friends headed south-east through mountainous Czech farm country along the eastern slopes of the Böhmerwald mountain range. With their marching papers in his pocket, their leader Hermann Pfrengle scanned the horizon ahead of them and kept his ears pricked for combat noise. The group members took turns towing their personal belongings on a baggage cart as they made their cautious way up and down the winding and less-frequently traveled, secondary roads.

Closing in on them, the Russians from the east and the Americans from the west were making their way across what had been the last-ditch efforts of Nazi strongholds. In the narrow corridor remaining between the Americans and the Russians, the Germans were preparing a hasty retreat while chaos reigned for everyone trapped in the middle.

Caught up in a grown up's war, the youngsters had been drafted into the Volkssturm (Home Defense Force) in support of the Wehrmacht, leaving behind their tasks in the Jungvolk (a junior branch of the Hitler Youth) for terse combat training and service on the retreating front. Now, knowing the cause was already lost and having finagled their marching papers from an army unit commander, they fled the war. Initially earmarked for Flakhelfer duty as anti-aircraft gun crew helpers—a Hitler Youth branch which supported the Luftwaffe—they wore the German Air Force uniform, but had turned in all their weapons.

The group had named fifteen-year-old Hermann Pfrengle, the eldest, as their leader, and he worried now, as they walked, over how he would transport himself and his buddies to safety. "Safety" was an elusive concept—one the group realized meant surrendering to the approaching Americans without interference by the SS or the Russians. The boys, the youngest of whom was thirteen, faced a dangerous hike through western Czechoslovakia with both the SS and the Russians close at hand.

For weeks Hermann had guessed Hitler was losing, and for the past several days his mission had been one of getting himself and his friends out of this losing war alive. Reaching home in the western part of Germany seemed out of the question; he and his companions focused instead on how they would go about a surrender.

As they rounded a curve on a country road approaching the mountains, hungry and tired of the war, they paused. Ahead of them, several SS troopers patrolled the road and had already set their eyes on the boys, watching them approach. There was no way to avoid these members of the most feared Nazi elite corps, yet the boys wished there was another way around them. To the SS, Hermann knew, their departure from the front lines would seem like treason.

With no alternative available, Hermann walked directly toward the patrol, resolving to show no fear—while his friends followed his lead. Julius, the boy closest to his own age and size, walked behind. When they came face-to-face with the patrol, the boys stopped, standing a head or more below the men who stared at them with derision.

"Let's see your papers," one trooper barked. Reaching into his pocket, Hermann quickly produced the group's marching orders; the trooper looked them over and then pushed them back in the boy's direction. "Where are your weapons?" he demanded.

Hermann shook his head as he responded, "We had to turn them over upon SS orders."

The trooper gave the boys a skeptical look, as if deciding whether to accept this story, and Hermann and his friends felt the tension rising as they waited him out. After a moment of consideration, the trooper motioned for the boys to come with him and hurried them toward the edge of the woods lining the narrow road. There was no sign of traffic in either direction; aware that there would be no witness to whatever happened next, they ventured on reluctantly with their heavily armed guide.

Hermann's and his buddies' eyes fell upon dark, shrouded objects swinging gently between the trees. As they approached the spectacle, the SS trooper came to a stop, and Hermann realized he was looking at the dead bodies of German soldiers—some of them in uniform, others dressed partly in civilian clothes.

"These men were deserters," the trooper said. "If it weren't for those papers you have . . . you would be joining them." Hermann and his companions hurried back to the road and their baggage cart and resumed their hike, shocked by what they had seen. They rumbled along, never looking back to see if they were being watched.

That moment had made Hermann's decision for him; when they had left the troopers far behind, he told his friends, "If we want to ever make it home alive, we'd better surrender to the Americans sooner rather than later." They had no experience with the American military, but they knew the options were worse: being captured by either the brutal SS or the vengeful Russian Army, which, they heard, was exiling prisoners to lifelong work in the Siberian coal mines. Hermann entertained some faith that the Americans, after a few formalities, might release them to return to their families in western Germany. Focused on their objective, the boys forged farther southeast into Czechoslovakia wondering how they would accomplish their goal of intercepting the American forces safely.

• • •

Hermann had been drafted into the Volkssturm on March 16, 1945, about seven weeks ago, following compulsory membership since the age of nine in the Jungvolk. Without any knowledge of Nazi fanaticism and excesses, he gained boy scout training with the group and was put to work on the Siegfried line, as well as digging bodies out of bombed areas near his hometown. After he completed some rifle training, the authorities of the Reich sent him to the front lines to take on America. This, he came to realize from the beginning, was a losing venture. The teenager spent much of his time with his comrades, all boys from his hometown, being chased back by the growing forces of the Americans.

Hermann and his chums, conspicuous in their blue-gray German Air Force uniforms, walked for three days in that part of Czechoslovakia known as Sudetenland since its annexation in 1938 by Hitler. Czechs and Germans lived there side by side, but Czechs were divided on their sympathy to Germany and the boy-soldiers knew it. They approached the Czechs with some hesitancy, aware of the suspicion aroused by their uniforms.

As they approached the town of Vimperk, Hermann and his comrades came across a farm run by a German family sympathetic to their plight. The farmer offered them shelter in his barn and brought them inside his home for a meal. It was the best meal they had eaten in days, and they did not know it would be the last meal they would eat for weeks to come. As they returned to the barn, they could hear the distant rumbling of American motors; they knew the U.S. Army was closing in.

American artillery rounds exploding in the small village sent them back into the farmhouse for cover, and they knew their fate was soon to be sealed, since the Americans must now be near the fringes of the village. The farmer's family and the young Germans listened to the concussions outside, unsure what to expect from these foreign troops. Finally Hermann, always the leader of his young group, made a decision.

"I'll go outside and look around," he said. "You all stay here." The family and the boys gathered together inside as Hermann made a wary excursion out of the house. This was his chance to receive the Americans; it was May 6, 1945, four o'clock on a relatively warm Sunday.

He knew the Americans were surrounding the farm, and he walked slowly and deliberately across the yard, toward the barn, and around the building's side. There he met the suspicious eyes of an American soldier and the muzzle of his submachine gun; Hermann could not tell who had spotted whom first. With the moment he had planned for finally upon him and with a weapon trained on him, he blurted out in his high school English, "We want to surrender." He counted on the soldier understanding his broken English, since he stood with his hands at his sides, a sheepish grin on his face. Out of pride, he had not raised his hands in the international gesture of surrender.

The solider shouted to his companions, drawing several more Americans who pointed their weapons at Hermann as they made their approach. When they saw that the boy was unarmed, they relaxed and asked him who was with him. It had been an easy afternoon for these triumphant troops; they had found a complete absence of German resistance in the village, and the Americans' relaxed faces reflected their good fortune. They searched the young prisoner and took his paratrooper knife, but overlooked his personal pocketknife, which he had tucked inside one of his boots. Then Hermann guided them inside the farmhouse and explained in broken English that the group was Volkssturm and the farmer's family was glad as the young soldiers were to see the Americans.

His captors searched his rucksack and took his map, his personal diary, his identification, and his marching orders, then gestured for the group to begin walking to a nearby collection point in a meadow near the farm. Hermann looked at his rucksack, preparing to take it with him, but he was immediately stopped. "Leave it," ordered a soldier to the young German's dismay.

The teenager, pointing to the rucksack, asked the soldier in halting English, "Can't I take this?" The American only shook his head and prodded him to move on; any joviality the Americans had shown a few minutes before seemed to have vanished as they began to transport the prisoners.

Hermann's high hopes turned to shock; he could see no reason why they were denying him and his group their few personal belongings. What was the point in refusing them the one thing that would help them survive their imprisonment? He fell into step with his captors, now worried that these Americans weren't going to be quite as considerate as he hoped. He was not completely without resources though; for when his new guard was distracted, he quickly retrieved a spoon from his rucksack and hid it inside his pants.

Several soldiers marched them to an area where the boys quickly lost track of the friendly family that had been their companions the day before. Here American soldiers milled around the meadow while groups of German prisoners were being gathered and questioned. It was a picturesque setting as the sun came down over verdant fields and pastures lined by heavy woods and a gurgling stream, but Hermann's eyes were on the Americans.

The sight of these foreign enemy soldiers was not without distractions to the boy. A truck for the motorized army supply company, which had surrendered with Hermann's group, had been hit by an artillery round, and the delectable aroma of canned meat wafted from the broken cans scattered around it, intensifying his hunger pangs. He had eaten little in the last few days except for the meal the farmer's family had served and the chunks of bread he stowed in his pockets.

When the Americans distributed German high-energy bars taken from another truck, Hermann took his with enthusiasm. He had heard stories of the deliciously sweet American chocolate bars, but they were nowhere in sight, and the German bar served only to whet the boy's appetite. In the meantime Hermann watched as an American tried one of the high-energy bars for himself. It was a sticky endeavor, and after a bite or two the GI grimaced and threw it away.

Waiting idly at the POW collection point Hermann began to study the Americans more closely; to him they seemed to be out of a different world. Their uniforms and equipment looked more practical and more comfortable than what the Germans wore, and the Americans moved swiftly in light rubber-soled boots with hardly a sound. Hermann recalled Nazi propaganda, following the 1944 Allied invasion, ridiculing those boots: "The Allies came sneaking ashore on rubber soles." But Hermann noted that those on rubber soles were winning the war. In contrast, the ubiquitous German "short Wellington" or "dice cup," with its stiff, nailed leather soles, worn by the German Army since 1870, made for a clumsy and slow gait and were torture to the feet.

Hermann also eyed the American small arms, finding the German equivalents lacking by comparison. Their carbines, submachine guns, and rifles were relatively light, small, and handy—in contrast to the unwieldy German K-89 carbine, the mainstay of the average German infantryman, which held six shots of single fire, and whose first model was fielded in 1898. The handy individual radio sets carried by many American soldiers also impressed the German boy. Their ability to communicate with each other by radio made messengers almost obsolete.

The multitude of vehicles, combat and otherwise, moving around the area made further comparisons futile. Hermann was awestruck by this sheer display of fighting power. No wonder most Germans had been kept in the dark about American ground combat strength. Had he known about it, Hermann thought, he and other Germans would have called it quits much earlier.

To the surprise of the teenager, the American soldiers interacted with each other and their superiors with a strange informality. There was no stiff saluting as a soldier passed a higher rank. Their loud voices had a distinct nasal sound; making it hard for the German prisoners to understand what they said or yelled. Most of them, he noticed, whether they were watching the prisoners, walking, or driving, seemed to be constantly chewing on something, although Hermann saw no sign of food. Months later the young German would learn of chewing gum and have a chance to try a stick for himself.

After a while, Hermann tried some English on one of the guards—a quiet, middle-aged man—and asked him about his civilian life. The American told Hermann he was a lawyer, but hastened to add that he was not supposed to speak to POWs. Refusing to accept defeat, Hermann approached another guard to practice his English. "Where are you taking us?" he asked. When the guard looked at him without response, he continued, "Will you discharge us at the destination? You are not taking us to the Russians, are you?"

The guard replied, "That's up to the commander," and avoided any further conversation.

Hermann and his friends were eager to know. If the Americans decided to turn the prisoners over to the Soviets, who were only about thirty kilometers away, the group would need to make contingency plans for an escape. But he didn't dare tax the guard's patience further. Because there was no useful information, he urged his friends to hang together and rest as much as possible. He also told the motley group to be on the lookout for food and any kind of cloth, not only for foot rags, but also for protection against the night temperatures that, in this mountainous area, still dipped into the freezing range.

Only a few hundred meters away stood the farmhouse where the prisoners had been forced to abandon their rucksacks, blankets, and extra clothing. Hermann brooded over this irony for several hours, his frustration and hunger breeding anger. Finally, as he watched the guards casually talking, he felt his outrage draw him to his feet, and he walked over to the men who had previously refused to talk. Now, keeping a polite tone, he asked permission to return to the farmhouse for his belongings. With a wave of his gun one of the guards chased him back to his group.

The hard ground and cold did not permit sleep. Through the night the Americans brought in additional groups of prisoners, from small units in the area. Others were stragglers retreating from the Russian front, Hermann guessed. He shivered through the dark hours and welcomed the warming rays of the morning sun as a gift from God.

This was not the treatment he had hoped for when he and his friends had discussed surrender to the Americans. They had counted on his leadership, and he wondered now if he hadn't made a mistake they would all regret. Julius, who seemed to question Hermann's decision, now grumbled a comment—why had they all agreed so quickly to turn themselves in?

CHAPTER 2

B y morning the prisoners learned just how much freedom their American captors had stripped from them. Hermann found he couldn't take a step without feeling suspicious eyes on him or without being called to order by the guards. Even relieving himself was allowed only by orders of his captors and did not always coincide with his individual needs. He had to control his desire to wash up at the nearby stream, yet overshadowing all desires was the craving to eat. As his stomach growled, Hermann heard distant firing noises come from the east. He couldn't care less; for him, the war was over.

As the sun rose along the horizon, the guards roused the prisoners, and Hermann and his friends stood to join several hundred POWs cramming onto trucks. Again, before boarding, the young prisoner ventured a conversation with the guards. "Where are we going?" he asked in English. Again, he was given no response. "Are we being taken to the Soviets?"

The guard waved to him to be quiet, and he stared at his captor in frustration before squeezing onto the crowded back of a military truck. It was going to be a tight ride, since there was no room to sit; the POWs clung to each other for balance as they pulled out onto the winding Czech mountain roads. Hermann watched the scenery whip by and realized as they passed an occasional road sign that the truck convoy was actually traveling west, not east toward the Soviets. The prisoners exchanged looks and words of relief.

But the rejoicing came to an abrupt halt when the truck directly in front badly negotiated a curve and flipped on its side, spilling dozens of men onto the road and the ditch beside it. The startled prisoners in Hermann's truck clamored to help, but the guards held them back. When his own truck sped past the scene, Hermann glimpsed a few bodies stretched on the road—they were fellow POWs and they weren't moving. The young prisoner stared behind him helplessly as the truck gained speed and hurtled on, bouncing them around tight curves as they left the accident scene behind.

The journey came to another halt, when two POWs from the truck ahead of Hermann's jumped off as the convoy slowed at a steep incline and darted up a slope beside the road. They had almost reached the top when the guards opened fire and began chasing them. Hermann watched as first the prisoners, then the guards disappeared over the top of the hill. More shots rang out before the guards returned alone, and the convoy rolled back into motion. Hermann could only guess the fate of the escapees.

Later that day, after crossing into Germany, the men were briskly unloaded—back in their own country, but feeling no closer to home. They stood in a vacant field awaiting the arrival of an American officer. When he appeared, he spoke to the men in flawless German.

His first order was for each prisoner to take off his clothes, with the exception of underwear, and spread his belongings on the ground. Hermann warned his friends to hide anything personal such as watches, then he sat to remove his boots and quickly tied his wristwatch around his ankle, tugging his long underwear over it. When he stood, he rested one foot over his pocketknife, where he had thrust it into the ground.

The officer warned the prisoners to turn over anything that could be used as a weapon, such as razors, knives, forks, scissors, mirrors, or can openers. If a later inspection revealed that someone was hiding such an item, the officer said, he would be executed immediately.

Hermann was stunned by what he heard. His hopes for American leniency now seemed dashed forever. This tough talk reminded him of some of the most unpleasant experiences before his capture and now seemed almost as threatening as the SS. It would not be the last time he would wonder if he made a mistake in being captured by the Americans. The harsh threats and abuse yielded the intended result though; hundreds of men shed a heap of "potential weapons." Prisoners then passed the subsequent individual inspections without major incident. All the while Hermann kept one foot over his pocketknife.

Thanks to the strong body odor wafting from the unwashed prisoners, display of soiled clothing, and the threat of body lice, the Americans were not thorough as they inspected the German prisoners. Instead, American guards walked away fast, with looks of disgust, after perfunctory searches.

Hermann listened to their English as they spoke to each other and picked up words such as "pigsty" and "animals."

Despite the absence of any bathing, Hermann and his friends never suffered from lice or other vermin. Hermann attributed that either to the lack of nutrition in their blood, or the fact that they maintained daily hygiene as best they could before captivity. As POWs, they kept separate from the others as much as possible.

The American officer began a dictation of POW rules. As he spoke he punctuated his language with threats and insults. At the end of his indoctrination tirade, Hermann realized there was nothing left that he and his fellow prisoners were allowed to do; everything was "verboten."

The verboten list seemed to go on for an eternity. Forbidden activities included: cooking, running, writing, congregating in groups of more than five (Hermann's group of friends numbered eight), talking in a loud voice, singing songs, communicating with any civilians, obtaining food from civilians, leaving an assigned area, conspiring to escape, and speaking of the Third Reich or Nazism in positive terms. The possession of matches and lighters was also prohibited.

"You dirty, lice-infested bastards," the officer shouted. "You all ought to be shot." He paused as they stood miserably before him. "I know there are war criminals among you, and you can be assured that they will be identified." He warned that they should help themselves now by giving him names of the criminals in their midst. "I don't know if you'll ever see your families again. . . . You are a human scrap heap like your Fatherland."

Many of the prisoners, stunned into humiliated silence, stood in rapt attention as the officer spoke. Hermann saw tears coming from the eyes of some of the older soldiers, who had developed firm mind sets and a strong attachment to their soldierly spirit, their cause, and their dignity. To hear it spoken of with such contempt hit them with cold shock. Hermann and his friends, still in their teens, looked around them with more equanimity than offense.

The sight of his comrades' tears generated a youthful block in Hermann's mind as he told himself not to let what he had just heard sink in too deeply. As the officer strode away, leaving them to contemplate his insults, Hermann turned to look at the ground. "Words!" he mumbled as much to himself as his buddies as he pulled his pocketknife out of the dirt with a sensation of sweet triumph—twice as sweet in the face of the degrading speech. Saving the knife saved him a modicum of self-respect.

CHAPTER 3

The next night Hermann and his friends joined between one hundred fifty and two hundred prisoners to sleep in a vacant barn that offered the comparative luxury of some straw lining the hard, lumpy dirt floor. The guards announced that they would grant the prisoners two latrine calls during the night. Hermann acted as interpreter, and the prisoners and guards agreed that following the sound of a whistle, a guard would yell the order "Piss!" and those in need would queue up to be taken outside.

About thirty POWs gathered at a time and formed a circle around a manure pit, generating clouds of steam in the night air illuminated by the guards' flashlights, reminding Hermann of a comical version of the ghostly scene from Richard Wagner's *Twilight of the Gods*.

With dawn, Hermann awoke to the sound of muted conversations. His heart quickened as he heard men nearby whispering their need for a can opener. "I might be able to help you with that," he hissed to the men talking beside them. They turned to look over this boy-entrepreneur. Reluctantly they struck a deal with the young prisoner: he would open their cans and they would donate one can to him in return. Protected from the sleepy eyes of the closest American guard or POWs, he went to work on the tins with the can opener on his pocketknife, and Hermann and his friends each enjoyed a spoonful or two of salty German meat.

Back on trucks again, the group arrived that afternoon, via the town of Freyung in eastern Bavaria, at the Tittling POW camp, twenty-five kilometers north of the city of Passau. As the men spilled out of the confinement of the truck, they came upon a new sight: black American soldiers watching them approach, derision on their faces. Facing this jarring hostility, the prisoners stepped off the trucks to walk a gauntlet of these jeering soldiers, some of whom were noticeably drunk. Hermann had never seen a black man before. The troops looked the Germans over with contempt and tried to remove anything shiny or decorative still worn by the POWs: rings, watches, military decorations, rank insignia, fountain pens, and the like.

As Hermann passed through their midst, they looked him over hastily but were disappointed, since the young prisoners had already been stripped of personal items and pins or were able to hide them. While the guards remained impassive, he saw some scuffles as POWs tried to resist. The ordeal was completed with kicks in the pants, and the POWs were ushered into the camp. Hermann thankfully left this sudden display of physical aggression. He would long carry a negative image of black Americans based on that first experience.

• • •

The large camp covered a grassy, soggy depression at the southwestern edge of the town of Tittling. When Hermann arrived, it held a few thousand POWs, and hundreds continued to arrive daily. As the camp expanded its population, the Americans widened the fences and moved the watchtowers outward several times to accommodate the men. Eventually there were about twelve thousand German soldiers in the camp.

The camp itself did not include a single building; instead the men would sleep, eat, and while away their time under the open sky. Despite the lack of buildings, some order evolved. The Americans immediately assigned the new prisoners to particular sections of the ground, and Hermann and his teenage friends were marched to a grassy section of the camp tightly surrounded by other prisoners. In these close quarters they were expected to pass both day and night in the swelling prison compound.

"Don't leave this area," the guards told Hermann and his friends. After the rigors of the trip and lack of food and water, Hermann listened to their words apathetically. It was unlikely he would go anywhere, since he felt too weak to do more than lie listlessly on the ground, feeling the sodden grass soak him from below while the sun warmed him gently from above. He was desperate for water and food, but he took some consolation in being assigned an area near one of the front gates, where he could easily watch the guards and the coming and going of vehicles and people. As the days passed it would be a welcome distraction from the daily monotony, waning morale, and hunger and thirst.

For the first two days, Hermann watched the gate and the comings and goings of the American guards. He slumped on the ground as he tried to hear what the men yelled and concentrated on the strange sound of their language. The longer he concentrated, he thought, the better his own English would become, helping him communicate with these people. But as time passed, his concentration faltered.

To keep his and his group's thoughts active, he engaged his friends in conversation. They comforted each other with comparisons of their lives before internment. "At least we weren't shot!" one of the boys pointed out.

Hermann determined to keep the boys talking, in a strained effort to keep up their spirits. He reminded them that they must remain alert, keeping on the lookout for any signs of food, drink, or clothing. He assigned each of them to alternating two-man watches while the others slept.

On the second afternoon Hermann wondered if he was hallucinating as he watched local women with buckets of water at the fence. They approached the guards, and he understood that they were asking to bring the water to the fence, but the guards turned them back. Despite the depressing sight, Hermann waited for the Americans to provide food or water. After two days, the boys became so weak they couldn't stand or walk for more than a minute without collapsing or even fainting. Each became more and more silent, engrossed in his own malaise. Dehydration was the most overwhelming concern as the first two days in camp passed with no water. Hermann watched the clear sky for clouds, hoping for a spring rainstorm to drop relief on and into his exhausted body, but instead the sun shone bright on cloudless days, drawing sweat and confusion from its parched victims. Early in the morning, before the sun began its hot, dry course across the sky, the men crawled on the ground, licking the dew from wherever it had collected, including the grass.

The young German prisoner was always aware of the watching Americans and could feel their stares as the hated defenders of Hitler's regime were reduced to crawling around on the ground like animals, desperate for water. He wondered if they took pleasure from the sorry spectacle. But Hermann reminded himself that matters could be worse; after all, the hot sun kept the prisoners dry from above while the moisture seeped into their pants. The bomber jackets the boys wore helped the sun in its task of keeping them dry and warm enough to avoid catching cold during the chilly nights.

Hermann mused about the irony of previous deeds that secured him the comfort of that jacket. Four or five weeks ago, he and his group had forced their way, over a German guard's protests, into an air force depot warehouse and retrieved their jackets just minutes before German demolition charges turned it into a heap of rubble. Well, he thought, the war was replete with idiotic and senseless acts, and by taking those jackets, he and his buddies had put a little sense into it.

Hermann joined the other men in not only licking the dew off the grass, but eating the grass itself to put something in their empty stomachs; their efforts stripped the field of its grass as thousands of POWs started grazing. The fifteen-year-old prisoner had another advantage over some of his neighbors; he took out his prized pocketknife and began digging up weed roots. They tasted bitter, and the foul taste reflected his thoughts as he considered that the Americans were indiscrimminately punishing them for things they had or hadn't done.

"If these guys are trying to break us by starving us to death," Hermann said to a friend as he pondered his soil-stained finger tips, "they are well on their way." Hermann felt degraded to an animal existence now, as he watched corpses being dragged away in the early mornings.

He heard of an armistice that went into effect on May 8, two days after his capture, but he was too lethargic to attach any significance to it. He had survived the war, but now the greatest challenge was to survive captivity. Hermann heard some of the adult POWs wondering why the American "liberators" didn't shoot the POWs instead of starving them to a slow death. "It would be easier on them and us," one soldier muttered.

CHAPTER 4

A round the third day in camp Hermann heard talk from the other prisoners of water. Speaking to some friendly, older POWs, he learned there was a small stream at the far end of the camp that other prisoners were already utilizing. The compound had been growing with the arrival of more POWs; whether the stream had just become accessible with this expansion, or some men had known of it and kept its existence quiet, no one could say.

The water was running at the lowest part of the terrain, they told Hermann, and as soon as he heard it, Hermann leaped to his feet, the fastest motion he had managed in days. He and several of his comrades staggered a few meters and collapsed while some more able prisoners who overheard the conversation forced their way past him, intent on finding water. As they watched the older prisoners stumble across the compound, Hermann mustered his dwindling energy. He called back his friends who were also moving toward the rumored run.

"Wait, we can't all go at once. You two," he selected the two youngest, smallest boys. "You go ahead, see what you can find." The two children staggered back to their feet, then walked and crawled away. Since they were the weakest, Hermann imagined, they were most in need of water; the rest could follow. Hermann knew it would be foolish to leave the campsite unattended, even though it was marked only by battered and threadbare German army blankets, one blanket per two boys, and some of the clothing they had taken off during the warm days. There were thieves among the prisoners who kept the compound residents jumpy and always aware of their neighbors, and the young boys were the most vulnerable.

It seemed like an eternity before Hermann's two young friends returned, mud soaking their fronts but seeming more stable as they walked. "There's water down there," they said. "Just a little run. We got down on our stomachs and just slurped some up." That was all Hermann needed to hear, and he was among the next group to make their way to the water. When he arrived, he found hundreds of POWs pushing their way toward and along the stream, most taller and stronger than he was. Through determination and perserverance he made his way over a bank, churned muddy with thousands of fresh POW boot tracks. There he found the water, dirt-brown and shallow as it bubbled along a dip in the meadow.

The muddy liquid was the most inviting sight the young prisoner had seen since his capture, and he dropped down on all fours, sucking it down in deep gulps, then crawled away to vomit before returning for more. This time he stayed where he was, keeping the water in his uneasy stomach and splashing some on his face, savoring the sensation before an adult POW began shouting. "Hey! The waters for drinking, not bathing," Hundreds of men continued to shove their way to the water and chased him away.

Not long after, the Americans finally allowed the prisoners their first food rations. The men formed lines in groups of five at a supply point set up about four hundred meters from Hermann's campsite. When Hermann got to the head of the line, a POW under the supervision of a German officer handed him a ration consisting of a 750-gram can of beef or pork in broth. The can was to be divided among five of them. The other three members of Hermann's group had to team with two other neighboring POWs to receive their portion. Since the three youngster's often lost much of their share to their adult counterparts, the oldest three boys, mustering a little more clout with the adults than the youngest boys, took turns taking their place in the food line. The daily ration was about three tablespoons per man.

"This isn't enough to live on," Hermann thought, but it was enough to keep from dying.

At the supply point Hermann noticed a heap of cans, and he guessed they had been provided by German trucks that were operating under American supervision outside the camp. There were several gates in the compound, and he assumed the trucks arrived through one on the opposite end of the camp, since he had seen no such activity. However the food arrived, Hermann was thankful for the small amount he now ate with his friends.

The meat, accompanied by water and grass, was enough to reactivate Hermann's bowel movements, which led to his visits to yet another section of camp. The latrine consisted of a narrow, open trench that POWs were assigned to spray regularly with chloride powder. But the powder could, of course, not mask the stench wafting from the pit, which was in full sight of the civilians who lived at the camp's edge.

Prisoners lined up at the latrine twenty-four hours a day. During the most active times, Hermann, standing in line to relieve himself, watched the homes on the other side of the fence and the families trying to live normal lives while, just upwind, hundreds of men relieved their bowels day and night. Hermann hoped the civilians there forgave the men this insult to the eyes and nose.

CHAPTER 5

S omewhat heartened, Hermann began to give the camp and its surroundings a closer look. He saw there were not only watchtowers set up around the camp's perimeter, but also quadruple machine guns mounted on half-tracks—to attempt an escape would be suicidal. Beyond the fence, parts of the town looked badly damaged by American artillery fire. The young German soon left his campsite, mingled with other POWs, and made brief, uninhibited strolls near the fences. The guards didn't seem to care if the prisoners stayed in their assigned sites, since it was nearly impossible to control each individual's movements, and the young friends moved around the camp more freely.

At the same time, several Americans sat at the gate smoking, chewing mysteriously, conversing, laughing, and periodically patrolling the outside of the camp's fence line. They struck Hermann as enjoying their role as war victors. They never entered the camp itself, as if to walk among the unwashed prisoners was beneath them; yet the prisoners appreciated this neglect, since few cared to be further harassed by the presence of Americans inside the camp.

Walking through the camp Hermann saw the sheer numbers and variety of prisoners sharing his home behind barbed wire. Everyone from foot soldiers to officers were represented. Because most of the rank insignia were gone from the POWs' uniforms, at first glance, the prisoners now all looked generally alike, save for the different colors of their uniforms identifying their military service branch. Despite an initial appearance of total equality, the prisoners could easily identify an officer by the quality and the cut of his uniform. These men, asserting some authority over members of their former units as well as other prisoners, provided a semblance of order inside the camp.

More than once Hermann watched soldiers who had smuggled their medals into the compound carefully bury them to protect them from the Americans. Days later, however, the same men were digging anxiously in the area to relocate them. By this time word had spread that the Americans would trade food or cigarettes for the medals.

The younger prisoners also noticed that some POWs seemed to have had an easier capture than their own, since some entered the camp still wearing backpacks containing their remaining provisions. Hermann mulled over this inequity and the unfairness of war in general, while his friends were quick to comment on what they saw, pointing out prisoner after prisoner who fared better than they did. Hermann now wondered at his role as leader of this group of juvenile soldiers, but encouraged his friends to take heart. "Something will come along for us," he said.

The boys seized on this forced optimism, asking him just when and how they could expect their lives to improve. "How will things get better? What are you going to do about this?" one friend asked.

With some reluctance Hermann responded, "I'll think of something."

With that utterance, Hermann determined to find some way out for his young companions. The Americans had paid little attention to their extreme youth, but he thought now he might use that youth to appeal for better treatment.

Hermann, in his narrow, ninety-pound frame, was dwarfed by most of the American soldiers. Knowing he looked young, worn, and beaten, the plucky youth planned to use that now to his advantage. His friends rallied around him for good luck, and Hermann stood up straight to slowly walk toward the fence near the gate where an American guard slouched in good-natured boredom, chewing gum and casting dull looks at the prisoners. Again, Hermann's high school English took over.

"My friends and I, we are very hungry," he said politely. The guard continued to slouch, his jaw chewing without missing a beat, but his eyes were trained on the teenager in front of him. "We do not have backpacks." He paused, then pointed at a rucksack one prisoner held under his head where he lay on the crowded field. "We came here with nothing." The American stared on, as if waiting for Hermann to make his point. "Maybe we can do some work for food."

Hermann waited to be chased back to his friends, but instead the guard stood straight and put one hand on his helmet thoughtfully. With a nod he waved Hermann away, saying, "I'll see what I can do. Report back here at this time tomorrow." Hermann's friends were elated when he told them the news, then skeptical. They argued into the night whether the guard would indeed come through for them.

The next morning Hermann appeared before the guard with his friend Hans, another of the older boys. The familiar guard spoke to a companion, and Hermann strained to hear. "Take these two over to the field hospital for KP." Hermann pondered what this "KP" could be as they were led away. He nodded to the guard in appreciation, without any idea what they were being assigned to do.

Within thirty minutes Hans and Hermann found themselves surrounded by mountains of potatoes, busily peeling with paring knives. It was better than anything Hermann could have imagined. The two friends devoured peels and occasionally an entire potato as they worked—KP, Hermann thought, was synonymous with paradise. Outside the kitchen they could hear the cries of the wounded in the hospital, which consisted of tents and tarpaulins set up among the walls of a group of destroyed buildings. As if a reminder that things could be worse, the moans of the injured kept the young friends busily peeling—and chomping on potato scraps.

The boys worked with alacrity while few adults stuck their heads in the door to monitor their progress. The guards had no reason to fear the boys would attempt to make a break for it—to walk away with so many Americans in the area would have been impossible—and Hermann and Hans knew all too well their own good fortune to be in the midst of this food source.

Several hours later a guard returned to the kitchen to escort them back to camp. They stood nervously with their hands on their heads as the guard searched them, then paused as he ran his eyes over the bulges in their pants, jackets, and overcoats. A quick investigation produced potato peels lining every fold in their clothing. "Hey, what's the big idea here," he said, pulling a handful of peels out and throwing them down.

"No one will eat these here in the hospital," Hermann blurted out. "Can we take them to our friends? They are just boys and very hungry. They will be very thankful." The guard nodded and led them out of the kitchen, the boys triumphant with their booty of potato peels.

As they arrived at the gate, Hermann turned a hopeful eye to the guard who said the words he had hoped but not dared to expect to hear: "Report back here tomorrow at the same time." The young prisoners surrounded Hans and Hermann when they returned and watched incredulously as the two pulled enough potato peelings from their clothing to constitute a feast. They formed a tight circle, sealed from the misery of the rest of the camp, and ate enough to fill their empty stomachs.

CHAPTER 6

In the morning Hermann awoke recalling the day before and the potatoes he had feasted upon, and he stood up with newfound enthusiasm. This time he chose another of the older boys to join him, since they were physically and mentally more mature, and he could never predict when they might need that maturity during the day at KP. The two eagerly walked back to the gate, and the same guard who had escorted them the day before was waiting. A young man, only a few years older than they, the guard nodded in almost a friendly way as they arrived. As the three set out for the hospital, the guard surprised Hermann by speaking to him.

"You speak pretty good English. Do you think you could write something in German for me?"

Hermann, eager to stay in good stead with this American, nodded hurriedly in agreement.

"Good, because there's this girl—my girlfriend—she's German and I want to send her a letter."

"I need some paper," Hermann said, considering the many uses paper might serve him and his friends in the camp, the foremost being written communication. When the guard complied, Hermann cleared a bare spot on a kitchen table and went to work translating the guard's draft in English, sharing as best he could, a complicity in a German-American love affair. It was filled with the standards of love letters: "I love you," "I miss you," and "I will see you soon."

When he completed his task, the guard happily signed the letter; and Hermann returned to work, perfecting his skill at peeling thick chunks of potato meat with the peels, then loading handfuls of the results into his pockets. Now and then a guard or German hospital staff member would come into the kitchen to check their progress, and the Germans, mostly military medics, were sympathetic to the young prisoners. Hermann, feeling his confidence buoyed, asked for bread or meat leftovers but was told that regulations did not permit it.

Finally a hospital staff member brought them two steaming cups of coffee, which they gulped down. It took only a minute before they stood bent over in the yard retching the brown liquid back out. They fared better with plain, clean water.

When the guard came to return them to camp, Hermann asked permission to fill some discarded cardboard boxes with peels for his buddies. The guard gave them a nod and shrug of approval, and they staggered home under heavy loads, more than a day's supply of food for their group and some left over for others.

The next day KP duty included some cleanup work around the kitchen. By now Hermann and his friends went to work with vast enthusiasm, finding their lives gaining a new meaning. Hermann continued to stow away peels and wolf down anything that didn't go into his pockets. When a German hospital orderly came by to visit the two during midday, he told them the Americans had relaxed the rules for POW treatment. "Things are going to get easier for you," the orderly predicted. Cheered, Hermann and his chum completed their afternoon tasks, considering new ways they could improve their lives in the compound now that prospects for survival seemed better than ever. When the guard appeared that afternoon, Hermann asked a favor with newly discovered confidence. He and his companion had flattened some cardboard boxes; they asked to take them home, since these boxes, headed for the trash, could insulate the prisoners from the damp ground at night. The guard not only allowed them this luxury, he accompanied them only part of the way back to the camp.

"I guess you know the way by now," he said abruptly and, with a grin, turned and left them to make their way to the camp alone. The guard's gesture, careless or trusting, suddenly offered them freedom. It was minimal freedom—but welcome. Although they weren't fenced in, they knew they were surrounded by Americans on the outskirts of this tiny German town, and to make a break for it would be futile.

Finding themselves suddenly alone, Hermann and his companion exchanged a smile and considered the route back. Rather than take the main path, they set off along a shortcut to the camp, which led them through a series of destroyed farm buildings. They came to an abrupt stop in front of a two-meter hole in the ground. The two boys froze in disbelief when they saw the contents of the open hole: knives, daggers, scissors. Hundreds of potential weapons, confiscated from the prisoners by the Americans, lay before them. Hermann and his friend looked at each other, then around them for any sign of an American watching. All was silent.

Hermann leaped into the hole, grabbing pocketknives and other "weapons," and handed about half the loot to his buddy, all of which quickly disappeared inside their pockets. Knowing they could be discovered at any instant, they worked with such speed they couldn't identify all the goodies cushioned in the handfuls of potato peels in their clothing. Then Hermann climbed out of the hole, and the two began walking on, glancing only furtively around them as they ambled toward the camp. It had taken them perhaps a minute; now they approached the gates of the camp with casual strides.

At the gate the two were looked over by the American guard. Each still carried several large flattened boxes under his arm, and Hermann hastened to explain that he had permission to bring the cardboard inside; the guard nodded, allowing them past. With their pockets bulging with potato peels, Hermann guessed the young boys had become a familiar sight to the guards by now.

That night Hermann was too nervous to hand out the "weapons" to his friends; instead he rammed them into the soft ground underneath the cardboard "mattresses." Among the weapons they retrieved from their pockets were about fifteen sturdy pocketknives, a pair of scissors, and a two-inch Fin knife. He especially liked the Fin knife and promised himself that this one he would keep.

Hermann slept fitfully, wondering if anyone might give him away to the guards or if someone might uncover his stash of weapons. Still he congratulated himself, knowing he had accomplished something meaningful for the first time since his capture and had managed to break the monotony and passivity of prison life. But despite the elation, he vowed not to take the same risk again; if the Americans caught him, he would be doomed.

CHAPTER 7

A t nightfall the next day, Hermann and his friend strolled into a section of the camp occupied by several hundred Hungarians. Hermann assumed these prisoners were members of the Mountain Artillery; here he could see what was clearly the better lifestyle enjoyed in this camp sector. The Hungarians had kept not only their backpacks but also some food supplies and even pup tents. Here there were no pallid faces of starving prisoners; rather, the prisoners seemed to have received preferential treatment from the Americans when they were captured.

Hermann surveyed all this with some envy, noting that, with all these amenities, the Hungarian prisoners were clearly the upper class in the camp society. After watching them carefully, Hermann cautiously approached several men. Ensuring they weren't officers, and speaking in German, he told the men he had something of interest to trade. "Do you have enough food to spare a few cans?" Hermann asked.

"That depends on what you have to offer," a Hungarian responded. Several prisoners had joined him, and they looked the young German over with naked condescension.

"A pocketknife." Hermann said. After a tense moment, he saw a glimmer of interest in the older prisoners' eyes. Following some negotiation, the boys returned to the disheveled crowds in the German section of camp carrying a can of goulash and two cans of sauerkraut in tomato sauce. Because there was no way to cook it at the campsite, the young prisoners devoured everything cold, a nocturnal feast under a starlit sky. Shortly thereafter, they came to regret their meal.

A stabbing stomach spasm sent Hermann running to the latrine and his friends followed close behind. They beat a path toward the latrine in the following days until their stomachs purged themselves of the canned food. The nightly trading visits to the Hungarian section continued, however, but canned fish took the place of sauerkraut. The arsenal finally dwindled to a few knives the boys kept for themselves as a last resort.

• • •

One afternoon, the boys were startled by the sound of voices yelling at the gate, and Hermann stood to see about six Waffen SS surrounded by shouting American guards. The elite German soldiers were being herded into a fenced off section of the camp where they stood, waiting. Prisoners gathered near the fence or stood in their area wondering about this new spectacle.

The Americans emptied the SS backpacks and threw their contents—packs of cigarettes, cans and packages of food—into the crowd of POWs; the prisoners instantly surged forward, multiplying into a hungry mob. The starving men descended like a hoard of wild animals on the goods and fought over each pack of cigarettes or item of food, grabbing at anything, clawing at their neighbors as they did so, and knocking others down in their excitement.

Hermann stood back in disgust, witnessing the complete erosion of the discipline and soldierly restraint that had been at the core of the German military tradition. That, the youth realized, had given way to the basest of instincts. He noticed the American guards were enjoying the public display, but they soon grew impatient with it since they had their own performance planned for the benefit of the POWs.

Several Americans led two men, dressed in what reminded Hermann of striped pajamas, into the corral with the elite German troopers. Hermann watched in disbelief as the pair began beating the SS while the guards ensured that the men did not fight back. With their fists and feet, the two men beat up the SS until they all were lying on the ground groaning or unconscious. At the end of this brutal spectacle, the two bullies walked away.

Witnessing an aspect of the war he had never known before—the infamous concentration camps—the youth tried to make sense of what he had just seen. He recalled the SS troopers who had hanged the German stragglers on the quiet country road, but he had no idea what he was witnessing now. Older POWs commented about anti-Germans being given a chance to vent their feelings on the SS; others added that this served the SS right.

Months later Hermann would learn that the two "bullies" who had beaten up the SS wore the uniform of concentration camp inmates, and he also learned about the Nazi brutalities in those camps. He would understand then that the Americans had given the two men the opportunity to pay back some of the misery the SS had inflicted on them and their fellow inmates.

After nightfall, Hermann heard a strange hollow pounding near the corral where the SS had been beaten. Guards shouted and floodlights beamed as Americans rushed toward the corral. "What's happening?" Hermann asked a prisoner who came from the direction of the corral.

"They escaped—at least some of the SS escaped."

Hundreds of Americans searched the fields adjoining the camp, their flashlights dancing across the ascending slopes. Hermann watched them until sleep overcame him. He woke the next morning to a strange calm. The corral was empty, but it revealed no clue as to whether the SS had been recaptured or had made a successful escape. There was only a pile of cardboard boxes that Hermann thought could have explained the thumps heard the night before; the troopers may have thrown the boxes at their guards as a distraction. The American response to the escape, swift and overwhelming, left the other prisoners uneasy. Those considering escape realized that it would take a miracle to elude recapture.

CHAPTER 8

The day after the incident in the SS corral, Hermann's KP duty ended. When he returned through the camp's gate in the afternoon, armed with his usual food scraps for the evening's feast, the guard motioned him through without comment. Hermann paused, waiting for his orders to return the next morning, but the guard was silent. Disappointed, Hermann walked back to his buddies. The next morning he returned to the gate as if reporting for work, but the guards motioned him back, signifying the termination of his days in the kitchen, surrounded by food, drink, and activity.

Boredom was his new companion. As the day passed idly, he stared at the other prisoners around him, wondering if someone else had secured his job or whether the loss of his job had something to do with the SS troopers' escape the night before. Since he began his daily excursions to the hospital kitchen, he noticed the envy and hostility of some fellow prisoners, who grilled him about his work and jeered as he walked by. "Oh, here he comes," he heard a prisoner comment loudly one evening. "This one—he likes to fraternize with the enemy."

Hermann resented the comment; he felt the hard stares the boys were getting from their fellow prisoners. Hermann stopped and confronted his adversary. "You should be happy," Hermann countered, "They let you bring your backpack in. At least we've found a way to feed ourselves without our provisions." A cutting reply prompted Hermann to hurl a scathing look. "Quit your griping," he muttered and walked away.

But if anything, his challengers became increasingly enraged by Hermann's continued employment in the kitchen, and one day the boy faced down some of them as they derided him for "fraternizing with the enemy." Smaller and younger, he braced himself for a fight until he heard the shouting of their officer. "It's better to have fraternization than fratricide," the officer commented as he led his men away. The bullies skulked away, and Hermann shrugged off the close call.

At night he recalled the feeling of food stuffed in his pockets and the sweet taste of raw potato peels that he had almost learned to enjoy. At these times he had to shake off his memories, chiding himself to avoid dwelling on the good life he had lost.

Having the days free again meant Hermann joined the thousands who idled their time away each day. Without American objections, some POWs had formed a choir to sing folk songs while others met for improvised religious services or Bible readings. The inevitable card games sprouted up throughout the sprawling camp, and two prisoners created a chess game with a makeshift set where prisoners took turns at the board.

Hermann observed all this as well as some of the more eccentric prisoners. One POW, so thin Hermann imagined he could disappear behind a telephone pole, proclaimed that he was Jesus Christ's disciple. The young prisoner watched this "disciple" trying to rouse a group of listeners or followers. The next day the same man claimed to be Hitler himself.

"Here comes the lunatic," men would say, nudging each other as he approached, but his presence seemed to entertain them so no one ever tried to chase him away. Hermann was impressed by the man's gift for rhetoric and would look forward to his passing through their section of camp. One warm May day, the man preached his way up to a guard at the gate. His arms outstretched, he slowly approached a guard at the gate. "Hey you, get back in da lager!" the guard shouted, using the German word for "camp."

One of the guards stationed outside the gate stepped inside to meet him, lifted his rifle, and knocked him on the chin, sending him into the dust. Several POWs rushed forward and dragged the man away. It was the first time Hermann had seen a guard venture inside the camp's boundaries. The inmates wondered now just how crazy this skinny "preacher" really was. "Do you think it was an act?" one of Hermann's friends asked as the man was revived.

"An act? Why would he do that?"

"Maybe he thought they'd discharge him for insanity." Hermann later wondered at the theater of the absurd that would cause a man to claim the identity of Christ's disciple one day, the identity of Hitler the other. He realized he shared his own moment on stage as a member of the Jungvolk.

The Third Reich and Nazi ideology, he thought, provided an incongruous script that brought the notion of the Fatherland together with behavior beyond the limits of any normal religious belief system. Hermann could only shake his head as he considered the naive and immature involvement of the Hitler youth in an insane ideology during the past few years, and the world they would return to if they survived internment.

Many of the prisoners suffered from depression, made worse by the installation of the American public-address system. The loudspeakers were mounted on poles along the camp's fence line; no matter where they stood in the camp, prisoners could not avoid the messages broadcast from them. Periodically, voices, some with American accents, spoke to the prisoners in their own language, sometimes telling stories of what Hitler had done, what the German military had done, and what they must live with now.

The stories were laced with insults and threats, and many of those listening became so despondent they withdrew from their fellow prisoners, eating alone and standing in isolation amid the POWs jockeying for their turn at the latrine. Hermann often noticed the questioning eyes of these more tormented prisoners, staring through the fence of the camp as if an answer or absolution lurked somewhere in the Bavarian hills.

Some men would break down and cry after the address system fell silent, and Hermann heard through rumors from his neighbors that a few POWs committed suicide. To be taken prisoner was shameful, but to lose the war and be blamed for staggering war crimes as well was too much for those with weaker spirits. Hermann tried to keep his inner strength, but during long restless nights he sat awake considering what Germany had wrought and what could be left of it now.

Nearly fifteen thousand men now resided on the soggy grassland, hoping each day that discharge might be near. According to rumor, some were later turned over to the Russians and those who did go to the Russians certainly saw their home country only years later, if ever. A deeply discouraging sight for Hermann and the others was the oxcart passing along the perimeter of the camp every so often carrying the bodies of those dead from disease or malnutrition.

Still, although Hermann and his comrades grew increasingly bitter toward the Americans, their greatest fear remained of the Russians. They knew the Russian army was only about thirty kilometers away in Czechoslovakia, and Americans used this fear as a form of discipline—any threat to turn the men over to the Russians brought immediate compliance.

CHAPTER 9

A s June approached and the days grew hotter and longer, the meager supply of water dwindled. The modest stream, which was drained by thousands of prisoners each day, was drying up under the sun's rays, and if that water source evaporated, the men would die. Each day Hermann felt the sun burn hotter and saw prisoners kneel above the trickle of water, desperation now in their eyes as they tried to satisfy a monthlong thirst.

The food had not improved in quality or quantity, and Hermann guessed from the increase of American personnel and the quadruple machine guns appearing by the fence that the rules would not be relaxed soon. Instead, the opposite was taking place. The announcements on the PA system grew harsher, and the guards offered no leniency to those brave enough to approach them. Hermann wondered if all this military buildup was the result of the escapes by the SS.

Stretched out idly under the ruthless heat of the late spring sun and shielding his head with a piece of cardboard, the youth longingly anticipated the coolness of nighttime. Then the sun would set and the sickening stench of the open pit latrine would ebb with the heat. At these times Hermann and his friends sometimes looked up at the starry sky and talked about a better life, their families, and their past happiness during KP duty peeling potatoes. Hermann silently cursed his surrender, and his friends began to do the same, verbally.

"We should never have gone to the Americans," his young friends said with irritating regularity. "That was your idea. Anything would have been better than this. I knew we shouldn't surrender. We should have gotten hold of some civilian clothes and found our way back home. We could be at home right now," they told him.

In self-defense Hermann raised the specter of getting caught on the way by the roaming SS, some Nazi fanatics, or the Americans. He strained to justify his decision not only to his friends, but to himself as well. Eventually the arguing gave way to a desperate silence, which was even worse for Hermann.

Soon he and his friends began to consider contingency plans in case the camp was turned over to the Russians. This desperate fantasizing always fell short of a solution, however, since their malnourished minds had become lethargic and unimaginative. Often they just stared at the stars, at a loss for plans, solutions, hopes, or fears. All agreed that if they were taken by the Russians they would be better off shot than dying in a Siberian coal mine.

Although Hermann's boyhood friends complained and criticized, they never stopped looking to their chum for leadership. It was a role Hermann no longer wanted, but still he tried to think of a way to help his friends. He was the eldest of the boys, he was the only one who spoke some English, and he felt their constant pressure to come up with an idea to rescue them from this experience, an experience they now wondered if they would survive. Hermann's frustration grew as he looked at the hungry and dying men around him—escape was impossible and the guards had no more work they wanted from him or his companions.

"But the guards know you," the youngest of his companions would say: "They'll listen to you. Maybe you could talk them into accepting some deal. It worked with the potato peeling. After all, we're just kids and we weren't regular members of the military."

Hermann shook his head at his friend. "Regulations are tighter since then," he said.

"This guy was full of ideas before we surrendered, but now he can't think of a thing," Julius commented.

Their fears heightened as they noticed the harsh threats and announcements over the PA system growing more adversarial; stringent rules again forbade prisoners from clustering in larger groups unless waiting for rations. It seemed the voice on the PA system was taunting them. "You all should be ashamed having fought for Hitler," the American voice would boom over the loudspeaker.

With this latest mood, Hermann had no wish to anger the guards or their commander. If he overdid it, he and his friends could be singled out for punishment, since speaking to the guards had become strictly forbidden.

His friends coaxed and complained to him more vigorously daily, and Hermann's frustration reflected their impatience. He had accepted leadership in the group before their imprisonment; now he wanted to be left alone. He couldn't avoid seeing the sardonic smile on his comrade Julius's face; but when he asked the boy for ideas, his friend would respond "You're the leader, not me."

After an argument one late spring night, Hermann stared at the stars, telling his friends to leave him alone to think. When a thought finally came to him, it was so simple and obvious that he wondered now why the idea hadn't come to him sooner. Since speaking to the guards was "verboten," he would have to write to them. The guards he spoke with in the past were reasonable and even sympathetic, and he imagined if he could communicate with them, they might deliver a message to the camp commander. He still had paper remaining from the love letter writing he had done for one of the guards.

That morning he sat down and carefully composed a petition for the boys' release to the camp's commander. He wrote that he and his friends, ages thirteen to fifteen, were not members of the Wehrmacht and therefore deserving of a discharge. He read it over several times before handing it to a guard, pleased with his best high school English. But his hopes were dashed when the guard looked at Hermann, then the letter, reading it over in a matter of seconds. He laughed suddenly, startling the young prisoner, and tore the petition apart.

Seeing their downcast leader, Hermann's friends realized that the petition had not been accepted. No one spoke for several minutes, and Hermann considered his next option. Stubbornness harassed him; he reformulated the request for discharge using the last piece of paper he had. Again he handed it to a guard, this time choosing one he hoped would be more sympathetic. As the man unfolded the paper and read it over slowly, Hermann stood by anxiously waiting. But his luck had not improved, and this guard didn't give him as much as a glance before crumpling the paper in his hand and throwing it aside.

Holding his head up, the young German turned to walk back to his friends, passing several older POWs who shouted at his departing back. They had seen him approaching the guards and they, like everyone in the camp, were nervous. "Don't make trouble you snot-nosed little boy," they warned. "Didn't you hear the warnings over the PA system? If you don't behave, we'll punish you before the Americans punish us!"

Hermann refused to speak to his friends as he seated himself and began to think. There had to be a way to get to the commander. The writing paper was finished, but there was still cardboard underneath their battered blankets. He peeled back a thin layer of cardboard for writing paper and went to work for a third time. Then he waited until most of the POWs were queuing up for food rations before he approached a third guard, sliding the paper in his hand. This time he accompanied the petition with one spoken word, "Please!"

It was not the same petition he had written the previous times—this one included any detail he thought would help: their ages, unit designations, hometowns, and the fact that they had not committed war crimes. He believed his English was at its best, and he knew this was sure to be his last chance. The guard looked at the paper, folded it up and put it in his pocket. Hermann returned to his friends with visible relief; yet, afraid of another disappointment, the group spent the next two days in nervous suspense.

Around noon on one of the last days of May, the PA system came on with the usual warnings and announcements. The boys sat frozen in disbelief as their names were read suddenly over the system. The names were read twice, and the announcer then followed the list with the statement they had hoped for and also feared, "Report to the front gate."

"Do you think it's a trick? Do you think they'll turn us over to the Russians?" one of Hermann's friends whispered, but the others brushed the thought aside.

"If nothing else we'll have a chance to make a break for it now," Hermann said.

The group headed for the gate, and this time the walk seemed to be an endless one. Hermann didn't notice his fellow prisoners as he headed single-mindedly toward the guards. The boys were ushered into a building outside the camp, where they were told to stand near the open door, probably so as not to offend the staff inside with their foul odor, Hermann guessed. There they watched American soldiers typing, writing, and telephoning in a large office room, ignoring the boys' presence.

The wait seemed unending before a soldier came to speak to them, asking for personal data: unit designation, home addresses, and ages. An American officer fired questions at them, which Hermann did his best to understand and answer before the officer handed the paperwork to a typist. The young German looked outside at the freedom that seemed so close at hand. He would have liked to sit on the floor, but he stood without complaint, frowning at his friends when they squirmed and appeared prepared to sit themselves. A sense of growing excitement overcame them. Hermann guessed that with the formality of paperwork it was unlikely they would be turned over to the Russians. He said as much to his friends in German; and a soldier walking by snapped at him, "Shut up."

Hermann gladly obliged. Finally the American officer returned to stand before them and handed each of the boys a typed sheet of onionskin paper. The top of it read "Certificate of Discharge." The grin on Hermann's face told his friends the good news. He stammered a few words of thanks, but the officer cut him short with an impatient sweep of his hand toward the door. He instructed them about the general curfew of 6:00 P.M. to 6:00 A.M. and dismissed them with the admonition "forget that you have been Hitler's soldiers."

As they filed out Hermann couldn't help thinking their departure was a great relief to the Americans' noses. They moved away in silence, each trying to grapple with the idea of what freedom meant before the moment was broken by sheer joy. Happily, they rushed to the nearest public water fountain in Tittling to savor the most delicious water they had tasted in months. Hermann may or may not have given the POW camp a look of farewell—later he couldn't remember.

More memorable for him was the taste of that cold, clean fountain water, something he would appreciate for the rest of his life. As they drank, children and locals congregated around the woebegone figures, watching them curiously, giving the boys the sensation of being strange animals who had escaped from the town zoo. Some friendly people brought them a bite to eat, and with their help they turned a shed into a bathhouse.

None of the small group had spoken more than a word since their release, as if speaking would wake them from an unbelievable dream. But eventually pent-up emotions bubbled forth, and the group broke into laughter and cheerful talk, eyes gleaming with the joy of freedom. Finally Hermann said, "We'd better get out of Tittling as soon as we can. I'd like to put some space between us and that camp."

They could see that the town's destruction at the end of the war was more extensive than they had realized from within the camp, and they were eager to escape this depressing reminder of the war and their imprisonment. At the edge of town they were stopped by men in uniform, this time Americans who demanded to see the papers showing their discharge from the camp. Their joy turned to anxiety when the patrol abruptly refused to let them pass and, instead, took them into custody. Hermann felt his heart sink as once again he was at the mercy of the American military. The arresting soldiers radioed a message, waited and received a message, then sent another, until one nodded curtly and handed them back their papers. "You can move on," an American soldier said.

The boys moved slowly as they continued their hike, their exhaustion forcing them to take frequent breaks. Within two hours they were stopped again by a second group of American soldiers. It took another exhaustive series of questions and radio transmissions before the Americans returned them their papers.

"These guys are as bad as the SS," one of Hermann's companions, complained and as they walked on Hermann heard another respond, "Maybe so, but at least they don't string people up on trees."

As the 6:00 P.M. curfew approached shortly before sunset, the boys found themselves near a Catholic convent, which operated a makeshift field hospital that was treating only a few patients. Nuns invited the boys inside and fed them a supper of bread and smoked bacon. Almost immediately Hermann felt a churning in his stomach as the food, especially the bacon, took his stomach, used to a more spartan diet, by surprise. This new insult to their innards soon sent him and his buddies racing outside to a manure pit and outhouses behind the building. Most of the evening the boys lay in the comparative luxury of soft bedding—dry, cozy straw. For Hermann Pfrengle and his friends, this first night of freedom, was spent with a roof over their heads—not sky—but God's roof all the same.

PART FIVE

Aftermath: Soviet Revenge

CHAPTER 1

Helga Wunsch was seventeen when the Russians poured into her hometown of Frankfurt an der Oder in eastern Germany in 1945. Unlike the more well-known city of Frankfurt, this small town bordering Poland quickly fell under the control of the Soviet government following on the heels of Hitler's defeat.

Until the war came to its close, Helga had managed to live her life in the river town as any young schoolgirl, making plans for going to university the next year. But the Soviets took her by surprise. They began their occupation in 1945 by reorganizing the East German government and abruptly closing her school doors after the battle actions. The war itself had touched her life in the peaceful town only by depriving her of her father for a time, who was sent with the military to fight the Allied Forces in France. But when the Soviets swept through in 1945, she was to learn the wrath of the men who had spent six years fighting her country. Without her father home from the war, she, her mother, and grandmother faced the strange enemy alone, hoping the occupying presence would eventually fade away. Instead, Helga helplessly watched the Soviets loot her town, removing railroad tracks, closing all shops and sending all food to the Russian effort. The Wunsch family had to wait in line for weekly rations provided by the Soviets: a loaf of bread and a cup of jam per person.

As fall turned to winter, thousands of Germans died of starvation, and Helga's grandmother was one of them. On November 7, 1945, the seventy-year-old woman, weak and malnourished, slipped away from her long life while the Soviets celebrated a national holiday. As she overhead the troops in their barracks laughing and drinking, Helga made preparations for the funeral of her mother's mother. But with worries about feeding themselves, they had no time to mourn. Helga envied her grandmother, but concentrated on survival as she and her mother began sneaking to area farms, rooting through the unharvested fields for potatoes and green beans. This was dangerous work since farmers were forbidden to provide produce to their fellow Germans, knowing that such infractions led the Soviets to shoot them on the spot. Potatoes, used to manufacture vodka, were especially valuable.

Still, Helga and her mother found enough vegetables to keep themselves alive. After harvesting potatoes or beans during the dark nights, the mother-daughter team left money in the farmer's mailbox to compensate him. They continued this form of survival while they awaited the possible return of Helga's father, who was hiding in the Alps and waiting for a safe opportunity to reappear after the full impact of Hitler's loss had reverberated throughout Europe. It was three months after Hitler's defeat before the Soviets allowed the bakers to reopen their shops for the German population in Frankfurt an der Oder. Although rationing would continue for years, life slowly returned to normal.

But the rage of the town's teenagers did not ease with their most severe hunger. Helga's friends railed against the injustices heaped upon them under Soviet rule, and they began to realize how much their lives were to be changed. It began to look like the Soviets were not going away.

Helga's friend Hans gathered several of his male friends around him with a plan for action. In 1946 they climbed aboard a train one day, headed for Berlin; once there the teenagers casually walked across the east-west line and entered the American Consulate. They approached the American officer there with a report of the troubles in Frankfurt an der Oder, and the officer nodded sympathetically. He knew they were suffering, but there was nothing either he or the boys could do about it. East Germany had become a Soviet state.

Nevertheless, Hans refused to give up. When he offered his services in espionage, the American officer laughed. Spies were adults with special skills and training, he told Hans. "Come back when you've grown up."

Hans and his friends returned home, disappointed but not defeated, and after several weeks they decided to try again. Because train travel was erratic, with only one rail entering and leaving most East German cities, when the train stopped short of Berlin the boys spent the night with a man named Mr. Vogel. Vogel was a German who had established a Red Cross shelter for people traveling East Germany. Although he was completely ignorant of the boys' anticommunist mission, he welcomed them into his home. The boys then continued on the next day, and again they came before the American officer. Again the officer sent them home.

For a year Hans and his chums continued their visits to West Berlin as life went on for Helga, who knew nothing of their clandestine actions. Her school reopened, and she began preparing for her graduate exams. Her father returned from the war unharmed, and with the help of a bicycle, was able to get out of the house and work for food for his family. Meanwhile, unbeknownst to Helga, her friend Hans was making headway with the Americans.

The officer there finally capitulated after three visits from the determined East German teenagers. If they really wanted to do something to hurt the Soviets, perhaps they could do a little spy work, the American said. The officer assigned them to work along main roads connected across the Oder River, which separated Poland and Germany. Each young spy was poised near a major road or railroad track with a book shrouding his pen and paper, onto which he recorded license plates of Soviet cars and large military vehicles or train loads crossing into Germany. The license plates, identifying the military units of the vehicles, would help the Americans monitor the movement of the military; if the Soviets began bringing in large weapons or troops, the boys would be able to quickly notify the Americans of their movements.

Hans and his friends wrote down the license plate numbers of Soviet cars and recorded which direction the vehicles took. Soon they were keeping the Americans well apprised of much of the Russian movement between that part of Poland and East Germany. The Cold War had begun.

Evenings and spare time still found the boys being teenagers, however, gathering with their friends, studying for exams, and dating. Helga spent days with the boys, went to parties, and developed a romantic relationship with a boy she called "Gebi." Life returned to normal for Helga, and she was happily ignorant of Hans and her friends' double lives.

But jealousy soon halted the spy activities of the young agents. When one of the most active members, Nethe, heard rumors of another spy flirting with his girlfriend, he went to the boy with a warning. "Stay away from her," he told the boy, "I have enough information on you to have the Soviets put you away for life."

The boy, not taking Nethe's warnings seriously, started dating the girl, a student in town whom Helga later learned about but would never know. Nethe was furious, and he took his rage to the KGB secret police. He told them of his friend's activities, but was soon surprised when the Soviets refused to allow him to leave. They held him there, subjecting him to a series of interrogations until he named several members of the small spy ring. The Soviets moved quickly. Hans was seized in the late summer of 1947.

Helga soon discovered that the Soviets had arrested some of her closest male friends. She met with her best friend Inge, and they tried to guess what could be happening. It was the talk of the town.

"I heard the Soviets are taking boys for slave labor in the mines in Siberia," a friend told the girls. They wondered at the thought.

"Who will be next then? Why did they pick those boys—all our friends?"

While they talked, Hans was transported to the Linden Street offices of the KGB at Potsdam—the former military prison of Frederick the Great. Ironically, the boys were being held, interrogated, and beaten in cells not far from Berlin, where they had first begun their espionage. In Frankfurt, Soviet officers rifled through Hans's belongings in his bedroom in his parent's home. With delight, the officers located an address book in his drawer filled with the names of his relatives and friends. As they pored through the ordinary address book, several officers agreed they had the key to more arrests; they believed they had discovered his "spy organization membership book."

Meanwhile, Helga was writing for her exams. She had five subjects to complete, and the papers she wrote on each would determine whether she could advance to the oral exams. If she did and she passed, she would be on her way to university. She began with English, then Latin and German, sitting in class for five or six hours to write each subject. By Friday she had completed three of five courses with only math and science remaining. On Tuesday morning, October 14, 1947, with only a few days to prepare for those two exams she planned to spend the day in study. Her three completed exams sat in her bedroom on a bureau top.

She was jolted from her sleep at 6:30 A.M. by a pounding at the front door. To her, the harshness of the knock was an ominous sign, and she listened as her father walked to the front door, which stood next to her own bedroom door. When he opened it, she sat up in horror as she recognized Russian voices. There were several, with one acting as interpreter, speaking German with a Russian accent to her father. Helga stayed in the bed as she heard, incredulously, her name shouted out by the visitors, their voices laced with contempt. Her father tried to protest, but she heard them enter the house. When they swung open her bedroom door without knocking, she saw that there were two officers of the KGB as well as a silent

German policeman waiting to take her away. She was under arrest, but she had no idea why.

"You will be coming with us," the officer translated for her from Russian to German. "You may pack three blankets, three pillow cases, and three sheets. Get dressed warmly."

Her father begged the men to step out of her room while she got dressed. At first they refused, then conceded to his continued pressure and left her alone in the room to listen to her hammering heart as she considered her options. Quickly she walked to the window and looked out at the street in front of her. Any fleeting thoughts of escape were dashed when an Asian-looking guard peered back at her from his post in front of the house. He was there with another soldier watching the front door and the windows, should she attempt to flee, and he pointed his bayonet at her face in the window, then grinned a mocking warning. She pulled back with a start and stood frozen as she heard one guard come into the house and speak with the officers inside. They returned to her bedroom. "I can assure you there is no chance of escape. Because you cannot be trusted we will have to wait for you here."

"I have to get dressed," she told them, but they only nodded and stared at her with bland faces. While both officers stood waiting, she took off her nightclothes with her back to them, trying to hide herself as she pulled on long underwear, a thick skirt, and stockings. Over her blouse she put on a cranberry pullover that she imagined would be the warmest, wherever she was going. Her parents waited nervously outside her room, and she could sense, if not hear, their worried conversation. She packed a few personal items, then motioned toward the family bathroom.

"Can I at least use the lavatory?" she asked, and the officer motioned for her to go, then one officer followed. Realizing that any argument was useless, she went into the bathroom and seated herself on the toilet before his stare. When she was finished she brushed her teeth, packed the toothbrush, and found herself only one pillow case, sheet, and blanket, assuming that the Russians would steal whatever she brought anyway.

As she went about her preparations she felt a strange sense of detachment and clarity of thought, reviewing what she would need and what she should leave behind. She left her watch on the bureau top, knowing it would be safer there, and then she spoke briefly to her father. "I borrowed ten marks from Monica yesterday because I didn't have enough money to pay a bill—please give it back to her," she told him.

Meanwhile, the other officers were searching her bedroom. They went through drawers and closets, peered under her bed and behind pictures on her wall. The officers gathered around one photo in her room and nodded with obvious pleasure, looking at the smiling images of herself and her classmates, including Hans. For the officers, it was all they needed, and they triumphantly gestured to faces in the picture that were nothing more than school chums to Helga. They took the photo with them for evidence, along with other photos, and her diary.

When it came time to go she walked to the door with a numb feeling. "They must be using girls now, for slave labor," she thought to herself. She put on a dark blue, wool winter coat and brushed past her distraught parents in the doorway to a cold and sunny October morning.

Four guards waited outside: the two who had been posted at the front door and two more who had been waiting in the back. Surrounded by uniformed men, Helga began her march to the street, then dared to looked back at her parents in the doorway. She was chilled by the look of desperation in their eyes. She was their only daughter, their only child, and they had no idea where she was going or why—there was nothing they could do.

"Don't look back! Look at the ground!" The officer screamed at her, and she turned to face forward as they marched her away.

CHAPTER 2

The group marched her a few blocks toward the KGB administration building, a German home turned into Soviet headquarters. As they proceeded down the street Helga spotted a classmate fifty feet away walking toward them. His eyes met Helga's, and swiftly he dropped his gaze to the ground ahead of him as if he had never seen her. He casually glanced behind him, then ahead, and crossed the street to give the group a wide berth. She didn't resent his refusal to acknowledge her, knowing she would have done the same.

Once inside the Soviet headquarters, she was ushered downstairs to a cellar, which the Soviets had fashioned into holding cells. A board was built into the wall about eighteen inches above the ground in her cell, and she sat on it, staring at the door in front of her. As she heard the heavy footsteps of her captors retreat upstairs, she was met with silence for the first time since her sudden waking at 6:30. It was now midmorning and she had no idea what to expect next, but she was surprised at her own calmness. Rather than shed any tears, she considered what might lie in her future with the deliberate curiosity of a disinterested spectator.

After some time had passed, she heard voices overhead and eventually approaching the stairs. More boots stomped the floorboards as they descended toward her, and she could easily make out the words of men talking. She recognized the name they spoke: Joachim Stern. Helga rushed to the door to listen more carefully, wondering if she had heard them right. Joachim Stern was another classmate of hers, called "Sternchen" or "Little Star" by his friends. Listening at the door, she realized that he was with these arresting officers and that they were bringing him down to another one of the holding cells. "Sternchen!" She called through the door. "Is that you? It's Helga. I'm here too."

"Shut up!" A voice shouted in Russian and she fell silent. She had studied enough Russian in school to understand the order. After the slamming of several doors, an officer burst into her cell. "If you ever speak a single word I will kill you on the spot," he barked before leaving her alone again.

Eventually they brought a cellmate to Helga. It was an elderly man who came in under guard and gave her a sympathetic glance. Before the door again slammed shut, the two Germans were told to sit on opposite ends of the board and not to speak. The man, who eventually introduced himself in a whisper as Mr. Vogel, was the same innkeeper who had taken in the boys on their way to Berlin. In keeping with Soviet law, he had required each overnight guest to register his or her name and address, and the KGB found the boys' names in his registry book.

The elderly man went through his pockets with unassuming resignation and pulled out a small package of cookies. He slid the package toward Helga, nodding and smiling at her, but she slid it back to him with her own smile. Uncertain when they would receive food, she was reluctant to take anything from him. Instead she watched him as he slowly ate one cookie himself.

When the two were finally moved out of the building, Helga noticed that the sun had crossed the sky, and it was, she guessed, now late afternoon. There in the yard before the house, she saw gathered a group of twenty-five to thirty people standing at nervous attention before armed guards. Most of them were her friends, and among them was Inge. She saw Sternchen and Annaliese—both from her school—and Rudi and his mother, as well as the Müller brothers, Kurt and Eddi, and Heinz Blumenstein, a classmate she had once entertained a crush on. All were under arrest. Ordered not to speak, they were herded onto two open trucks with benches facing each other. Several guards armed with bayonets climbed on each truck while the prisoners seated themselves and stared at one another with big eyes as if to say, "You too?"

Helga expected them to head across the bridge over the Oder toward Poland and ultimately Russia. Instead they turned west to the Autobahn and made their way toward Berlin. Could they be going to the airport? she wondered. But the group landed in Potsdam and the infamous interrogation site on Linden Street.

Upon arrival, they were stripped naked and searched before being escorted into their new cells to await endless months of questionings and beatings. After Helga redressed she entered cell number 81 on the fifth floor, which would be her home for the next five-and-a-half months. The steel frame of the bed—a dirty straw-filled sack—was attached to the dark green wall, and the bed filled most of the cell space, approximately eleven square meters. Opposite the bed, a tiny folding table and seat were fastened to the wall and a bucket with a lid, intended for use as a toilet, decorated the corner next to the door.

Her cellmate, Mrs. Finke, was an older woman who had been under arrest for weeks. She regarded Helga with both sympathy and resignation. After she was shoved into the cell behind Helga, she told the younger girl what she could expect at the interrogation station: repeated hours of questioning and beatings, very little sleep, and a piece of bread about five inches long per day. With the bread they were served two cups of black sweetened coffee and a clear bowl of "soup" twice a day.

The soup, Helga discovered, was actually a bowl of greasy water that occasionally included a fragment of overcooked potato or carrot, if she was lucky. If she was in interrogation at the time of meals, she would not eat. Mrs. Finke looked Helga over as she talked, and she stopped suddenly when she saw Helga's hand. "What is that, did you sneak something past the Soviets?" she burst out.

Helga looked down at the simple gold ring with a single ruby stone that had been her mother's confirmation ring, given to her as a gift from her godfather and eventually passed on to Helga. She had forgotten all about it. She hurriedly pulled the ring off, looking at Mrs. Finke and around the cell and wondering over her luck at getting it this far. The Soviets would take it as soon as they found it, she knew that.

"You had better find a good place to hide that ring if it means anything to you," Mrs. Finke said. Helga opened her mouth and thrust the small band under her tongue when she heard the boot steps of a guard approaching.

Feeling the contours of the ring in her mouth, she stared at the door as it swung open and an officer shouted at her to come out. She followed him down the hall to the interrogation building, then was seated before an officer known as Mr. Tobartchikov. He and his female interpreter turned their scornful attention on her. Many of Helga's beatings would be at the hands of the woman interpreter.

"What am I being charged with?" Helga asked.

"You are being charged with spying. We have proof."

"Spying? I have never spied. I don't know what you mean. Is there some kind of mistake?"

"Stop lying," the officer screamed in her face. "We have the membership book, your name is in it."

"Membership book? What are you talking about? Membership to what?"

"To your spy organization, we have already arrested the leaders of your group and they have given us your name. We have a written confession that you must sign."

Helga looked at the officers in disbelief, then shook her head. "I won't sign. I didn't do anything wrong."

"Give us the names of the people you worked with."

"I don't have any names. I'm telling you I don't know anything."

The officer struck her across the face and waited for her to regain her stability on her chair. "You're lying," he said.

After staring at her for several minutes in frustration, he walked out of the room. She remained on the rickety wooden seat for what seemed several hours, while the sharp pain in her jaw dulled to a vague throbbing.

Finally he returned and they began the same process again. She asked who had given them her name, and they told her it was her friend Hans.

"Hans would not say such a lie. He knows I haven't done anything," she said.

"He gave us your name and said you worked with him as a spy."

"That can't be. I want to speak with him," she retorted, but the officer stood to lead her back to her cell. More than five hours had passed.

"You will not be speaking with any one of the other spies. If you will not sign the confession, I will have to send you back to your cell to think about it."

After several days of the same routine Helga became increasingly sick and despondent, even though her sense of detachment grew wider. She wondered in amazement how they could think that she was a spy. Her cellmate could sympathize. Mrs. Finke's own problems started when her husband began having an affair. The man's mistress, wishing to do away with the wife, had informed the Soviets that Mrs. Finke had been speaking against them. For that she had ended up on Linden Street in Potsdam.

The older woman and the schoolgirl spent months together in the cell, always wary of the eyes of the guards pacing outside and glancing through a small window on the door. Mrs. Finke had smuggled a needle into the cell and, when no one was looking, she used it to repair her clothing with thread she had pulled out of her clothes or from the straw sack. Helga began to consider whether she could use the needle to send a communication to her family.

Complaining of skin problems, she persuaded a guard to hand her a blob of petroleum jelly on a piece of paper. She tore away the gooey remedy, leaving a two-by-three-inch piece for writing. Then she wore down the end of the straw pulled from her bristly mattress on the floor of the cell, always watching for a guard to pass. When she was finished, she had a reasonably sturdy pen and paper. Now she needed only the ink. Using Mrs. Finke's needle, Helga pricked the tip of her finger. As a drop of blood oozed out she caught it in the end of the straw. She quickly wrote a careful "M," then "E" to begin her letter with the word "Meine," but the wound on her finger went dry, and no more could be squeezed from it. She paused when footsteps passed and the guard glanced in the window; then she pricked herself again in the same spot. With the resulting dark red bead, she was able to write the "I" and "N," and again she had to stop—there was not enough blood.

"How do you intend to send this letter home?" Mrs. Finke asked.

"Maybe someone will be released and I can slip it to them," she answered, preferring to concentrate on her project rather than consider the likelihood of seeing it completed successfully.

After her daily interrogations, Helga returned to the cell and worked on her letter, which would take several weeks to finish.

The Soviets, in the meantime, were making no headway with their questioning. Each day they brought up the same charges, and each day she refused to sign a confession. Often the officer or interpreter would strike her across the face by hand or with a ruler, but she assumed her confession would mean she would never be released. Instead she tried to break down their evidence.

Helga understood now that Hans had been involved in espionage and that her name in his address book convinced the Soviets of her involvement in the spying affair. She had heard the rumor that Nethe had turned his friends in over a jealous fight with another of the boys, but she wondered if it could be true. What she was certain could not be true was the story the Soviets shouted at her repeatedly—that Hans had named her as a fellow spy.

She repeatedly demanded to speak with Hans, and just as often, they told her she could not. They did say, however, that he had confirmed to them that she was a spy.

"He would not do that. That can't be true. I have to speak to him," was her reply.

Instead, the Soviets warned that if she did not cooperate, she would be banished to "Kartzer." In January, after several such threats, the officer abruptly stood from his seat and said "All right, you will go to Kartzer then."

They took her to a specially designed cell and ordered Helga to strip, though they allowed her to keep on her underclothes. She found herself standing in a tiny room with one high open window. A cold winter wind blew in, numbing her bare skin. On the opposite side of the dividing bars the Soviet guards stood and stared at her, laughing.

With a subzero wind blowing directly on her, Helga looked around her for shelter, but there was none. She finally chose the dividing bars for some exercise. She could grip the bar above her head and pull up, then do a few knee bends. She tried these calisthenics once, then again and again, stopping to wrap her arms around herself, then continue. With the increased blood flow she felt herself warming up.

At one point, a Soviet guard entered the cell before she could drop down from the bars, and he shouted at her in rage. "Stop that, let go of that bar and stand in the middle or I'll take the bra and panties." She obeyed, but when she saw him retreat she continued her calisthenics until she heard the next guard coming. After awhile the guards lost interest. They had seen her and the other German prisoners enough times, with and without clothing, and they were bored with it. They watched her only to ensure that she was behaving herself by standing motionless in the middle of the cell.

She stayed in the cell for what she guessed was three or four hours before the door opened and she was allowed to leave, put on her clothes, and return to Mr. Tobartchikov, her interrogating officer. She learned later that she had been lucky—some prisoners were required to strip naked, and the guards would then turn an ice-cold waterhose on them. Many died from illnesses that had begun in the rigors of Kartzer.

Helga never saw her friend Inge, who was being held in another women's cell. Still, she communicated from cell to cell through a knocking system: one knock represented the letter "A," two knocks indicated the letter "B," and so on. A scratch on the wall meant a word had been completed. With this pounding and scratching she learned that about a dozen of her friends were being held at this Soviet interrogation headquarters. All the boys and girls who had been arrested in Frankfurt were there, and none had been released.

CHAPTER 3

The winter seemed endless in the unheated cells, and Helga was on the border of starvation and exhaustion. Her frequent interrogations continued, and she often lost a night's sleep as well as a meal because she refused to confess or reveal names. Finally one day the Soviets caught her by surprise—they granted her the wish she had asked for so adamantly. They would allow a meeting with Hans.

On the appointed day she waited in the interrogation room with exhilaration for Hans to be led in. She would talk to her school friend, she thought; he would tell them she was innocent, and she would be sent home. She could barely hide her excitement as she sat in the corner with a guard on each side, knowing they were about to be proven wrong.

When they brought Hans in she stared in shock—at first thinking that there was some mistake. The figure in front of her was a broken, middle-aged man that she would never have recognized as Hans. His face was smashed with bloody scars and his shaved head bore open wounds. She stared into his dimmed, swollen eyes, wondering if it was really him when he was pushed into a wooden chair facing her.

"Here is Helga Wunsch," the interrogator said to Hans. "Was she a member of your spy organization?"

Hans seemed not to even look at his old friend. "Yes." he said.

As soon as the word was spoken he was grasped by both arms and the guards dragged him out of the room.

Helga sat is silence. She could not believe what had happened. After the door slammed behind him Helga stared at the place where the broken version of Hans had been until the Russian officer's voice broke her spell. When he looked at her, his eyes flashed with a combination of contempt and triumph. "Now will you sign your confession like Hans signed his?" he asked. Stunned, Helga could only shake her head, no.

Back in her cell she felt for the first time that she would give in to despair. As she told Mrs. Finke about Hans's betrayal, she realized she could not blame or hate her old friend. He was not the friend she had known and grown up with any more, and the empty look in his eyes revealed to her that he was no longer a normal boy. They had tortured him to insanity and he could be held responsible for nothing. Mrs. Finke sat forward as Helga spoke, shaking her head. "You can refuse to sign that confession but all it will mean is more interrogations, more kartzers, possibly your death."

"Are you saying I should confess when I'm not guilty?" she said.

"That is exactly what I am saying."

"If I sign that confession they will never let me go."

"Do you think they will let any of us go no matter what we do? We have seen and heard too much, we know too much, they will never let us out to talk about Linden Street. Do yourself a favor and sign the confession. Then probably, they will at least leave you alone. That will be the end of the interrogations and the beatings."

Helga spent the night considering Mrs. Finke's words, although she knew almost immediately the woman was right. The Russians had shown no hesitation in bringing her in again and again, and there was no sign that the interrogations would ever end.

The next time she was called in, Mr. Tobartchikov asked his usual question. "Are you prepared to sign the confession?"

"Yes," Helga said, and she signed it. No further word was spoken.

Mrs. Finke's advice proved correct. From that date in the winter of 1948, Helga was left alone.

CHAPTER 4

Helga learned that a classmate was being held in the neighboring cell—her school friend Heinz Blumenstein, the boy she had once harbored a crush on during more carefree times. But the wall was not the only way to reach her friend. The small window admitted a narrow strip of pale sunlight into the cell each day, and that window, well above the prisoners' heads, could be pushed open.

One afternoon, Mrs. Finke clasped her hands together while Helga stepped into her palms and pushed the window open a crack. Heinz had managed the same next door, and the two friends actually stood below their windows and talked to each other. It would be suicidal if they were caught by the guards, but Helga and Heinz had planned their communication system carefully. She and Mrs. Finke waited until immediately after a guard passed to open the window. Guards standing on the roof would hear the voices, but it would be impossible from their position to determine from which cells the voices were coming. To ensure that a guard in the hallway didn't discover them, Mrs. Finke stood with her back against the door to listen for the pounding of the booted guard's approach. If a guard did look through the peep hole, all he would see was Mrs. Finke's back.

"Heinz, Heinz, do you hear me?" Helga hissed near the window once her roommate nodded her to go ahead.

Heinz was waiting at the other window, as they had arranged, and they had the luxury of speaking to each other for several minutes.

Are you all right?" Helga asked, thankful to hear his voice.

I'm all right, more or less, beaten up of course. But, my pants are falling down," he answered.

"Your pants are falling down?"

"The button on my pants broke off. If I could, I would pass them over to you; maybe you could sew it back on." Even here in the prison he was teasing, and both of them laughed.

But since Mrs. Finke did have a needle, Helga guessed that it wouldn't be hard to sew the button on if she had the chance. But she considered a different approach. If he had a needle and thread, he could sew the button on himself.

Every morning the prisoners were let out of their cells for a "potty run." At this time the prisoners would be taken, one cell at a time, to carry the full pot to the toilet at the end of the hall, dump it and, if lucky, wash up quickly at a sink installed next to the facilities. Here Helga had her only opportunity to wash herself and occasionally her underwear when the guards allowed her the time to do it.

Helga understood Mrs. Finke would never part with her needle, fearing the loss of her most valuable possession, so she went to work on making several needles of her own. She drew out pieces of straw from her mattress until she found one of a proper size, then pulled a thread from the mattress cover. She broke a short split into the top of the straw with her fingernails and slid the thread into place. The needle would be good for only one stitch, after which it had to be "threaded" anew, but it would be a help to her friend. On her next trip to the toilet, she stowed the threaded needles with her and hid them behind a shelf near the sink. Heinz, on his own toilet run, picked them up and was able to repair his pants.

• • •

Now that the Soviets left her alone in her cell following her "confession," she had more time to contemplate her future and her family. Her letter to her family was complete, but she now realized that she would have no opportunity to deliver it. Her earlier hopes that someone would be released who could post the letter for her proved to be naively optimistic. No one was leaving this place alive.

She had addressed the letter to her mother and father and her boyfriend Gebi, whom she hoped had been lucky enough not to be arrested. The finished letter read:

My three beloved ones. Stay healthy like I am. I am fine. We are all in Potsdam for investigation, then probably some time in a camp. Don't worry, it's peaceful and warm here, food good. Mom should go and see doctors for arthritis. Is Dad home? Do you still have contact with Gebi? Don't leave Mom alone so much. Please give Gebi emergency address in West Germany. Did you give Monica her 50 marks? Did you get my three papers from the school? Dear Daddy, can you help Gebi along financially? Be courageous, never give up hope, like me. I am living on hope, memories, and faith that I will come home. We must wait. Thanks for all your love and being so good to me all my life. Forgive me the worries I sometimes gave you and forget the bad times. I am here totally innocent. They don't believe me. My loving thoughts are with you always Mom, Dad, Gebi. Greetings, kisses and all my love and keep me in your love.

She wrote a postscript on March 1. "I am still here in Potsdam—Helga." As she looked the letter over, she saw how many lies it included. She was close to starvation and had lost so much weight her menstrual cycle had stopped. There was no peace and no warmth in this place, and she had long ago lost hope of ever being released. Her only hope was getting this letter to them to offer some relief from their worries. She wondered if her own father might have been arrested.

The Soviets continued to require regular strip searches and occasionally moved prisoners with no warning to other cells. Helga's greatest fear now was that the letter would be discovered. Her ring, which she still sometimes kept hidden in her mouth or bra, along with the letter, was also in need of a permanent hiding place. She had occasionally left the ring inside her mattress, attached to a thread of the mattress cover, but she feared that she would be transferred to another cell at any time and not given the chance to retrieve it. She had tried hiding the ring in her vagina but she feared it would fall out. She finally found a spot for it in the tip of her boot, held in place by a piece of cotton she had requested for menstruation she claimed to have, but it was a risky hiding place as well.

During one strip search a guard decided to investigate her boots. He stood waiting with impatience, ordering her to take them off and hand them over one at a time. She pulled off the first and handed it to him as he shoved his hand inside, looking for any hidden treasures. He then he motioned for the second boot, the one holding her letter and ring. She handed it to him with her heart hammering in her ears. He grabbed at the boot, but it slid from his grasp, bouncing heavily on his foot. In annoyance the officer kicked it out of his way and continued with his search of her cell. Helga couldn't believe her good fortune.

Afterward, she decided, with the help of Mrs. Finke's needle, to sew the ring and letter into the center of the shoulder pad of her top coat. There it was safely hidden from the inquisitive hands and eyes of the Soviets.

Although Helga and her roommate continued to grow weaker from lack of food, Helga noticed some women seemed quite well fed and more comfortable than the others. They had access to warmer clothing and were obviously fleshier. Mrs. Finke had noticed their condition as well. "I suppose some women will do anything for some extra food," she commented. "Why do you think the guards never rape us?"

Her young roommate shook her head. "I would rather starve to death than sleep with a Russian," she said.

To confirm their suspicions, the two women began listening for strange activity. Helga's hearing had become sharp enough to detect any sound from the hallways, since listening was one of her most constant activities. She listened for the movement of the guards as they paced the length of the hallway, and she knew each cell by the number of footsteps it took for the man to reach it. She and her cellmate counted the footsteps, heard the guards when they stopped, and knew just where they were. They heard the keys coming from the guards' belts and they heard the cell doors open. Regularly the guards would arrive at certain cells and stop, unlock the door, and enter. For an unusual length of time the guard would remain inside, then come out again to continue his patrol. Helga calculated which cells were being entered and who resided in those cells. Invariably, they held healthy and well-fed young women.

"I will never be that hungry," Helga said again, although she was relieved that these sexual volunteers kept the male guards satisfied and uninterested in the other imprisoned prey.

CHAPTER 5

On the morning of March 29, 1948, Helga was taken from her cell for the occasion she had been awaiting. Her trial was scheduled for that day and finally she would face a judge regarding the charges against her.

Helga did not hold much hope for the trial. No lawyers had ever come to her cell, and when she and the other defendants arrived in the military courtroom, a large hall, there were no signs of defense attorneys or a jury. Instead the twenty-eight defendants, among them eight women, sat on wooden benches facing a dozen Soviet war tribune officers behind a raised podium.

Two other trials would follow, as she learned much later, but many of those arrested with her sat beside her now to learn their fate. Among those was Nethe, the boy who was rumored to have informed on the entire spy ring out of jealous rage. She stared at his face, trying to discover some sign of the truth. An officer announced to the hushed group that they would each have a chance to stand and face the panel, at which time they would be permitted to speak in their own defense, with the help of a translator. Helga knew this would be pointless.

When her time came, she stood to face the row of eyes that evaluated her. An interpreter explained that she was being charged with spy activities in Frankfurt an der Oder, and he listed a series of invented evidence as well as her signed confession. "Do you have anything to say in your defense?" the translator asked.

"No," she shook her head bitterly.

The panel then sentenced her to twenty-five years imprisonment.

Only a few defendants spoke in their own defense, but all but one were given the same sentence of twenty-five years. When Nethe stood, the Russians asked the same, predictable questions and he, like most of the others, offered no defense for himself. "We sentence you to fifteen years," one of the panel members announced and Helga shook her head as he sat down. There now seemed little doubt that the rumors had been true: there was no other reason, she thought, for his earning a shortened sentence.

No one contested his or her conviction, except one man who chose to speak when he was offered to do so. "I would like to ask for a longer sentence," he said, "if my wife could have a shorter one. I would like to take as much of her sentence as possible—"

He was cut off by the pounding of the gavel. "If you don't have anything to say for yourself then shut up!" one of the officers shouted.

Several women in the following trials were charged with having relationships with Soviet soldiers who deserted to West Germany. The women were accused of trying to influence the thinking of their Soviet boyfriends, and they too received twenty-five-year sentences. In other cases, people were charged with providing civilian clothing to Russian soldiers intent on fleeing their service in the military. These people also were sentenced to twenty-five years.

Mrs. Finke, who had been turned in by her husband's jealous mistress, was sentenced to twenty-five years. During the trial she learned that her husband had asked for and been granted a divorce based on her "anticommunist activities," and immediately after the divorce, he married his mistress. Mrs. Finke fell into despondency, eventually leading to her death.

In the evenings a bell rang, and the defendants returned to their cells. The trial went on for three days and after it was over, on April 1, Helga wondered if she had just been the object of a perverse April Fool's joke.

CHAPTER 6

With the conviction and sentencing, the Soviets allowed all women of the Frankfurt an der Oder "spy ring" to remain together in a larger, fifth-floor cell. With a thrill of relief, Helga now was reunited with Inge and her other friends from school. On April 5, 1948, a soldier came to the cell door and informed the group that they would be moved to a new place of confinement. It was the day before Helga's twentieth birthday. She was about to experience what she would later call her "most unique birthday." She took comfort in being reunited with Inge who had also lost at least a third of her body weight and looked frail and aged. Still just teenagers, they faced the loss of their youth behind bars. Expecting hard labor, starvation, and death, Helga and Inge were certain they would not survive the twenty-five-year sentence, but they concerned themselves only with their immediate condition.

With all the men from their trial as well as other unfamiliar prisoners, Helga and her best friend climbed aboard a prison train of the East German railroad with no idea where—or if—they would ever climb off. The women were given no water or food until one warmhearted Soviet secreted them a bowlful of cooked macaroni, which the women divided among them. The train heaved sluggishly into motion and began a two-day trip that should have taken only a few hours. The train would constantly have to stop and back off the tracks to allow another train to pass on the single track. In many cases, the Soviets had stripped the rail lines between major eastern German cities, leaving only one set of tracks to connect them. The prisoner-laden train took a lower priority and was stopped constantly on its cumbersome journey.

Through cracks between the slats in the car walls, the prisoners watched passing scenery and occasionally glimpsed a station sign. From the position of the sun they saw they were traveling southeast—not toward Russia. They felt as if they had been traveling for weeks before the train finally reached their destination.

When, on April 7, 1948, they were finally ordered to disembark, the women stumbled out into the light and blinked at the streets of an unfamiliar small German town. It was not Russia! Waiting for them were Soviet guards armed with straining German Shepherds and rifles. The guards hurried the hungry and exhausted group into a line of two women, side by side and surrounded by barking dogs and armed guards. They began a long march through what appeared to be the center of a village they learned to be Bautzen. They were to make their way through town to the Bautzen high-security prison, once used by the Nazis and now to be their new home.

Ahead of the procession, the Soviets had cleared the road, sending everyone in the busy downtown street inside or home so they would miss the spectacle. The Soviets planned to spare residents the sight of fifty to one hundred of their countrymen being led by armed guards to prison and, thereby, protect themselves from any anticommunist backlash.

The downtown street was eerily silent as Helga walked through, with only the shouts of the guards and the barking dogs to fill the void. Looking at the closed shops and the vacant road, she guessed the town had been bustling with activity only minutes before the prisoners' arrival. The Soviets seemed to have cleared the road entirely. But still Helga felt eyes on her. As she walked, the young prisoner glanced up toward the windows of the homes and saw faces there, peeking out from behind curtains. The looks from these windows were furtive but sympathetic, but before she could catch anyone's eyes, the onlookers drew back from the windows, intimidated by this sign of Soviet force.

• • •

Though she did not know it yet, Helga's life was about to improve. She was led into a relatively large cell with three other women. Each had her own bare wooden bed with a straw sack for a mattress, and each still carried the bedding she had brought with her from home. At the end of the room sat a chamber pot, which the women would be allowed to dump once a day at a community washroom. During the pot emptying, the entire cell was allowed to go to the washroom, where prisoners could rinse out their underclothes or wash their faces in the ample time allowed by the fellow prisoner guards. When Helga finally was able to put to use the toothbrush she had brought with her from home, rinsing and spitting in the cold tap water, she could see blood disappear down the drain. Her gums were shrinking away from the teeth, yet another result of her malnourishment.

She was weighed by a Russian doctor in a perfunctory exam in which all the prisoners were declared healthy, even though she now weighed eighty-nine pounds. Here at the doctor's office she had her first opportunity to look in a mirror, and she stood frozen in shock as she met her reflection. The face that stared back at her was wan, thin as a corpse, and years older than the face she had last seen before her capture. But at least her lifestyle soon proved a vast improvement over what she had grown accustomed to at Potsdam. Here, she could shower once a month at a communal showering.

The guards gave Helga and each of her fellow prisoners a wooden bowl and spoon of her own to keep, and the food rations improved. The soup was more than just water—there were vegetables and potatoes swirling in an actual broth. For three days the prisoners were each given ten grams of margarine, twenty grams of sugar, and thirty grams of jam, as well as regular supplies of bread.

Despite the slightly better conditions, this was the place where many of Helga's male friends died, as the degenerative effects of tuberculosis and the occasional other diseases finally took their toll. Though all the girls were still alive, more than half of Helga's male friends had died. Helga heard of their deaths, one following another. Among them were Hans, Nethe, and Heinz. Helga felt saddened by Hans's death and could feel no bitterness toward him. Despite the fact that it was his betrayal that kept her there, he had no choice. She only hoped he would find peace in death.

Every day a fellow prisoner guard came to the cell and ordered the women out. They could then begin a thirty-minute round of exercise of walking, talking, and socializing in front of the women's building. April gave way to May and June, and Helga's emotional condition improved with the weather. One Soviet guard was always posted at the building entrance, but often the cell doors were left open during the day, and the prisoners were allowed to wander from one to another, visiting with friends within the women's building. Helga met other prisoners who had been involved in spy activities, and they told her the clandestine organization was still thriving with new members.

The guards first assigned Helga and Inge to separate cells, but they convinced them to place them together by insisting that they were cousins. However unlikely that relationship might have been, the guards were usually relieved to grant their wishes. Since the guards were often short of beds, the two chums agreed to share a bed so they could be placed in the same room. The guards were stern but humane, and Helga felt thankful each day when she woke up in this new place, where there were no more interrogations and she would be allowed to eat a little more and spend time with her friends.

The women at Potsdam who had offered sexual favors for food were forced to eat the same diet as the other prisoners now, since the guards rarely came in personal contact with the female prisoners. A liaison between the German women and the guards was appointed; the women rarely saw their captors. Women who had appeared well fed at Linden Street began to shrink away with the others, and an inevitable equality returned to reign among the political prisoners.

As the days passed Helga dared to hope they would stay where they were indefinitely. This life, she thought, was almost tolerable.

CHAPTER 7

One day the guards came to the female prisoner building and ordered the women there to pack. Bautzen was to become a camp for men only, and the women would begin another journey to an unknown home. This time Helga and Inge climbed onto cattle cars, empty except for two barrels in each car. In one barrel sloshed rancid water, filled with rust. Helga resolved herself not to touch it, knowing it would make her sick. The other barrel was empty and was intended to be the only toilet for a group of fifty or sixty people.

Lining the car walls were four wooden platforms designed for sleeping extending the length of the car. There was room there for only some of the women on board, and those who got on the car first hurried onto the platforms to assure themselves a place. Inge and Helga were among those who scrambled onto one of these makeshift beds, with Helga in front, pulling her friend by the hand while others squeezed in to join them. They lined up like herrings, allowing five women side by side on each of the four platforms. The others were left to lie on the floor of the car, if they could find the space.

As the train lumbered out, Inge suddenly let out a gasp, running her hand over her wrist. "Oh Helga my bracelet!" She too had forgotten to remove a precious piece of jewelry when she was arrested, and she, like Helga, had made it a daily project to protect the jewelry from detection. But seated in the crowded railcar as she ran her hand over her forearm, she realized it was gone. The clasp must have loosened, Helga thought.

"Where is it, I had it when I got on the train!" she exclaimed.

"Well it must be here," Helga responded, kneeling and running her hand across the board of the thick platform where they sat. They fumbled in the dim light for ten minutes, but found nothing. Other prisoners agreed to help with the search. Women knelt throughout the box car searching for the tiny delicate strand of gold, but no one found anything. "It must have fallen through the slats," Inge finally said, and Helga silently imagined she was right.

Inge cried inconsolably and Helga listened to her, holding her hand for comfort but with nothing to say that would soften the loss.

The train barreled on through the German countryside, ground to a stop, then heaved forward again. Two days passed, and although the train stopped several times, no one ever came to the door to assist the women. Many of the undernourished and sickly prisoners began to waver between life and death, and the car was filled with the rattle of tubercular coughing.

The toilet barrel filled to the top and began to slosh its contents onto the floor with the movement of the train, coating the floor of the car where the women who had not been fortunate enough to get on the platforms now lay. There was nowhere to go and the poor women became drenched in human waste.

Toward the end of the second day the women discovered a death among them. An elderly prisoner had died from illness and hunger. The women left the body lying on the car floor, backing away to give it some room as they waited for the train to stop again. When it finally did they pounded on the door shouting with all the noise they could muster. An irritated Soviet guard slid open the wide cattle door only far enough to peer inside.

"There's a dead woman in here," someone shouted in Russian. The guard shut the door again and returned with several companions armed with rifles. They pulled the door wide open and it yawned over the yellow fields of a German farm.

"Where is the body?" the guard asked and the women pointed. "Back away from the door!" he barked at them, and they all obeyed nervously, watching as the man stepped forward. With the help of another guard, he lifted the woman's limp and wasted body and walked to the door with it. Then, with a perfunctory swing, they tossed the body off the train into the field, where it fell like a piece of wood. The guards shut and locked doors, and the train moved on, leaving the body in the field.

Helga peeked through the cracks between planks of the cattle-car walls and watched the pale light from windows high on the car. Women took turns standing on each other's shoulders to see out the windows, which were secured with heavy metal bars. Even so they allowed a glimpse of the beautiful countryside and the freedom the women had left behind.

By watching for and reading the signs of the passing train stations, the women discovered that they were headed back toward Berlin. At the end of the three-day journey they disembarked in Oranienburg, a section of the city. Here they were sent to a former Jewish concentration camp known as Sachsenhausen, complete with gas chambers and the related ovens and smokestacks.

Once inside the camp Soviet guards assigned prisoners to their new barracks, dividing the women alphabetically. Inge, whose last name began with "P," gave Helga a disappointed look over her shoulder as they followed the guards' gestures in separate directions. They had become accustomed to being separated, but they never knew if it would be for the last time.

Helga was ushered into a barrack filled with rows and rows of narrow beds that once held Jewish concentration camp victims—now the Germans were to sleep in those same beds. The camp was divided into sections, and within each section stood approximately twenty barracks. Each barrack held about 150 women. Surrounding each section were electric fences, and beyond those barbed wire fences. Finally, wooden walls ultimately separated the various portions of the camp.

Once inside the barrack the women put their belongings wherever they found room on the length of beds and watched as the guards walked out, leaving the door standing open. Through the opening, they could see the gray sky that followed a setting sun.

Nervous at first, the prisoners stayed where they had been put, until a few wandered toward the door. Helga followed, standing just inside the barrack door, where she could see the other buildings, also open with prisoners milling near their doorways. She stepped outside and looked up at what was becoming a starry sky; no one stopped her. At the corners of each fence stood a watchtower, but there was no sign of distress. Finally a prisoner crossed from one barrack to another, and the women realized that they were free to roam throughout their section of the camp any time of the day or night. Helga walked to Inge's barrack and found her inside, wondering whether to make the same walk. Once again the two friends were reunited.

In the morning the women were awakened by the clang of a bell ringing outside the building. They leaped out of bed with military haste and ran to the door, where several Soviets waited, waving their hands and issuing orders. The officers sent the women into lines, ten people deep, and began counting. In this way, twice a day, the guards kept track of the prisoners despite their relative freedom within the camp section.

The women quickly adjusted to their new routine. Their long days were uninterrupted by anything other than three meals and "appell," when they lined up for the Soviets, once in the morning and again in the evening. Rarely did anyone appear to be missing. But the harsh conditions, lack of food, separation from family, and hopelessness still occasionally compelled a prisoner to give up and run into the electric fence, where she would meet instantaneous death.

With winter approaching, Helga began to wonder how she would survive the harshness of the weather in nothing more than the sweater and coat she wore the day the Soviet officers came to her door in Frankfurt. The cranberry sweater was showing signs of wear after several years of daily use, and she pondered how she would make it last for the remainder of her sentence. As she sat with Inge looking through the thinning strands of wool in her sleeve, she came upon an idea. "I wonder if I could reknit this together with some thicker thread," she commented aloud.

"Thicker thread?" her friend asked with skepticism.

"I could unravel the sweater, wrap the wool with a thicker thread and reknit it that way," she said.

They looked at each other and smiled at this tedious but enlightening idea. It was an idea Helga would never have entertained years before, but now she was happy to have the activity to occupy her time. She pulled sturdy, white threads from the mattress of her bunk, removed her sweater, and went to work unraveling.

Several women in the barrack had carved wooden knitting needles from firewood for the pot belly stove, using the knives they had been given to divide bread rations. Helga borrowed a set and began the formidable task of reknitting her sweater. The project consumed her days for more than a month until the sweater was completed. When she pulled it back over her head she was pleased to feel the added weight and insulation.

What had once been a pretty and feminine sweater, purchased by a school girl, had become a thick, shapeless garment that would serve as her most important life preserver. Helga had been a pretty girl, but now her appearance was the least of her concerns. What she had seen in the mirror in Bautzen—the wasted and aged girl who had stared hopelessly back at her in the reflection—was who she was now, and she concerned herself only with staying alive.

CHAPTER 8

The monotony was broken one day when the women were called out for an unscheduled appell and two unfamiliar officers met them outside. "We have decided to allow you to write letters home. We will supply you with writing material and you may write one letter to whomever you wish among your family and friends."

The officer then paused after speaking, looking the women over and awaiting a joyful response. The women stood silently in disbelief. Finally, a prisoner standing near Helga let out a laugh, and soon the rest fell in with her, giggling and then laughing loudly as the officer stared at them, dumbfounded at their reaction. The laughter swelled around them, expressing their disbelief that the Soviets would suddenly offer them this luxury. It had to be a cruel joke. They had been treated with savage contempt since their arrest, and this startling announcement was obviously an attempt to tease them. The officers turned on their heels and walked away. Helga wiped tears from her eyes as she realized it had been years since she had really laughed.

Several days later the women were shocked to see boxes containing paper and pencils delivered to their barracks. As fellow prisoners handed out the material, the women accepted them with looks of suspicion. "You may use these to write to whomever you choose," they were told. "But the letter must be no more than fifteen lines in length. You are also allowed, from now on, to receive mail and there is no limit to how much mail you can receive."

After the guard walked away the women huddled together, sobered by this latest gesture. "It's a trick," a woman said to Helga and Inge. "We write these letters and they read them to see what we are thinking. They're trying to trap us into saying something about the conditions we are kept in, or saying something political, and they'll give us a new trial, adding a few years!"

Everyone nodded in agreement. They doubted the letters would ever be sent, but still they were willing to give it a chance. Helga sat down to write a letter to her parents and her boyfriend Gebi, without knowing, after more than two years, if all three were still living or in what condition they might be.

She wrote the letter with only a modicum of seriousness. She sat beside Inge, first pondering the joy the letter might bring her parents when they saw it, then pushing the thought from her mind. "I am well," she wrote in the letter, telling her loved ones that she was in good health, well fed, and thinking of them constantly.

Although she had little hope, the exercise occupied the majority of her day. The prisoners were in good spirits as they handed their letters and pencils back to the guard that evening, all carefully addressed to the homes of their families. For Helga, so much time had passed that she could not be sure if any of her friends or family had stayed in Frankfurt an der Oder, and she had long ago given up hope of communicating with them ever again.

Two weeks later the guards arrived with more boxes, announcing that these were filled with letters back from their loved ones. The prisoner-appointed guard pulled out an envelope and called out a woman's name. With a nervous laugh the prisoner stepped forward and hesitantly held out her hand to accept the letter. Helga felt her mouth go dry as the guard took out another letter and called out another name.

Soon she heard Inge's name, and she gave her friend's hand a squeeze in excitement, watching her step forward to receive her letter. Finally Helga heard her own name read, and she took a letter in her hand without looking at it, unaware of even walking back toward the barracks. The women had scattered to read their mail. Unwilling to go inside, Helga sat down on a bench in front of her barrack and felt the letter between her fingers. Her feet were trembling so hard they would not stay flat on the ground.

With a deep breath she lifted the letter before her to see the address written neatly on the unsealed envelope. She recognized the handwriting of her father, and with shaking fingers, she looked the letter over, turning it again and again as she stared at her name. The fact that her father had touched the same letter she gripped in her gnarled hands now overwhelmed her. She felt a flood of love for her father and relief that he was still alive and free. Yet she couldn't bring herself to open the letter. Inside, she feared, would be bad news about her sickly mother.

Around her some of the other prisoners, with their letters read, were telling others about their families. For some it was the hardest blow since their imprisonment—their family members had died, had been arrested, or were no longer able to be contacted. Helga dreaded such news. Finally she reached into the envelope and pulled out the letter, reading with careful concentration. Her father wrote to say the arrival of her letter had been the greatest moment of his life. With joy he marked the calendar for this "blessed day" when he first learned that his daughter was still alive. But her mother's handwriting was missing in the letter.

Her mother, Helga knew, was suffering from severe arthritis, and her father wrote that she had now left town for treatment. But the week before he had telephoned her with the news of their daughter's letter. Gebi was still waiting and hoping for Helga's return. He had not taken another girlfriend and he planned to write her a letter.

Her father enclosed a photo of himself and her mother; Helga was shocked at how much they had aged. The vital couple she remembered from the time of her arrest looked tired, old, and discouraged. Though the letter itself had been censored, she still determined from his words that her father was attempting to persuade Soviet authorities that they had sentenced her unfairly and that she must be released.

On August 22 the prisoners received their second piece of paper for writing, and this time Helga sat down with relish, composing a letter that abundantly communicated her love for her family and friends. At last she had a moment of brightness in her days.

CHAPTER 9

As fall came Helga watched as many of her fellow prisoners disappeared from illness. Although some never returned, those who came back from the camp's hospital barrack regaled the others with stories of a luxurious place where the food was good, the beds were soft, and the doctors and nurses were kind.

By the fall of 1949 Helga had her own medical problem. Her undernourishment had manifested itself in skin ulcers, causing festering sores that dotted her arms, legs, and torso. As the sores spread the itching became intolerable and Inge finally commented, "You ought to have a doctor look at that. I think they'd let you go to the hospital, you lucky girl."

Helga quickly put her name on the list, asking to see a doctor for her open sores. A few days later a guard handed her the permission slip she had been anticipating, allowing her entrance to the hospital barrack for consultation. When she stepped into the hospital barrack, she immediately saw that life would be easier here. The doctor was a male German prisoner, and he was sympathetic as she told him the sores were spreading quickly. He gave her a cream to treat them with, wrapped her heavily with bandages, and put her to bed at the makeshift medical center.

Helga could hardly believe her luck. As she considered the probable length of her stay and wondered when she would eat, the woman in a bed beside hers introduced herself as Hillo. "Hello, what brings you here?"

"Bad skin," Helga responded, pointing to her bandages.

"Well you're fortunate. This is not such a bad place to be. I'm glad to have your company. If you can, stay as long as possible because it's better than anything you experienced in the camp," Hillo said.

Helga was pleased. When the food came it was given to the women in bed, and consisted of a generous portion of thick potato soup, bread, margarine, sugar, and jam. The staff was comprised of German prisoners and only occasionally did a Soviet officer drop by to examine the appearance of the hospital and the condition of the patients in it. The doctor said she could be in bed for a week or more until the sores healed, so she lay back in the narrow bed with a feeling of luxury.

Hillo soon became her best friend in the hospital. They talked of their lives in Germany before their arrests, and eventually about their schooling. Helga was pleased to have her first chance to consider the five classes for which she was taking exams more than two years before.

"Do you like poetry?" Hillo asked her after two or three days.

"Yes, I love it," Helga replied, and the woman recited several poems she had learned before the arrest.

"That's beautiful," Helga said, and her companion offered to help her learn the poems. They soon got to work on the most challenging poems, then pursued their education further by reflecting on what they recalled of the Chinese philosopher Laotse's writings from 600 B.C.

Each day a doctor or nurse would unwrap Helga's bandages, examine the thirty-two oozing sores, and apply another layer of cream. Eventually her skin began to feel better and, to her chagrin, Helga watched them smooth and shrink away. "You'll be finished here soon," a nurse told her one day as she looked over the sores.

When the nurse left the room Helga carefully unwrapped the bandages. She ran her blanket over her arm experimentally and frowned at the sting of pain. Sharp fabric threads broke off against her festering skin with the abrasion of the coarse, filthy blanket against her arm. She rubbed the blanket into her sores, oblivious of the pain, feeling the delicate new growth of skin break away as she rubbed dirt back into the wounds. Then she rewrapped the bandages.

The next time the nurse unwrapped Helga's skin she looked at the sores with alarm. They were nearly as bad as they had been when Helga arrived. Discouraged, the nurse went to work cleaning them and reapplying a healing cream; Helga felt confident that she would be there at least another week.

At the same time, letters from her parents, friends, and former teachers came in on a daily basis, often many arriving on one day. Gebi wrote nearly every day. The young man, ever devoted to her return, offered to share his calculus course from the University in Rostock so she could stimulate her mind. She greedily opened his letters and completed the mathematics exercises he included. His later letters would then tell her if her answers were correct.

She could send him only fifteen-line letters, but the letters he sent in response covered many pages and often took her an hour or more to read. He told her he would wait for her return from the camps so they could marry, despite the fact that she had a twenty-five-year sentence. He remained optimistic that she would get an early release, while she worried that he would waste his life waiting for her.

Nevertheless, she was happy to receive his letters. Every second or third day he sent another series of questions in trigonometry and calculus, and she carefully went over her answers.

With the newly opened sores Helga was able to extend her time in the hospital first to several weeks and eventually to two months. It was past Christmas when the sores healed, and she was proclaimed ready to return to the camp's mainstream.

Helga was saddened to say goodbye to Hillo, who had helped her pass so many dull hours. She had been there when Helga arrived, but still was not well enough to leave the hospital. Several years would pass before Helga would see her again.

CHAPTER 10

Inge greeted Helga with a relieved embrace in January 1950 when the two women saw each other again for the first time in several months. The days were growing colder, and they spent their time inside the barracks, huddled together to stay warm. The letters continued arriving from friends and teachers, and rarely was there a day when Helga's name was not called during mail delivery.

She pasted pictures of her parents and Gebi above a shelf she built at the foot of her bunk. On the shelf she collected the many letters she received and reread them during the long afternoons. Gebi told her that he spent every two or three days with her parents, and was hoping she would soon be returned to him. Finally she wrote him the letter she had dreaded sending, telling him not to wait. "I know I have written that I was not giving up hope, but I know that I will never make it out of here. You will ruin your life waiting for me," she wrote. "Please consider someone else." Gebi's return letter surprised her. "You're crazy," he wrote. "You'll be released from there and I'm going to wait for you until then. We will still be married."

Helga's father wrote of his own ventures into a new business. He dealt in chemical cleaners, which were used to remove the rust from machinery damaged by the bombing of World War II. He also used the chemicals to clean farming equipment and other machines rusted out after they had been exposed to the elements. As Helga's father expanded his business he hired Gebi's unemployed father, a handicapped, elderly man.

But letters were not the only solace at the prison. To pass the time in the barracks, prisoners kept track of the calendar and celebrated each other's birthdays—even the birthdays of their mothers, fathers, sisters, or other loved ones. Helga and Inge often worked together to make birthday cakes for other women in the camp. Despite the fact that their daily rations consisted only of a small piece of bread, they managed to use some bread to make special cakes by soaking the loaf in water just long enough to make a thick mash. Inge then stirred sugar, margarine, and jam into the mash, beating it until it could be remolded into the shape of a cake. Some women further perfected this technique, sculpting tiny intricate floral designs from margarine and sugar to place on top of the celebratory cakes. Helga became one of the most sought-after cake decorators in her barrack.

• • •

Prisoners consisted of both political "violators" and criminals, guilty of everything from theft to murder. These Soviet guards held the criminals in much higher esteem and saved their mercy for them. Helga and Inge watched bitterly as the criminals were offered better treatment, including the luxury of work outside the barracks, where they had access to extra food. Each day a guard would take these more fortunate women to do tasks in the hospital or kitchen. Some went to the most highly regarded of all jobs—working in the Soviet administrative building.

Occasionally all the criminals would be at work, however, and assistants were needed in the camp. Then the political prisoners cast their names in hopes of being chosen. Eventually Inge and Helga got their own assignment—peeling potatoes in the camp kitchen.

On that spring day, the guard took them out of their barracks and walked them through the gates and toward the large kitchen complex. As they walked they saw parts of the camp that had previously been shrouded behind the wooden walls. Their escort pointed as they walked to a smokestack that rose up from a large building within the camp. "Do you see that?" he asked as they turned to stare. "That's where the Germans incinerated people." Helga looked at the smokestack. She had vaguely known of the existence of concentration camps and had even recalled her parents mentioning them during the war. "Be careful what you say about the Nazi government," her father had often told her, "or you will end up in one of those concentration camps. They are supposed to be awful." But he seemed to have little information about what was happening in those camps, where strict secrecy was the rule. Now, indeed, she was in one of those very camps but under circumstances she had never expected.

At the kitchen Helga and Inge were put to work peeling and chopping potatoes and other vegetables for the camp soup, which boiled in large open vats. As they worked they busily munched on all the food they could stuff into their mouths. With luck on their side, they continued kitchen duty for a week before new prisoners were sent in their place.

In the meantime the women received their first newspapers with their mail. The papers were often inaccurate propaganda pieces by the burgeoning East German government, but occasionally information appeared that interested the prisoners. One day a front-page story proclaimed that the Soviets intended to hand over its political prisoners to the East German government. The story claimed that 5,504 people sentenced in military war tribunals would be going home.

Several days later the outdoor bell rang for the prisoners, and they gathered outside, full of anticipation, to await the arrival of a Soviet officer. The man announced that the East German government was doing so well in its integration into the new Communist system that it would take over the holding of the political prisoners. What would this mean to them? Some would be released; others would continue their incarceration under the East Germans. There were eighteen thousand German political prisoners in Soviet-occupied East Germany and in camps in the Soviet Union, and they could only guess which would be the ones to be liberated.

Helga and Inge discussed this latest excitement and agreed that it was not good news for them. They learned that 3,432 prisoners were to be handed over for a second trial, and 10,513 would go to East German prisons, while 649 would remain under Soviet control and be taken to the Soviet Union. The newspaper confirmed those figures following the officer's announcement.

"Well we didn't do anything against the East German government," Inge said. "So maybe they'll release us or shorten our sentence."

They could guess, however, which prisoners were most likely to be among those freed. Women who were charged with dating Russian soldiers would surely be released by the German authorities, as well as others who had received lighter sentences, such as ten years. Helga and Inge did agree, though, that they were not likely to be among those going to the Soviet Union since they were small-time offenders.

"It looks like we'll be taken by the East Germans," Helga said. All they could hope for was that East Germany, feeling sympathy for its fellow countrymen, would release them soon. Nobody in the camp knew that the East German government would never be granted permission to release anyone. Instead, the only tasks the Soviets conceded to the Germans was to watch, guard, and feed the political prisoners.

Soon after the announcement the discharges started. Prisoners were called up to start packing, and with overjoyed faces they prepared themselves to go home. As Helga had expected, the prisoners with lighter sentences were on their way out. The women excitedly went through their few belongings and gave away almost everything, including their most treasured possessions—mirrors, pencils, knitting needles, playing cards, or crochet hooks.

Only one woman with a twenty-five-year sentence was called out for release. Helga and her friends agreed that this woman must have been released by a bureaucratic mistake.

CHAPTER 11

S oon the women to be sent to the Soviet Union disappeared from the camp, and those remaining knew they would be in the hands of the East Germans. Still, Helga felt a great sense of relief. The constant fear of being shipped to the Soviet Union was gone forever. Instead, she hoped, the East Germans would either soon release her or offer better treatment.

On February 11, 1950, Helga and her coprisoners left the camp for good—a year and half after their arrival. They were given a package of food, and when Helga opened it she was surprised to see a piece of salami, bread, margarine, and cheese. Again the women climbed onto cattle cars but this time the cars were not overfilled. The women did not have to fight for a spot to sleep on the platforms, and they enjoyed their meals with a sense of positive anticipation.

The women soon arrived at the small unknown town of Stollberg. As they walked away from the station Helga saw her new home awaiting her on the top of a hill; she shuddered at the uninviting spectacle. Known as the Castle of Hoheneck, this place would become her most hated place of imprisonment. Dark, windowless, and sprawling, it appeared ominous and struck a worrisome cord in Helga's previously optimistic thoughts.

The series of buildings, constructed in a rectangle, enclosed a gravel and brick courtyard without any trees, plants, or grass, and served as a prison for both criminals and political prisoners. Gone were the barracks, the fresh air, and the freedom of movement Helga had come to know in the former concentration camp of Sachsenhausen. The castle had once been a monastery and its austere structure formed the setting for Helga's worst prison life. The women found themselves locked in large attic bedrooms at night, in dayrooms during the day, or in tiny cells in the south wing. Each day they would file out to meals and, once in a great while, for brief calisthenics in the brick courtyard that centered the complex.

About half the prisoners were locked in the small cells all day, and only those on the north wing had the comparative luxury of the attic room, where they had one hundred companions with them to help pass the days and nights. The guards kept the prisoners moving regularly, so Helga spent about half of the days in the cells and the rest of her time in the dayroom. Some criminal prisoners worked in various shops in the building, while others bore their days under the watchful eyes of the East German guards.

Helga's hopes of better treatment were dashed as soon as she passed through the Hoheneck castle doors. As had the Soviets, these new guards watched their prisoners with contempt. Helga Wunsch was assigned her new name: Prisoner Number 1247. The prisoners stood at attention as they listened to their new orders: they must remember to use their prison identification number. If Helga had to speak to a guard or an administrator, she would be known only by her number and she must announce herself by saying, "May I respectfully present myself as Prisoner Number 1247."

"Get back in line, you piece of trash!" one of the guards barked at Helga when she stepped back from the group momentarily. Inge, standing beside her, tensed in anger. "Murderers," another guard muttered. "You don't deserve to be treated like animals. Get moving." They were quickly marched forward to relinquish their belongings.

The guards ordered the prisoners to strip off their clothing, boots, and any remaining personal effects. For the first time since 1947, the women shed the clothes they had been arrested in and donned uniforms of gray slacks and flannel underwear shirts covered by button-down blouses without collars. Helga learned that the collars in previous uniforms had been used by prisoners to strangle themselves. Colored stripes ran down the slacks, the sleeves, and the back of the blouses. Political prisoners like Helga wore green stripes, criminals wore yellow, and dangerous prisoners who had attacked guards wore red.

Helga turned over her own worn boots with a painful reluctance. They were replaced by East German prison-issue boots with thick wooden soles and foot rags to wrap around her feet in place of socks. Normal walking in these shoes was impossible, and instead the prisoners stomped forward in an awkward gait.

"Your uniform and appearance must always be immaculate, you pieces of trash," the guards told them. They often seemed poisoned with an outrage that Helga didn't understand. She couldn't comprehend the constant insults that included calling the political prisoners "murderers." After all the abuse she had suffered from the Soviets, she never imagined this from her own countrymen. But the guards did not consider themselves and her to be of the same race, and she simmered with rage over the constant insults and humiliation.

Helga was happy, however, to have her clothing finally sent back to her parents. After years of waiting, the thread-bare, blue overcoat carrying her tiny ring and the letter written in her own blood would be safe in their hands. She handed all her clothing to the guard, providing an address for shipping, and hoped that the filthy clothes would return home after three and a half years of constant wear. She wondered what her parents would think of the cranberry sweater she had reknitted with heavy cream-colored string.

The prisoners learned that any violation of the rules would lead to a reduction of privileges, already fewer in number than they had enjoyed with the Soviets. There would be no mail to or from the outside world and no newspapers. There would be no freedom of movement within prison walls, and the inmates would be strictly monitored at all times. Any friendships that grew in the prison would be broken up, and existing relationships like the one Inge and Helga had formed would be sharply discouraged.

Meals consisted of the ubiquitous watery soup and bread, but often the soup would be replaced with plain water in the case of any infraction. If a button on a shirt was not properly buttoned, or if the end to a foot rag was hanging out of a boot, privileges would be removed.

Helga sometimes saw Inge during the day while she was being shuttled from one sleeping room to another and occasionally she was allowed to share a cell with her, but they had little opportunity to visit with each other. Instead, they learned to keep quiet.

Three prisoners usually shared small quarters the size of a walk-in closet. The bell woke them around 5:00 or 6:00 A.M.. But without a watch or clocks, Helga could never be sure of the time. In the morning, the prisoners could take their chamber pot to the wash room and dump it, as well as wash hands and faces quickly at the sink, but they were always rushed and pushed by the police guard.

The criminals among them in the cells or dayrooms were permitted to work in one of the shops during the day. Whenever a woman guard unlocked the door for attendance, Helga and her cell mates knew what to do. All cell mates stood straight in perfect posture as the assigned person immediately reported, "This is cell number 584 with three convicts present." The representative would then advise the guard which prisoner was working in the shops and identify all the prisoners present by their ID numbers. Those who were housed in the dayroom in the north wing were ordered to take off their outer clothing in the evening and leave it folded on a bench in the dayroom. Stripped to their underwear they would then file across the yard for the night.

Some afternoons a guard would come to the door and shout for them to "Come out for your walk." The political and criminal prisoners then fell into line and filed out the door into the cold winter air for their only opportunity for fresh air. These walks in Hoheneck, unlike those Helga had almost enjoyed as a Soviet prisoner, were ordeals at best. Each prisoner had to leave three yards between herself and the prisoner in front. The group walked in single file with their hands behind their backs, always looking at the ground as they walked. In this way Helga and her comrades made their way around the inner courtyard of the castle whenever a warmer-hearted guard was willing the leave the comfort of the guards' quarters. No speaking was allowed and those who violated the rule were sharply punished. No one spoke even a whisper with these harsh rules. Instead they would walk in silence with their heads bowed.

• • •

One cold day Helga noticed a guard giving the prisoners a particularly scathing look. The women seemed to have committed no violations of the East German rules, but the guard eyed them all carefully anyway. As they neared the doorway into the building the guard shouted, "I heard talking. You stay!" and her arm gestured at them to halt in the courtyard. They undressed, their breath steaming in the chilled air, then stood while the guard walked inside and slammed the door behind her.

Once inside the guard peered out at them through the window, laughing and shouting insults as the women shivered. Helga believed she could strangle the guard with her own hands if she was given the chance. She saw the pleasure the guard derived from watching someone else suffer. Though she had at first rationalized the guards' behavior, assuming they had been brainwashed in compulsory political workshops that ran almost daily, she could find no excuse left, nothing to explain someone gleaning such sadistic pleasure. She turned away in disgust.

But it was not the only time Helga was the object of indiscriminate punishment. She was always prepared for a verbal assault; despite how careful she was with her uniform and her behavior, it didn't take much to infuriate the guards. One day a guard made a point to tell her what she thought of her and her fellow political prisoners. "You all are garbage compared to the criminals in here. They may have killed somebody, but they only killed one or two or five. You and your people killed millions, you filthy Nazi."

Helga was no longer surprised by this charge. She learned quickly at Hoheneck that an anticommunist was synonymous with Nazi in the minds of the East Germans. In their view, her ideology made her responsible for the Holocaust, the deaths of all the Jews, and the other atrocities committed by the Nazis. Arguing with the guards was pointless and would cause further punishment, so as time passed Helga adjusted to her new identity—Number 1247, Nazi, and murderer. She finally succeeded in building an impenetrable wall around herself that could deflect the insults and humiliation. Still, she doubted she would survive long in this place.

Depression was one of the greatest problems at the sprawling castle. Not only was the winter weather harsh and unforgiving in the Erzgebirge Mountains, the thick stone walls seemed to absorb inhospitality, and with the gray uniforms, it seemed that there was no color left in the world.

Finally the following spring the first word of good news came to the prisoners. The prison governor announced to the gathered women that they could send a letter to their families. Each woman was allowed to write one letter of ten lines only each month. They were also permitted to ask for packages, which they could receive at the compound if there were no violations of conduct or rules.

Inge and Helga exchanged looks of delight. Not only would they have contact with their families again, they could actually receive gifts. It was not hard to decide what to ask for since most items such as food would probably be stolen by the guards anyway. Helga made her decision within minutes. "I'm going to ask for a facecloth," she told her friend. Until now she had washed without such a luxury. "I'm going to ask for the brightest, most colorful facecloth they can find."

Inge laughed at the idea. "That's fantastic," she responded. "That's what we need here—some color." Both the friends wrote letters home, both asking for the same thing—color.

While some of the criminals spent their days working in various shops at the prison complex, the political prisoners usually idled the day away sitting in their cells or in the large dayroom with their one hundred companions. Their meals were sparse, and diseases were common. Helga was in moderate health physically, but her mental state declined. With nothing to engage her intellectually in this dank and cramped confinement, there was little to keep her mind from miserable thoughts.

When the packages arrived Helga was overjoyed. Her parents wrote to her regularly, and she learned that her beloved Gebi had not yet given up hope: he was still waiting for her return. She learned this with a mixture of joy and sadness, and thought how different her life had once been.

Underneath the letter in her small package were the items she had asked for. Her mother had sent her facecloths with the most brilliant colors and fanciful designs. One was fashioned with vibrant red, yellow, and orange and included the smiling face of Mickey Mouse. Another depicted a squirrel. Laughing with delight she raised the cloths up to show Inge. Inge had her own bright cloths, and they smiled then giggled as they pressed the cloths to their cheeks.

In their excitement they talked and laughed loudly before Helga noticed Inge's expression change. Inge's eyes were trained on the doorway behind Helga and her face turned suddenly grim. Watching them in the doorway was one of the East German police guards. The woman had her arms crossed over her chest and her eyes burned with hostile intensity. As their gaze met, she began walking toward them. Helga felt her heart sink, knowing that she and Inge had made a fatal mistake; they had allowed the guard to see them happy. She could see that their delight infuriated her.

"Give me those!" the woman barked at them.

"These came in our package from home, we were told we could have them. . ." Helga began as the guard ripped the cloths from their hands.

"Shut up you Nazis before I take away your meals."

Helga shook with rage when the guard walked away with the bright splashes of color peeping through her tightly gripped fingers. Once again they were enfolded in gray.

CHAPTER 12

Helga came to know a few guards who did not have the sadistic streak she had come to expect. One light-haired woman, known as the "Good blond angel," was fair with the prisoners, did not dole out punishment, and even smiled at those political prisoners who were beginning to feel like the dogs they were told they were.

One morning this blond guard came into the closet-sized cell where Inge and Helga shared their space with a third girl, Waltraut. The three were giving each other facial massages when the door swung open. "Can any of you do needlework?" the guard asked.

Helga felt her hand going up almost as if with a mind of its own. Though she knew very little about needlework, this sounded promising. "Yes, I can," Helga called out.

"Oh good, I'm looking for someone to make me a tablecloth with embroidery, something very pretty. Do you think you could do it?" Helga nodded enthusiastically.

When the guard left, the triumphant prisoner beamed at her friend Inge and they laughed together as Inge said, "What do you know about needlework?"

"Not much," Helga responded, "But I have nothing but time to learn it as I go along. Now we'll have needle and thread and scissors to cut our nails with."

The young prisoner imagined all the stitch work repairing clothing that she could do, and she waited with heady anticipation for the next few days until the blond guard's return.

When the guard returned she brought with her a new white bedsheet that was intended to become a table cloth, a needle, white thread, and scissors. She piled the material in front of Helga on the bunk where she sat and asked, "How long do you think this will take you?"

"I don't know," Helga responded, "but I ought to be able to complete it in several weeks." She then began work, looking the fabric over, and considering borders, center designs, how she could use different stitches. She began her task through guesswork, often taking a stitch back out and pondering how she could best decorate this simple cloth. She worked through the afternoon, ignoring her tiring eyes and stopping only to eat. At the end of the day, she bundled up the cloth and mulled over it as she lay in her bunk that night.

The next morning she returned to her work with an excitement she hadn't felt in four years. She worked slowly and deliberately, talking to Inge as she stitched and, occasionally pausing to spread out the entire tablecloth and consider her progress. After about a week, the blond guard asked to see how the work was coming. When Helga held it up for her appraisal the East German slowly smiled, nodding warmly. "That looks beautiful. Keep going," she said.

Soon the guard returned with another question, "Can either of you do crochet?" Inge's arm shot into the air. I can," Inge called out.

"Oh that's great," the guard said, "because I need something made for a baby."

Inge knew less about the art of crocheting than Helga knew about needlework, but she understood the value of a crochet hook in the prison and she had been watching enviously as Helga had worked away at the tablecloth. Soon Inge was holding a crochet hook in one hand and pink yarn in the other. Following advice from other prisoners and from Helga, she tied a knot on the hook and went to work, connecting tight sections of yarn to make the bodice of a baby jacket. Each time she got to a difficult stitch she would experiment before stopping in exasperation and pulling out the yarn to start again from the beginning.

For Helga, the tablecloth became a piece of art. She was amazed at her own handiwork, and she would pause after moments of hard work, admiring what she had done. The stitches were tiny and painstaking. Experimentally, she measured two inches in from the border and removed threads to open a strip along each edge, where she invented a new stitch to create a delicate spidery design. That design she made more elaborate in the corners.

When the guard came back to retrieve the tablecloth, Inge was beginning to master her crocheting. The blond angel was delighted with the work they were doing. The tablecloth was beautiful. As she examined it her eyes shone with pleasure, and Helga felt her heart sink. The tablecloth had been her only source of amusement for more than a month, and she had come to love it like a family member. The thought of giving it up left her with an aching sadness.

"I have an idea that might make it prettier," Helga said quickly as the guard began folding up the piece to take it away. "I could add some stitchwork in the center . . . four identical designs with stitches taken from the border pattern. I promise you will like it, see here in the middle where it looks so empty now?"

She took the cloth from the guard and opened it again, trying to make her point. The guard nodded and patted the cloth as she set it back down on the table.

"You do good work. I trust you can make it even nicer."

Helga was granted unlimited time with her creation. When she finally completed her work, there was nothing more that could be added. She knew there had never been such patient and intricate needlework and she cast the tablecloth one last look before handing it over. Soon Inge had completed her baby clothing as well. The good-natured guard took their handiwork home, congratulating them on their talent, and leaving them suddenly with nothing to do. Later she would secret small pieces of food into their cell, pulling them out of her pockets when she was sure no other guards were watching.

Months later the guard became a convict in Hoheneck herself. Charged with being too friendly with the political prisoners, she too was now an "enemy of the country."

But the blond angel was not the only guard who was known for occasional acts of kindness. One morning another guard came to the cell neighboring Helga's and Inge's. She was looking for a helper to unload bread from a truck parked in front of the prison. Gerda Shumacher, a girl of Helga's age, eagerly volunteered and left her cell for the rare privlege of doing a day's work. All morning she walked back and forth under the weight of boxes of bread, passing from the truck across the pavement, up a set of stairs onto a doorstep landing, and through the door into the kitchen. The guard watching her spoke as she passed once, saying curtly: "There's a sandwich in the paper bag on the landing. It's for you."

Gerda stiffened nervously, continued unloading the bread, and glanced down at the landing as she passed, where a small paper bag sat neatly tucked beside the door. When she was certain no eyes were watching, she bent down, picked up the package, and pressed it into her pocket. When her work was completed another guard came for her, ushering her back inside through the courtyard. The guard immediately noticed a slight bulge in Gerda's green-striped jacket. The police woman reached under the jacket and removed the package, never taking her eyes from Gerda's face. She slowly opened the bag and peered inside, then shut it, her mouth pressed into a frown. "Where did you steal this sandwich?" she asked.

Gerda stared back, shifting her weight from one foot to the other, not speaking a word. "Speak up, you stinking thief! Where did you get it?"

When the prisoner still refused to answer the guard she threw the sandwich down on the ground in rage. "You stole this from one of the guards didn't you?"

Gerda hesitated, then slowly nodded. The guard slapped the hapless prisoner across the face, knocking her off her feet momentarily; then she shoved Gerda into her cell for unlimited solitary confinement.

The next day Gerda was put on public display in the Hoheneck courtyard where prisoners of the large community attic room passed. She stood in the center of the courtyard while the other prisoners stood at attention, sympathetic and miserable as they listened to the prison chief chastising the "dirty thief."

"You know this girl," the chief announced. "This is Gerda Shumacher. She is a thief. She stole a sandwich from one of our distinguished guards. This girl is not worthy of any respect. Let her punishment, unlimited solitary confinement and no food or water every third day, be a warning to all of you."

The insults continued as Gerda stood silently and the prisoners looked on in pity. After that, Helga heard Gerda being pushed back into the cell beside her own; it was the cell used for solitary confinement. When the guard left, Helga began knocking on the wall to her, asking her if she was all right.

"I couldn't turn in the guard, that would mean she would be arrested and sentenced, and I would be punished anyway," Gerda tapped back to Helga. "But I can't stand being called a thief. What am I going to do?"

Helga had consoling words but no advice for her neighbor, and she sat by the wall in silence, fearing for the woman's future.

The next morning Helga heard the guard making her rounds from cell to cell, and was so accustomed to the sounds of this morning watch that she could anticipate each footfall and the jingle of keys on the woman's belt. She was then startled to hear the footfalls stop suddenly and the guard utter in German, "Oh my God!"

The guard was standing in front of Gerda's solitary-confinement cell. As the guard ran back in the direction she came, Helga and her cellmates hurried to the door, straining to hear through the walls. The prisoners tried to tap a message to Gerda, and tension grew when they received no response and the guard returned with the camp leader. Helga listened to the fragments of explanation she could glean from their dialogue, and her heart sank. According to their anxious conversation, over the night Gerda had torn her sheet into long strips, which she then tied together to hang herself. The guard had found her hanging from the heating pipe in the back corner of the cell—dead. Much later Helga would learn that Gerda's parents were informed that their daughter had suffered a fatal heart attack and was cremated in Stollberg, her ashes buried.

CHAPTER 13

Helga was growing from a teenager into her midtwenties. She had lost her youth overnight with her capture in Frankfurt an der Oder, but the aging process had beat a slow and torturous path over her body and spirit during her years of imprisonment. Wearily accustomed to life at Hoheneck, she knew she would not be transferred out again. But she tried to focus on the immediate and to find new ways to occupy her unchallenged mind.

In the letters from her parents she learned that her beau Gebi had finally given up waiting for her. He had finished his studies, earned his university diploma, and was teaching at the Rostock University. He also was engaged. As a teenager, before her arrest, Helga would have been devastated. But reading the words before her as she sat in her cell, she could feel only relief and a dull sense of loss. For years she had suffered the guilt of knowing he was wasting his own life waiting for her and now the crushing weight of that guilt was lifted from her narrow shoulders. There was no emotion left for the boyfriend she had once hoped to marry and no point in mourning the end of their dreams. Instead, she folded the letter carefully and placed it back in its envelope, her eyes dry. She would have to glean what happiness she could by hoping that his own life had found meaning.

In the meantime, the East German government was searching for ways to make the prisoners more useful. The guards offered Helga and Inge their first real break from the monotony of prison life—nail production. This manufacturing chore could be done outdoors with little contact with

East German guards. The guards provided thick cables for the girls to unwind for two weeks to produce thin wires. Here, breathing fresh air and enjoying a modicum of freedom, they worked happily, reciting and memorizing poetry to occupy their minds. When they had completed unraveling the wire they were sent to the prison shop to cut, pound, grind, and hammer it into nails with sharp points and thick heads. In the shop they again were able to talk freely and were given better food. It was another high point for Helga, the likes of which she hadn't known since she had given up her tablecloth to the blond guard. But nail production did not prove to be lucrative for the prison system. Soon they dropped it entirely in lieu of a more productive endeavor—sewing.

Helga and Inge went from the outdoors to a small sewing area that would encompass the entire second floor. The high-ranking police chief explained their duties. "I am going to allow all of you to begin work at the sewing room in eight-hour shifts. I would hate to see you suffer from boredom."

The sewing began that day and continued operation twenty-four hours a day to produce aprons, uniforms, and various women's and children's clothing that was sold in stores outside the prison walls. The guards assigned one small task to each prisoner, such as sewing hems, seams, or, for the more advanced, attaching sleeves or collars. "This will help you occupy your time," the chief said.

The irony of this work and the presentation of it as a favor to the prisoners was not lost on Helga. Nevertheless she was happy to have more work. The guards assigned to the sewing room soon grew tired of their work and found prisoners with sewing experience to instruct and supervise the workers as well as repair machines. After that guards idled away the shifts in their lounge. Helga and Inge persuaded their fellow prisoner supervisors to allow them to rotate tasks, thereby learning, step by step, the entire sewing process. But even this added challenge did little to relieve the monotony of the factory. The sewing-room managers drove the prisoners hard to keep up production, but the threats meant little since no one worried about losing her job. Instead, the managers' pressure only made the prisoners nervous.

CHAPTER 14

In the spring of 1955, while Helga's world remained unchanged, Europe was expanding its economic influence. West Germany was enjoying a booming economy as East Germany became more closed and the government more restrictive. In this climate, West German Chancellor Konrad Adenauer made an unusual proposition to his cold-war adversary to the east. He offered to pay for the release of the longer-term political prisoners, allowing more potential laborers in his country, which was now encouraging immigration of foreign workers.

On May 5 Inge was released. Helga watched her pack, overwhelmed with relief that Inge was not the one being left behind. The two women loved each other as sisters and Helga couldn't bear the thought of leaving Inge alone in the prison. But Inge cried hopelessly as she prepared to go. "I can't stand leaving you here," she sobbed, clutching her emaciated friend.

"I'll be released too," Helga assured her, "and then I will be able to join you in Berlin." To ensure that she was granted a ticket to West Berlin rather than East German Frankfurt an der Oder, Inge had reported that her mother now lived there. Helga watched her friend walk out of the dayroom where they had languished for so long, and, through a window, saw her old friend pass from the administrative building to the outside where she would turn in her prison uniform. Tears poured out of her eyes as she smiled a final farewell.

She continued her work at the sewing factory and waited, while her thoughts were occupied with her friend and her new life as a free woman—perhaps working somewhere, dating and enjoying a social life.

One day Inge Schulze, a friend in the prison, came to her with her eyes large and serious with grief. She took Helga by the arm, guiding her away from the other prisoners. Helga felt the familiar fear of bad news as she gazed at her friend's eyes. "I got a letter from my mother," Inge Schulze said. The woman's mother, Helga knew, was friendly with her own. All the parents and relatives of the imprisoned Frankfurt youths had formed close friendships. "Your mother wanted me to be the one to tell you . . . your father has been arrested."

Helga felt her eyes fill with tears as she looked at her friend in disbelief. "Why? What can they possibly be charging him with?"

"My mother said the agents had been pestering him to turn his business over to government hands and he was refusing. They said he made anticommunist remarks."

Helga would learn later that her father had branded himself as a black sheep with the communist government by hounding them for the release of his daughter. Not only had he gone to the Russian Consulate to plea for her, he had sent letters, translated into Russian, to the Kremlin insisting that she was innocent. He had even gone to the KGB headquarters in Frankfurt. When he then refused to relinquish his fledgling company to the East German government, the Stasi, an East German version of the Soviet KGB, sent an agent to him posing as a potential client. In an effort to coax Wunsch into antigovernment statements the agent began criticizing the East German system and communism. Helga's father was reserved in his response.

"You should be careful about saying this sort of thing against the government," he warned.

Though the agent had not managed to get an anticommunist statement from him, he had enough to charge the man. Helga's father had not refuted what the agent said, they charged, proving he was in effect, a political enemy. He was sentenced to one-and-a-half years.

In December the Hoheneck guards held a surprise search of the cells while the prisoners labored in the sewing factory. They found in Helga's belongings a one-inch pencil and a sewing needle. She braced herself for the worst when they left her in her cell, as they had with Gerda Shumacher. Helga expected the solitary confinement and public spectacle that her friend had received and resolved to take it without any weakening. The next morning, December 28, 1955, she received no comment from the guards, so she went to work at the sewing factory as usual. She was interrupted several hours later by one of the guards.

"There is someone here to take you to your cell," she said. Helga followed the guard to her cell. The guard swung the door open, nodding in the direction of her bunk and saying, "Pack your things." Helga was certain she was to be moved to solitary confinement, and with shaking hands she packed her few belongings—her blanket and sheet, toothbrush, hairbrush, and pictures of her parents. Helga was dumbfounded then, when the guard led her to the administration building.

As she turned in her uniform and accepted new women's underwear and clothing, she realized she was really leaving. Suddenly she felt her heart plunge in terror. She had been in prison for more than eight years. When she was arrested she was a teenage school girl, now she was a wasted 27-year-old woman with no high school diploma and no idea what she would do with her freedom. For eight years she had not even gone to the bathroom without someone telling her when and where. Decision making was a long-forgotten concept, and freedom now loomed ahead of her like an ominous thunder cloud. Prison officials took the uniform from her perfunctorily with no more respect than she had seen or expected for eight years and sent her away under police escort with a ticket back to Frankfurt an der Oder. Nervous, hollow, and nothing like her original self, she stepped onto a train back to her hometown where her mother now lived alone.

Her mother had an inexplicable vision that day, knowing instinctively that Helga was on her way home. She asked several neighboring friends to accompany her to the station as her daughter's train approached. At thirty minutes past midnight Helga arrived in Frankfurt an der Oder and passed through the gate to see the happy face of her mother and five friends. Instantly Helga's fear evaporated. Although her father was still imprisoned, she saw that she would not have to face her future alone, and she looked ahead with confidence, prepared to begin rebuilding her life even as Europe was still rebuilding itself.

EPILOGUE

OSCAR SMITH

At the end of the war, Oscar "Smitty" Smith recuperated at San Francisco's Letterman General Hospital, having spent four years in captivity. For his service in the military, Smith earned a Bronze Star medal, a Purple Heart, an American Defense Service Medal, a Good Conduct Medal, and a Distinguished Unit Badge, as well as a Philippines Defense Ribbon.

After returning to his home in Pennsylvania, he earned a bachelor's degree in engineering at the Pennsylvania State University in 1953. He also studied human relations at Temple University and took human engineering testing courses from Johnson O'Connors in Philadelphia. At Lebanon Valley College he studied industrial engineering.

From 1936 to 1976 (minus his years serving in World War II) he was employed at Bowman's Department Stores, Inc., where he was named store superintendent and training director.

In 1976 he joined the Dauphin County Commissioner's Office as director of security and safety until the commissioner appointed him to chief clerk maintaining security and safety.

Smith is past president and lieutenant governor of Optimists International and a member of the American Society of Safety Engineers. He also is active with the American Society of Industrial Security and vice chairman of the POW Committee of the American Legion. He was past president of the Crime Clinic of Greater Harrisburg and executive director there for nine years.

He was licensed by the Atomic Energy Commission and was an instructor for the State of Pennsylvania Radiological Defense.

Smith also served as chairman of the property committee and deacon at the Salem United Church of Christ and presented the Humanitarian Chaplain Citation to four chaplains in Philadelphia.

He lives in Harrisburg with his wife, the former Elsie Irene Fry, his daughter Barbara Jean, and his son William David.

His companions in prison camp, Vince Grayson and Revere Matthias, have not been heard from based on Smith's investigations. He believes that they did not survive their internment.

ROBERT SALMON

While he was interned, Robert Salmon's wife Frances King Salmon joined her sister Etha in Minneapolis, where she secured a job at the Glen Lake Sanitarium—a tuberculosis treatment center. After his release he joined her in Minnesota. He secured a position at the University of Minnesota Hospital pediatrics department as a biochemical researcher.

In November 1946 he took his family to England for several months to study for the certification exam for the Royal Institute of Chemistry in London. He passed that exam, making him a Fellow of the Royal Institute of Chemistry—one of the highest ranking honors for scientists in England.

In 1947 missionary work reopened in Shanghai, and Salmon's colleagues began sending letters, petitioning him and his wife and family to return to China. When he refused, another letter came from the church, assuring him his salary would be generous and the children well provided for.

He wrote back a short letter to explain: it wasn't the money now, but his attitude. The war was over, and for him Shanghai and the people living and working there would never be the same. The Chinese had their own battles to fight among themselves, and this communist struggle was one he wanted no part of. He also rejected a suggestion that he become ordained as a minister. "My experiences 'in camp' have made me feel that preaching is futile, and that the only way of sowing the seeds of true Christian spirit is by living a Christian life and dying a Christian death."

Salmon continued his biochemical research at the University of Minnesota Hospital in Minneapolis where he retired in 1965. He died in 1975 at the age of seventy-five.

Salmon's comrade Ellis Tucker settled in West Virginia following the war and remained a close friend of the family until his death in the late 1950s.

EDWARD UZEMACK

One month after his liberation, Ed Uzemack was back to reporting at the *Chicago Times*—later to become the *Chicago Sun Times*. He had returned home to a wife and small child he needed to support, and was eager to return to work. Several competing newspapers vied for his POW experiences, which he eventually offered to the *Times*. As he had in the Stalag, Uzemack worked long hours to keep his mind occupied. He remained with the newspaper until 1951 when he joined the Office for Price Stabilization as regional director. Following that, he joined the American Medical Association as speechwriter for the association's president. While working there he wrote for six AMA presidents.

He then joined the Illinois State Medical Society as assistant to the executive, where he ran conventions and was an agent to the press. After years of working seven days a week, he suffered a heart attack in 1957.

Continuing to work, he next took on public relations as director at the Portland Cement Association coordinating regional public relations offices. In 1966 he returned to the AMA as director of officers' services.

In 1974 he took on a position at the Pennsylvania Osteopathic Medical Association working, in part, to increase public awareness of osteopathy as a medical practice. He retired in 1979.

After retirement he found himself unwilling to end his working career, so he joined the Pennsylvania Association for Home Health Agencies and started his own newsletter-writing business.

His first wife died in 1971, and he then married Patricia Sebourne. He and Patricia live in the Harrisburg, Pennsylvania, area and will be celebrating their twenty-fifth wedding anniversary.

Fellow newspapermen John Dunn and Denny Murray also returned to the United States after the war. Dunn became feature editor for the "Today Show," and Murray went on to write for the *Chicago Tribune*. Both have since passed away.

Despite his months at the Stalag, Uzemack has remained unincumbered by troubling memories. Instead, he says his busy lifestyle has always kept him vital and healthy. "I don't brood," he commented, "I annoy people instead by waking each morning so chipper."

HERMANN PFRENGLE

Pfrengle's trip home took about eight weeks, mostly on foot. "Romantic, patriotic dreams, and the boyscoutish adventure of saving the Fatherland," Pfrengle said, "had given way to the joy of survival and a new outlook on life without the ideological ballast of Nazism, its perverted ideals, and war machine." Food continued to be rationed in Germany, and the population grappled with the aftermath of the war's devastation and misery.

Following a twenty-one month "vacation," Pfrengle continued his high school/junior college education in 1946 and graduated in 1949. After his studies in architecture and motivated by a sense of rebuilding and reconstruction that led to a bachelor's equivalent degree in 1953 from the Technical University of Stuttgart, Pfrengle finally won his chocolate bar in the form of U.S. government employment. The dawning of the Cold War made him realize that continued survival, peace, and freedom necessitated more than designing houses. His professional interests turned to international cooperation.

In 1955 he started work for American consulates in Germany and after completing a U.S. government course program and graduating from the Language School in Munich, he entered the diplomatic arena as a scientific translator and interpreter at the American Embassy in Bonn. In 1964, he was promoted to Assistant Research and Development Coordinator. The American reeducation effort had come full circle for Pfrengle.

Involvement in the first major U.S.–German cooperative program gave Pfrengle the opportunity in 1966 to work in the United States with the U.S.-FRG Joint Engineering Agency in Detroit.

In 1969 he became an FRG liaison officer in the field of defense cooperation within NATO. From 1972 he was assigned in the Washington, D.C., area and was instrumental in establishing and operating international acquisition liaison activities. His work also involved contacts with the U.S. Congress and several departments.

Being a lifelong learner, Pfrengle earned a B.A. from Michigan State University at Oakland, an M.L.A. and an M.A. from Johns Hopkins University in Sociology and International Politics/International Economics, and completed Ph.D. course work in International Relations at American University.

Pfrengle was appointed guest lecturer at the Defense Systems Management College in 1978 and Honorary International Professor in 1988. He has written numerous articles and made contributions to books on national and international acquisition management and economics, focusing on transatlantic cooperation.

Since his retirement from FRG service in 1994, some of his latest writings, ranging from politics and management to literary issues, have been published in American newspapers and in a professional magazine. Other retirement activities focus on voluntary work for a local amputee support group and chess. Now living in Herndon, Virginia, Pfrengle remains active in the international arena.

He is completing a book collaboratively with Franz Frisch about his World War II experiences called "Forget That You Have Been Hitler Soldiers."

HELGA WUNSCH

Helga Wunsch returned to Frankfurt an der Oder in 1955 to find her mother ailing and her father in political prison. She was denied permission to return to high school to study for the examinations for her diploma. Having been a political prisoner, she ranked as an outcast who would never receive permission to pursue any work but manual labor, such as street sweeping. She found herself continuously watched; her mail arrived opened. That same year she fled to West Berlin, and her parents followed her after her father's release from prison.

The West German government and private organizations supported Helga and her parents, and she went ahead with reviewing and then taking her exams. In October 1956 she enrolled at the Johann Wolfgang Goethe University in Frankfurt, majoring in English and geography. Four years and 211 credits later she graduated and began teaching at the Wallschule in Langen.

While a student she lived in England for three months and began pen pal relationships with other English speakers. One of those pen pals was an American named Rist, whom she later married. She joined Rist in America in Camp Hill, Pennsylvania, on February 23, 1962. She immediately began teaching German at the Lower Dauphin Senior High School in Hummelstown, Pennsylvania. She taught there for thirty-three years and received countless awards as an outstanding teacher. In 1995 she began teaching at Wilson College in Chambersburg, where she instructs students in German as an adjunct professor.

Helga Rist feels no resentment toward the Russian and East German people, but admits she will always feel strong bitterness toward the Soviet and East German governments. "I can't say I have any regrets," she says, reflecting on her life before and after imprisonment. "Because I had never committed the crime [for which she was wrongfully sentenced], there is nothing I could have done differently." It is this irony that she has come to peace with, but that she still occasionally shares with her young students who now learn of the Cold War as only a part of history.

In 1995 she received a statement of exoneration from the Russians admitting that the Soviets had been wrong in arresting her for espionage.

BIBLIOGRAPHY

Bard, Mitchell G. *Forgotten Victims: The Abandonment of Americans in Hitler's Camps.* Boulder, CO: Westview Press, 1996.

Botting, Douglas. *From the Ruins of the Reich.* New York: Crown, 1985.

Brown, Raymond. *The Diary of Raymond Brown, interned in Stalag IX B, Bad Orb, October 9, 1994 through April 2, 1995.* Private Collection.

Collar, Hugh. *Captive in Shanghai.* Warwick House, Hong Kong: Oxford University Press, 1990.

MacDonald, Charles B. *A Time for Trumpets: The Untold Story of the Battle of the Bulge.* New York: William Morrow and Co., 1985.